Leading Merchant Families
of
Saudi Arabia

Leading Merchant Families
of
Saudi Arabia

J. R. L. Carter

Scorpion Publications
in association with
The D R Llewellyn Group

First published in 1979 by
Scorpion Publications Ltd
in association with
The D R Llewellyn Group

ISBN 0 905906 22 5

Editor: Leonard Harrow
Design and Art Direction: Colin Larkin
Design Assistant: Rhonda Larkin
Set in Compugraphic Times Roman
Printed on Bedford Antique Wove 90 gsm
Originated by Colourwise Litho Ltd, London
Printed in England by Butler & Tanner Ltd, Frome, Somerset

Contents

Acknowledgements

It would have been impossible to write this book without the encouragement and assistance of the following people and I very much wish to thank them all for their help. His Excellency Shaikh Ghazi Gosaibi and His Excellency Sh. Yusuf Hamdan, Sh. Saleh Toaimi, Sh. Hamad Nasir al Rajhi, Sh. Ahmad Abdalmuhsin Fraih, Sh. Ghiath Muhammad Kaaki, Omar Aggad, Sh. Abdullah Muhammad Jomaih, Sh. Umran Muhammad Umran, Sh. Khalid Yasin al Fitani, Mr Muhammad Rashid Abu Nayyan, Sh. Yaqoub Yusif al Rashid, Sh. Abdullah Abdalaziz El Khereiji, Sh. Abdalmuhsin Abdalrahman El Khereiji, Sh. Muhammad Abdulrahman al Fraih, Sh. Abdalrahman Muhammad al Sania, Sh. Ghazi Muhammad al Gosaibi, Sh. Muhammad Khalifa al Gosaibi, Sh. Said Salah, Bassem Said Salah, Sh. Muhammad Abdullah al Mutluq, M. S. Hindi, Sh. Fahd Saad al Mo'ajil, Sh. Abdalkarim Abdalaziz El Khereiji, Sh. Abdullah Abdalaziz Mo'ajil, Sh. Khalid Abdullah al Zamil, Sh. Hamad Abdullah al Zamil, Sh. Ibrahim Hasan al Gosaibi, Sh. Khalifa Saad al Gosaibi, Sh. Hasan Muhammad al Saidi, Sh. Ghazi Ahmad Zainy, Syd. Hisham Ali Hafiz, Syd. Muhammad Ali Hafiz, Sh. Adnan Abdalrahman Abdalmajid, Sh. Abdalkarim Zaid al Quraishi, Sh. Hisham Ahmad Ka'aki, Sh. Sami Mahmoud Attar, Sh. Abdalrahman Abdullah al Abbar, Sh. Khalid Ahmad al Abbar, Sh. Abdullah Ibrahim Silsilah, Sh. Walid Ahmad Juffali, Mr Muhammad Baheej, Mr Sami Odeh, Sh. Uthman Muhammad Salih Nassif, Syd. Ahmad Muhammad Baroom, Dr Hasan Yusif Nassif, Sh. Adnan Taha Samman, Sh. Abdalwahab Zinada, Sh. Abdalra'ouf Abu Zinada, Sh. Ahmad Hasan Fitaihi, Sh. Umr Ibrahim Sani'e, Mr Amal Aghaby, Sh. Abdalrahman Abdalaziz al Rajhi, Sh. Ali Muhammad al Rajhi, Sh. Muhammad Batati, Dr Solaiman Faqih, Sh. Abdullah Said Binzagr, Sh. Nizar Abdulmajid Jamjoom, Sh. Sulaiman Ibrahim Howaish, Sh. Mozhar Musallim Nowilaty, Mr Gordon Ambridge, Sh. Abdalatif Jamil, Sh. Yusif Jamil, Mr Khalid Habash, Sh. Ali Shobokshi, Mr Jean Pierre Gaspar, Sh. Abdalghani Abdullah Mofarrij, Sh. Abdalaziz Al Abdullah Al Solaiman, Abdalmajid Ahmad Mohandis, Sh. Hasan Khazindar, Mr Said Baaghil, Sh. Ahmad Muhammad Salih Baeshan, Mr Hasan Hawarneh, Sh. Mahfouz bin Mahfouz, Sh. Muhammad Abdullah bin Mahfouz, Sh. Salih al Esayi, Sh. Ali K. Kadi, Mr Henry Mueller, Mr Clyde Leamaster, Sh. Sulayman Abdullah El Khereiji, Sh. Ibrahim Abdullah El Khereiji, Sh. Talal Dhulaimi, Mr John Cross, Mr Tim Sisley, Sh. Hisham Alireza, Sh. Said Ahmad Noman, Sh. Saif Noman Said, Sh. Salih Ibrahim Zamil, Sh. Muhammad Ahmad Zaidan, Sh. Wabel Pharaon, Syd. Fadl Al Husseini.

Foreword

I very much welcome the opportunity to commend this important and timely publication. The position of Saudi Arabia in the international community and its significance as a trading partner to so many Western nations is obvious.

British exports to Saudi Arabia may shortly exceed a billion pounds a year and a further expansion of our trading links there represents a prime aim of this Committee.

The difficulty of choosing an appropriate Saudi partner, particularly for industrial joint ventures, is a major preoccupation for businessmen, and I believe that this book will make a substantial contribution to overcoming that problem!

The general reader too, will find much of interest in the historical development of the various business houses, which despite their rapid growth still remain very much 'family' orientated.

The gathering of so much information in such a short space of time speaks much for the energy of the writer as well as the tremendous co-operation of so many businessmen in Saudi Arabia itself.

Lord Selsdon
Chairman of the Committee
for Middle East Trade

Introduction

This book has been designed to assist businessmen active in the Saudi Arabian market, as well as those planning to enter the market for the first time.

The selection of the companies included has been arbitrary and has been dictated by the need to reflect the activities of companies in various areas of business and in different parts of the Kingdom. Those familiar with the country will notice some obvious omissions. The author apologises for this; some are due to requests for anonymity, others because of pressure of time. We have attempted to achieve a balanced view of the market and the order of entry in the book is designed to reflect this spread of interest rather than to imply any order of size or excellence.

The importance of the Government role in the market cannot be overstated. We hope that the inclusion here of details of the Saudi Industrial Development Fund and SIBC will be found useful.

The presentation has concentrated on finding a method of presenting as much information as possible in the shortest and most accessible way. At the same time, it is hoped that the reader will obtain an idea of the historical development of the market from an understanding of the origins of some of the major business houses. To an extent, the accounts which are included also provide an insight into a society which has solid and ancient origins but which has, nevertheless, absorbed Western ideas and has moulded them to its own use with startling rapidity.

It is hoped that the structure of Arabian names will be apparent to the reader and that the family tree will guide him to the right person in the family. The question of the transliteration of Arab names and words is one which involves endless wrangling unless an academic system is used. This makes matters difficult for the non-academic reader, so this book uses the spelling in English used by the people themselves. At times this will result in the same name being spelt in different ways in the same family!

Any errors are the author's, but every effort has been made to ensure that details are both up to date and accurate. The author will be glad to consider recommendations for additional companies to be included in the next edition.

Ahmad Al Firaih Co.

Address head office P.O.* 128 Riyadh

Telephone 24317

Cable address RADWAN

Proprietor Sh. Ahmad bin Abdalmuhsin Al Firaih

Company History
The family company was established in 1949 and the office occupies a central position in the capital between Batha and Wazir St. opposite the Arab Bank.

Business Activity
Their activities concern the import and supply of spare parts for air conditioners as well as general trading.

Agencies
Ranio Controls of Plymouth, UK
Pleuger Unterwasser Pumpen GmbH, West Germany
Imperial of USA
J. B. Industries, Illinois, USA

Turnover 1.5 million Saudi riyals

Bankers Arab Bank

*for Post Office Box *passim*.

Ibrahim Al Khamis & Sons Company

Address head office Riyadh

Telephone 26256

Telex 201532

Cable address AL TASSHELE

Subsidiary offices in Jiddah, Qasim, Ta'if, Beirut and Cairo

Proprietors Partnership between Abdalrahman bin Ibrahim and Muhammad bin Ibrahim

Company History
The company was founded by Ibrahim al Khamis who was a confidant of H.M. King Abdalaziz al Sa'uwd. He was the first person to import goods to Riyadh from Syria which he did by camel in the twenties and thirties. It is related that he was also the first person to build a stone house outside the walls of Riyadh which he did with the aid of Syrian masons he also brought back to Riyadh. The story goes that hearing the masons at work the citizens of Riyadh were at first fearful that Ibrahim was making idols and they reported him to the King. Today the company has a licence to import from the USSR and holds the agency for Lada, Moskavitch and Volga trademarks in cars, heavy agricultural equipment and tractors.

The Family of AL FIRAIH

They originate from Ushayqar in Najd and are representative of the smaller family with whom it is often better for the Western business man to make contact because they will have time to devote the necessary energy to his needs. Whilst in the past they will share roots with other people of the same name they do not nowadays share a family relationship and the Westerner should be careful about associating people with the same last name.

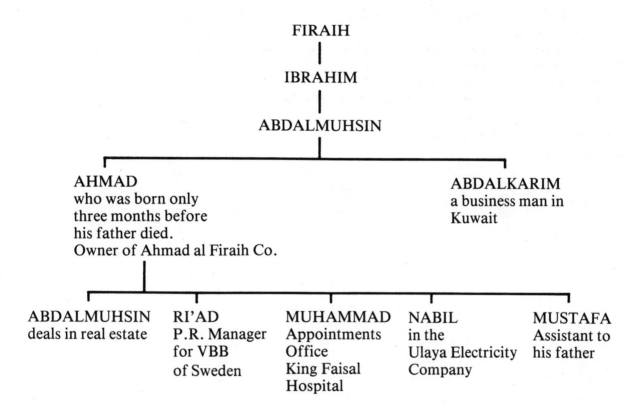

FIRAIH

IBRAHIM

ABDALMUHSIN

AHMAD
who was born only
three months before
his father died.
Owner of Ahmad al Firaih Co.

ABDALKARIM
a business man in
Kuwait

ABDALMUHSIN
deals in real estate

RI'AD
P.R. Manager
for VBB
of Sweden

MUHAMMAD
Appointments
Office
King Faisal
Hospital

NABIL
in the
Ulaya Electricity
Company

MUSTAFA
Assistant to
his father

The Family of AL KHAMIS

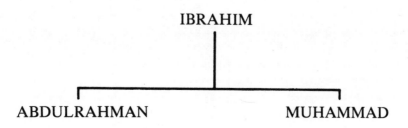

IBRAHIM

ABDULRAHMAN   MUHAMMAD

The Fuzan Muhammad Al Nassar Establishment

Address head office P.O. 2254 Riyadh

Telephone 33124

Telex 2001435 FUZAN S J

Cable address NASSARCO

Subsidiary office Zilfi, 300kms south-west of Riyadh, tel. (from Riyadh) 06422-1343.

Proprietor Sh. Fuzan bin Muhammad Al Nassar

Company History

Sh. Fuzan returned from employment in Kuwait twenty-five years ago and settled in Riyadh with his family to start the business. At present his company operates as commission purchasing agents and specialises in crockery and building materials. However, he is anxious to expand into the domestic appliance field and is actively seeking agencies for refrigerators, television sets and washing machines.

Turnover 2 million Saudi riyals

Bankers Riyadh Bank

The Family of AL NASSAR

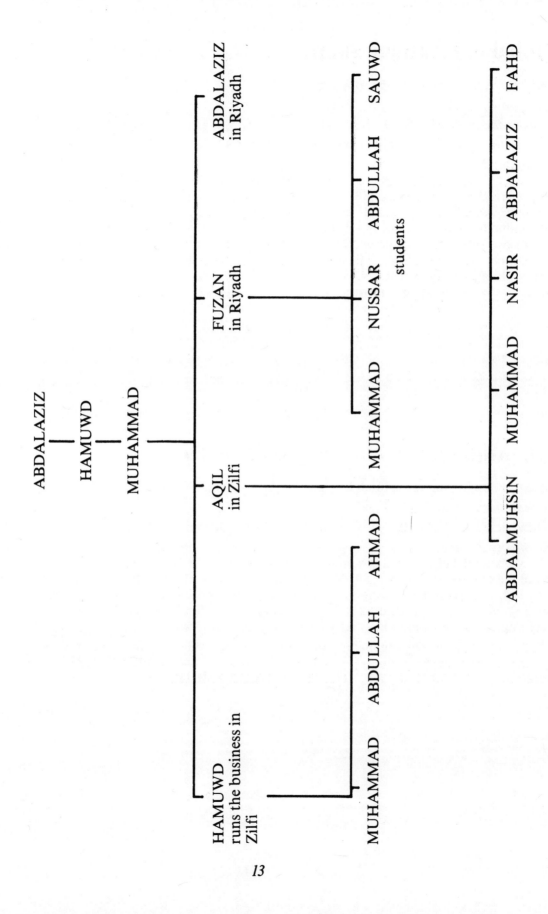

ABDALAZIZ
HAMUWD
MUHAMMAD

HAMUWD
runs the business in
Zilfi

AQIL
in Zilfi

FUZAN
in Riyadh

ABDALAZIZ
in Riyadh

MUHAMMAD   ABDULLAH   AHMAD

MUHAMMAD   NUSSAR   ABDULLAH   SAUWD

students

ABDALMUHSIN   MUHAMMAD   NASIR   ABDALAZIZ   FAHD

13

Bohaimid Antique Shop

Address head office P.O. 252 Al Khobar

Telephone 44189

Cable address BOHAIMID

Proprietor Abdulrahman bin Sulaiman Bohaimid

Company History
This successful small business was established in 1968 and four years ago moved to its present larger premises. Abdulrahman Bohaimid started because a bedouin asked him to sell a chest for him. Abdulrahman was able to do this quickly and easily and the consequence was that he was inundated with antiques. Sadly this source of supply has now been exhausted and this shortage is reflected in the prices. However Abdulrahman takes a real interest in his wares and guarantees their authenticity. His shop is in any case the best place in the Eastern Province to see traditional Arabian artifacts.

Bankers Riyadh Bank, Saudi British Bank.

Sh. Muhammad bin Ahmad Al Sania

Address head office Asia Hotel, Riyadh

Telephone 26461, 35127, 35736

The Asima Hotel, Riyadh, is fully owned by Sh. Muhammad.

Company History
Sh. Muhammad bin Ahmad acquired the Asima Hotel in 1968 and began to rent the Asia Hotel from the Minister of Finance, Sh. Muhammad Al Ali Aba Al Khail, in 1972. Since then he has not wished to expand his business except to rebuild and redecorate his hotels which cater mainly for middle class Saudi nationals. Sh. Muhammad bin Ahmad is religious and his learning and humility are widely respected in a materialistic world.

Partnerships Sh. Abdalrahman bin Muhammad, besides managing his father's hotels is a partner in the Umaya Company for building, construction and the transport of heavy machinery. P.O. 8133, Riyadh, tel. 35736, tx. 200222 AMUDI SJ.

The Family of BOHAIMID

Originate in Manfuha Riyadh.

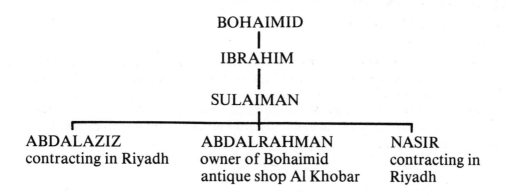

```
                    BOHAIMID
                       |
                    IBRAHIM
                       |
                    SULAIMAN
        _____
       |                 |                 |
   ABDALAZIZ      ABDALRAHMAN          NASIR
   contracting    owner of Bohaimid   contracting in
   in Riyadh      antique shop Al Khobar   Riyadh
```

The Family of SANIA

Originate in Majma'a of Najd some two hundred and twenty five kilometres north of Riyadh. Salih and Muhammad, the sons of Sh. Ahmad bin Nasir, were the first to come to the capital.

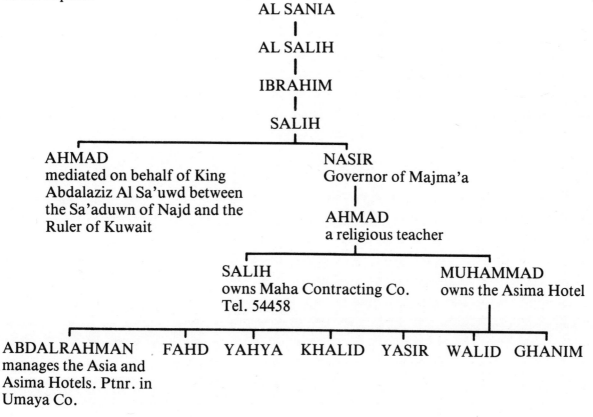

```
                         AL SANIA
                            |
                         AL SALIH
                            |
                         IBRAHIM
                            |
                          SALIH
        _____
       |                              |
   AHMAD                           NASIR
   mediated on behalf of King      Governor of Majma'a
   Abdalaziz Al Sa'uwd between          |
   the Sa'aduwn of Najd and the     AHMAD
   Ruler of Kuwait                  a religious teacher
                         _____
                        |                               |
                    SALIH                          MUHAMMAD
                    owns Maha Contracting Co.       owns the Asima Hotel
                    Tel. 54458
```

ABDALRAHMAN   FAHD YAHYA KHALID YASIR WALID GHANIM
manages the Asia and
Asima Hotels. Ptnr. in
Umaya Co.

Al Saidi Trading Store

Address head office P.O. 1501 Dammam

Telephone 22085

Cable address HASAN AL SAIDI

Proprietor Sh. Hasan Muhammad Al Saidi

Company History

Commenced operations in 1965 running a poultry farm having left Aramco. This enterprise was sold in 1971 and Saidi Trading founded. This business specialised in the import of foodstuffs and provided the basis of its present activity which is real estate. At the moment holdings consist of some six buildings which are all domestic accommodation. It is intended to expand into the manufacturing field and investigations are under way to establish a factory.

Bankers Riyadh Bank, Saudi Faransi Bank.

The Family of AL SAIDI

Originate in Najd at Al Shara west of Riyadh.

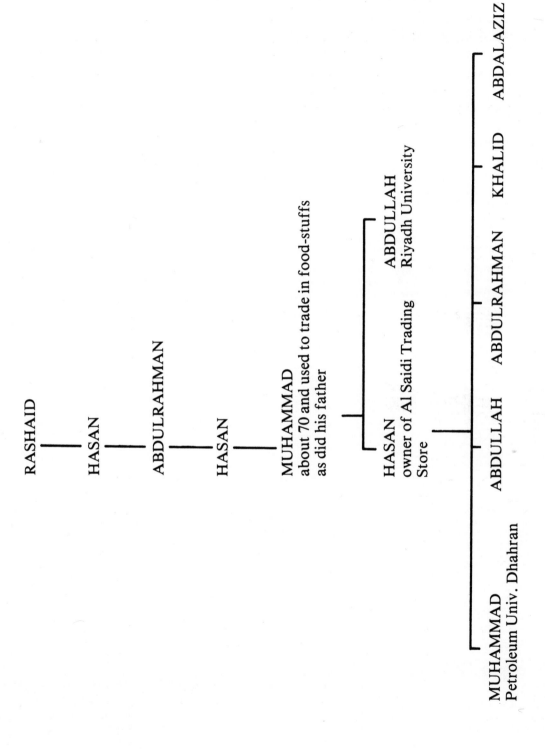

RASHAID

HASAN

ABDULRAHMAN

HASAN

MUHAMMAD
about 70 and used to trade in food-stuffs
as did his father

HASAN
owner of Al Saidi Trading
Store

ABDULLAH
Riyadh University

MUHAMMAD
Petroleum Univ. Dhahran

ABDULLAH

ABDULRAHMAN

KHALID

ABDALAZIZ

Al Hizam Al Akhdar Co.

Address head office P.O. 1527 Jiddah

Telephone 55741

Proprietor Sh. Abdalaziz Ibrahim Al Sanie

Company History

The company was formed in 1973 and its first contracting job was acting as a sub-contractor on a road project in Jizan. Today the company specializes in villa construction and house extensions and whilst it is small it is noted for meticulous and closely calculated work.

The Family of SANIE

Originating in Anaiza of Qasim some centuries ago and an old Jiddah family more landowning and professional in character than commercial. Sanie St. in the old city is named after them and its current value is estimated at three hundred million riyals. The streets of Jiddah can be confusing to the visitor, for instance some, like King Faisal Street, have more than one name. This thoroughfare is also called New Street and Gold Street as well. When it was built it was obvious to call it New Street; but the third name was given to it due to the habit of the old merchants of burying their gold. Much was found in forgotten hiding places when houses had to be pulled down to build New Street. The more cynical say that the epithet derives from the compensation paid by the government to the owners of the destroyed properties!

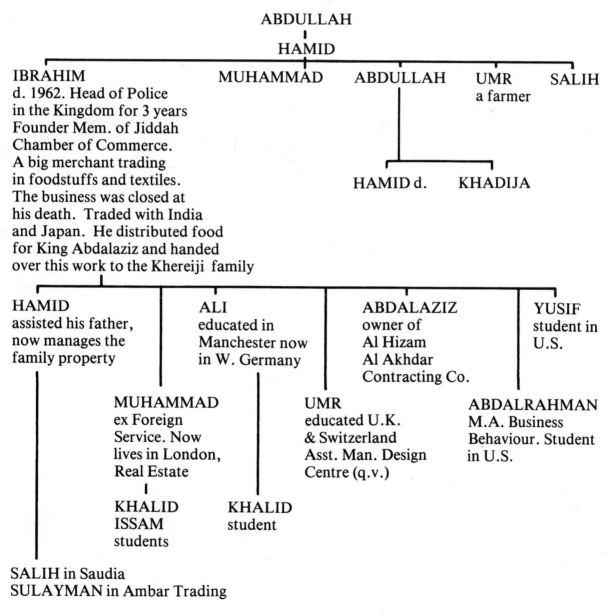

ABDULLAH

HAMID

IBRAHIM
d. 1962. Head of Police
in the Kingdom for 3 years
Founder Mem. of Jiddah
Chamber of Commerce.
A big merchant trading
in foodstuffs and textiles.
The business was closed at
his death. Traded with India
and Japan. He distributed food
for King Abdalaziz and handed
over this work to the Khereiji family

MUHAMMAD　**ABDULLAH**　**UMR**
a farmer　**SALIH**

HAMID d.　KHADIJA

HAMID
assisted his father,
now manages the
family property

ALI
educated in
Manchester now
in W. Germany

ABDALAZIZ
owner of
Al Hizam
Al Akhdar
Contracting Co.

YUSIF
student in
U.S.

MUHAMMAD
ex Foreign
Service. Now
lives in London,
Real Estate

UMR
educated U.K.
& Switzerland
Asst. Man. Design
Centre (q.v.)

ABDALRAHMAN
M.A. Business
Behaviour. Student
in U.S.

KHALID
ISSAM
students

KHALID
student

SALIH in Saudia
SULAYMAN in Ambar Trading

19

Abdalrahim Abdullah Mofarrij

Address Jizan. There is no formal address as the establishment is well known.

Telephone 1312, 1313, 1611

Subsidiary offices
Jiddah Main Office P.O. 1337 Cables MOFARRI,
tel. 33115, tx. 401423 MUFRIJ SJ
There are two other branches in Jiddah.

Proprietor Abdulrahim Abdullah Mofarrij

Company History
The business was founded in 1946 based on the importation of sorghum and grain from Jizan to Jiddah. Abdalrahim Abdullah had his own dhows and also carried money on behalf of clients to make purchases in the Jiddah entrepot market as in the early days there were no banks.
 Today the company acts as a general importer specialising in foodstuffs and building materials. Developments have included the addition of an ice factory at Rabigh, which is equipped from the UK, and the establishment of improved farming interests in Jizan. The company possesses considerable real estate assets in Jiddah and elsewhere and is represented by agents in Yanbu, Wejh and Tabuk.

The Family of MUFARRIJ

A family of Rabigh on the Red Sea coast. Originating from the tribe of Harb.

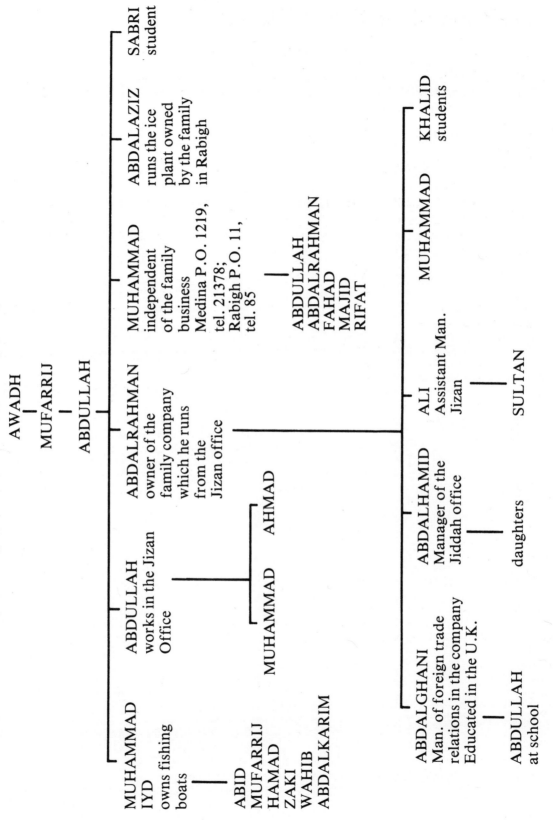

AWADH
|
MUFARRIJ
|
ABDULLAH

MUHAMMAD IYD
owns fishing boats
- ABID
- MUFARRIJ
- HAMAD
- ZAKI
- WAHIB
- ABDALKARIM

ABDULLAH
works in the Jizan Office
- MUHAMMAD
- AHMAD

ABDALRAHMAN
owner of the family company which he runs from the Jizan office

ABDALGHANI
Man. of foreign trade relations in the company
Educated in the U.K.
- ABDULLAH
  at school

ABDALHAMID
Manager of the Jiddah office
- daughters

ALI
Assistant Man. Jizan
- SULTAN

MUHAMMAD

KHALID
students

MUHAMMAD
independent of the family business
Medina P.O. 1219, tel. 21378;
Rabigh P.O. 11, tel. 85
- ABDULLAH
- ABDALRAHMAN
- FAHAD
- MAJID
- RIFAT

ABDALAZIZ
runs the ice plant owned by the family in Rabigh

SABRI
student

Sulaiman A.R.A.K. and Partners Co.

Address in Saudi Arabia P.O. 4066 Riyadh

Telephone 29454

Telex 202132 ATHLEH S J

Cable address ATHLEH

Head office Sulaiman Al Abdulkarim and Brothers Co., P.O. 675 Kuwait, tel. 432344, 431957, tx. 2259 OBTEH KT, cable OBTEH.

Subsidiary offices Riyadh as above. Dubai—Al Abdulkarim Trading Co., P.O. 4641 Dubai, UAE, tel. 221851.

This company is an interesting example of the mobility of people in the Peninsular and represents a Saudi business concern that has become largely expatriate. Naturally there has been a similar flow in the other direction. The company is concerned with the import and distribution of foodstuffs.

The Family of ABDULKARIM

Originate from Harma near Hawtat al Sudair of Najd.

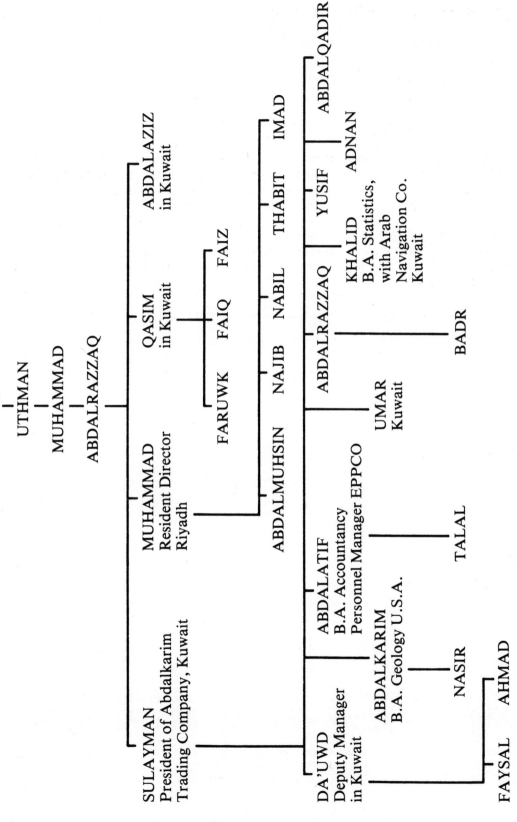

Al Ansari Establishment

Address head office P.O. 137 Al Khobar

Telephone 42849, 41218

Telex 620122 JALEEL SJ

Cable address JALEEL

Proprietor Sh. Abdaljaleel bin Abdalkarim Al Ansari

Activities

In Al Khobar the company is involved in construction and retails furniture from a large showroom in Amir Nasser St. In Bahrain the family holdings are controlled as a collective company between the four brothers Ahmad, Abdaljaleel, Abdullah and Ibrahim.

1. Al Ansari Lighting Co. Manama, P.O. 5182, tel. 714780, tx. 8848 ANSACO BN
2. Al Ansari Lights Co. Muharraq, P.O. 22395, tel. 325495, tx. 8848 ANSACO BN
3. Crystal Palace, Bahrain, tel. 254129
4. Bahrain Mattress Factory, P.O. 5648 Manama, tel. 243409, tx. 8472.

The above list is a partnership of 50% each between Sh. Abdaljaleel Al Ansari and Sh. Ali Hasan Mahmud.

The Family of ANSARI

Originated in Medina and descend from Abdullah ibn Abbas who is buried in Ta'if. The Ansari are so called because they assisted the Prophet Muhammad in his early conquests. This branch of the family migrated to Bahrain about 150 years ago, others having also settled in Iraq and Iran.

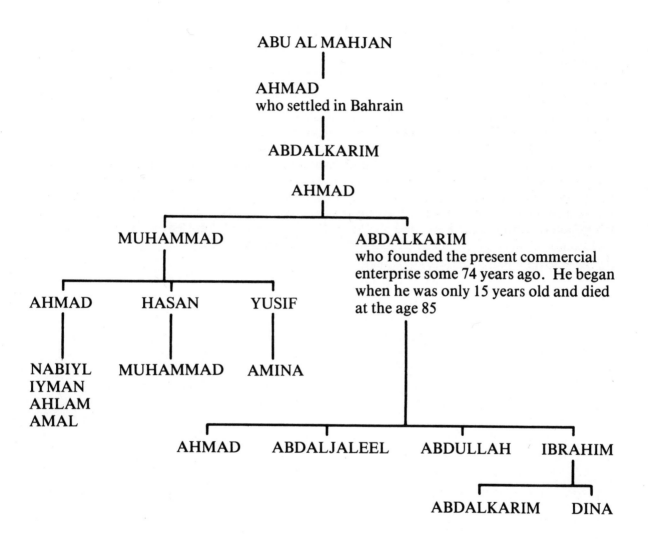

ABU AL MAHJAN

AHMAD
who settled in Bahrain

ABDALKARIM

AHMAD

MUHAMMAD

ABDALKARIM
who founded the present commercial enterprise some 74 years ago. He began when he was only 15 years old and died at the age 85

AHMAD   HASAN   YUSIF

NABIYL
IYMAN
AHLAM
AMAL

MUHAMMAD   AMINA

AHMAD   ABDALJALEEL   ABDULLAH   IBRAHIM

ABDALKARIM   DINA

Ahmed Hasan Fitaihi

Head office P.O. 2606 Jiddah

Telephone 21014, 42734

Cable AHMAD FITAIHI JIDDAH

Telex 401084 FTAIHI SJ

Branches
Main Showroom, King Abdalaziz St., tel. 34649, 42114
Queens Building Shop, tel. 42734
Gold Street Shop, tel. 21864
Al Zubair Street Shop, tel. 21864

Company History
Sh. Ahmed Fitaihi is the proprietor of one of the oldest jewellery businesses in Jiddah and the family business began in 1931. Whilst still retaining their interests in the traditional trade in gold in the old souq they have been able to build a flourishing modern business on this foundation. Sh. Ahmed is particularly enthusiastic about Arabian and Islamic design and always selects pieces that reflect the highest standards in this respect. He himself set up an independent business ten years ago and the faithfulness of his many customers demonstrates the quality and honesty with which he conducts his affairs. He represents leading manufacturers around the world and Sh. Ahmed's great personal knowledge of precious metals and stones enhances his company's reputation for integrity and quality.

Bankers Riyadh Bank, National Commercial Bank.

The Family of FITAIHI

A family settled in Jiddah for many generations and one which still maintains its place in the small goldsmiths' area of the old souq. Here they have two shops which give the Western visitor the feeling that he has really found Aladdin's cave.

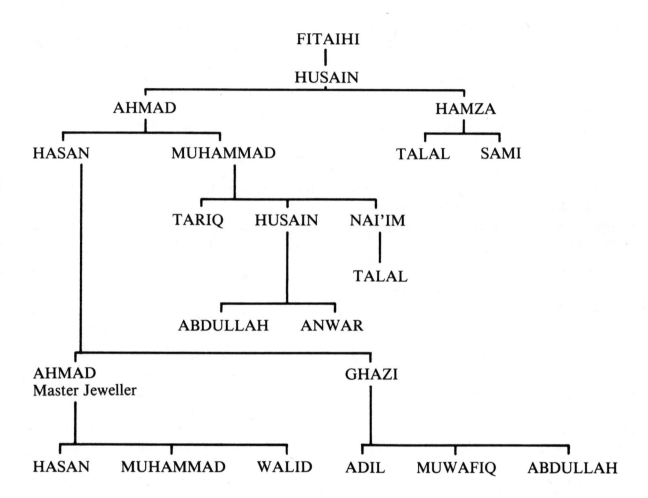

Associated Agencies Ltd.

Address head office P.O. 419 Jiddah

Telephone 22396, 23430

Telex 401025 ZINADA SJ

Proprietor Sh. Abdalraouf Abu Zinada

Company History

Associated Agencies began as a travel agency and is still outside the IATA due to the restrictions imposed by that body on operations for more than one carrier. Today it operates as a holding company to control the various interests which have developed since its inception. Sh. Abdalraouf now engages in the travel business through the Hatim Travel Agency, named after his son, and this is a wholly owned company (P.O. 419, tel. 31882, 31026, tx. 401025 ZINADA SJ). A second wholly owned company is the Arabian Establishment for Alimentary Products (P.O. 1450, Jiddah, tel. 22429, tx. 401025 JINADA SJ). In addition to these Sh. Abdalraouf has engaged in two joint ventures:

1. Al Sagr Insurance Co. of Saudi Arabia with the New Zealand Insurance Company, P.O. 419 Jiddah, tel. 31820, tx. 401025 ZINADA SJ.

2. The Jiddah Medical Center with Sh. Ibrahim Shaker, P.O. 419 Jiddah, tx. 401025 ZINADA SJ, tel. 53695, 57324, 690837/8/9/841/42

Bankers Citibank, Banque du Liban et d'Outre Mer, Al Jazirah Bank, National Commercial Bank.

The Family of ABU ZINADA

The family has been in Jiddah for centuries and some members still carry out their traditional function as auctioneers and superintendents in the vegetable and fruit market.

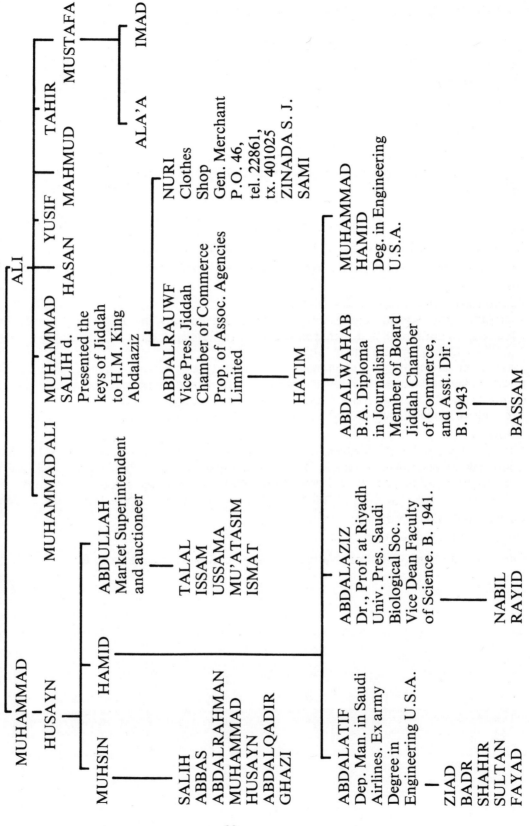

Abdulghani El Ajou Corporation

Address head office P.O. 78 Riyadh

Telephone 25709, 25710, 25749

Telex 201088 ELAJOU S J

Cable address ELAJOUTRADE

Subsidiary offices
Al Jeel Trading Est., P.O. 5012, Riyadh
El Ajou Trading Agencies, P.O. 3202, Riyadh
National Glass Factory, P.O. 404, Riyadh, tx. 201869 MODOFF

Proprietor Mr Abdulghani El Ajou

Company History
Established in 1962 as a sole proprietorship

Branches overseas London, Syria, Lebanon, North Yemen, Jordan

Local branches Jiddah, Al Khobar (Dammam) and Jubail

Business Activity
Agents/distributors/representatives for
1. complete photographic equipment—cameras (conventional and instant), movie projectors 8 mm and 16mm, sound and silent films, processing lab equipment, VTR and tapes
2. audio visual equipment and microfilm
3. complete ranges of office equipment—furniture, typewriters, calculators, planning boards, photo copiers, Diazo material and supplies, security paper-shredders
4. indoor decorative materials—tiles, wall tiles, false ceilings, lighting
5. complete range of medical and hospital supplies, including furniture and equipment

Agencies
Polaroid, Cutter, Jewett, Stryker, Dietzgen, Airshied, Cinema Prod. of USA; Eiki, Otsuka, Toitu, Stitz, Canon, Meito Shokai, Ishimitsu of Japan; Coulter, Pye Unicam, Bell and Howell, Kardex of UK; Alpia of France; Roth and Webber, Kindermann, Linhof, Arri, Ideal, Triumph and Adler of Germany; Riffe of Italy; Neustedler of Austria; Eskofot & Nordisk of Denmark.

Capital 30 million US dollars

Turnover 100 million US dollars

Bankers Arab Bank, Citibank, National Commercial Bank, Saudi Cairo Bank.

Said Al Ajou Trading Corporation

Address head office P.O. 435 Jiddah

Telephone 34054, 34641

Telex 401646 MODIRD SJ

Cable address AJOUCO

Subsidiary offices
Modern Trading Agencies, Jiddah, tel. 33775
Glass and Mirror National Factories, Jiddah, tel. 20245
Saudi Arabian Trading & Resources, Jiddah, tel. 55618
Nibal Trading Corporation, Riyadh, tel. 39835
Said al Ajou Trading Corporation, Al Khobar, tel. 41237

Proprietor Said Ahmad al Ajou, who is a shareholder in the Saudi Cairo Bank, the Arab Bank, the City Bank and the Riyadh Bank.

Company History

The Said al Ajou Corporation was established in 1975 and comprises three main divisions representing a consolidation and continuation of the original Al Ajou business interests. These consist of Contracting (ARCON), the Electronics Division, which handles television, radios and office equipment, machinery and furniture, and thirdly the Glass Division, which today is the largest importer and wholesaler of glass in the Kingdom.

The Corporation represents Glass Export of Czechoslovakia and French and Belgian companies in the same field. They also act for Celotex false ceilings and tiles of the USA. They are agents for Graetz Televisions from West Germany, Marantz audio equipment from the USA, J.V.C. of Japan for audio and video equipment and Imperial of West Germany for photocopiers.

At the moment the Corporation is investigating the contracting market and investing considerable resources in the acquisition of the best technical expertise to enable them to compete for the most major Government tenders.

Bankers Arab Bank, Saudi Cairo Bank, City Bank, Riyadh Bank, Jazira Bank.

The Family of AL AJOU

A family emigrating from Jaffa in Palestine where Ahmad Sa'id Al Ajou was in the glass business. This he continued in the Kingdom some twenty-three years ago, at first purchasing from wholesalers and cutting the glass himself. Ahmad was followed by his sons Sa'id and Abdalghani and the family was able to open a branch in Riyadh. At the present time, exhibiting the spirit of sturdy independence which led to their earlier success, the two brothers have established their own separate businesses.

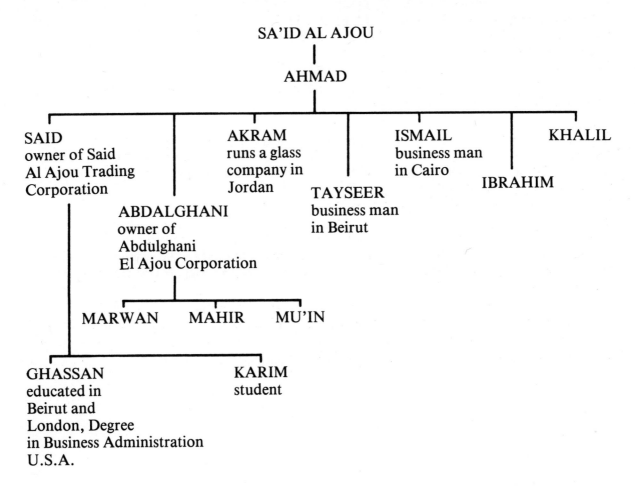

Binayti Development Company

Address head office P.O. 3305 Jiddah

Telephone 54240, 674406, 674410

Telex 400412 BINAYT SJ

Cable address BINAYTI

The Chairman and Board of Directors
Chairman:Sh. Umr M. S. Nassif
Sh. Ali M. S. Nassif
Sh. Uthman M. S. Nassif
Sh. Ibrahim M. S. Nassif
Sh. Nabil Abdulillah Nassif
Sh. Ussama Abdulillah Nassif
Dr. Bakhashwin
Mrs. Fatima Ibrahim Nassif
Mrs. Sadia Nassif
Mrs. Salwa Nassif

The company was established in 1975 as the Binayti Establishment and became a limited liability company in 1978. The Nassif family is not a purely commercial one but represents many generations of scholars and public servants and is one of the oldest in Jiddah. At the present time Binayti is a multi purpose company specialising in contracting for housing projects and their most recent expansion has involved them in a joint venture with an Italian company called Premo which will result in the setting up of a factory for pre-cast concrete. This venture involves Premo and Binayti as principals and other members of the Nassif family with Talaat and Wahib Lami. This company is called the Saudi Italian Pre-Cast Co. and is established in Yanbo. The Lami brothers are the owners of the Lami Trading and Contracting Company in Jiddah, established in 1979.

Bankers Riyadh Bank, City Bank

The Family of NASSIF

Originating from Harb between Jiddah and Medina. The first station on the Hidjaz Railway from Medina to Damascus was called Bir Nassif after the nearby well.

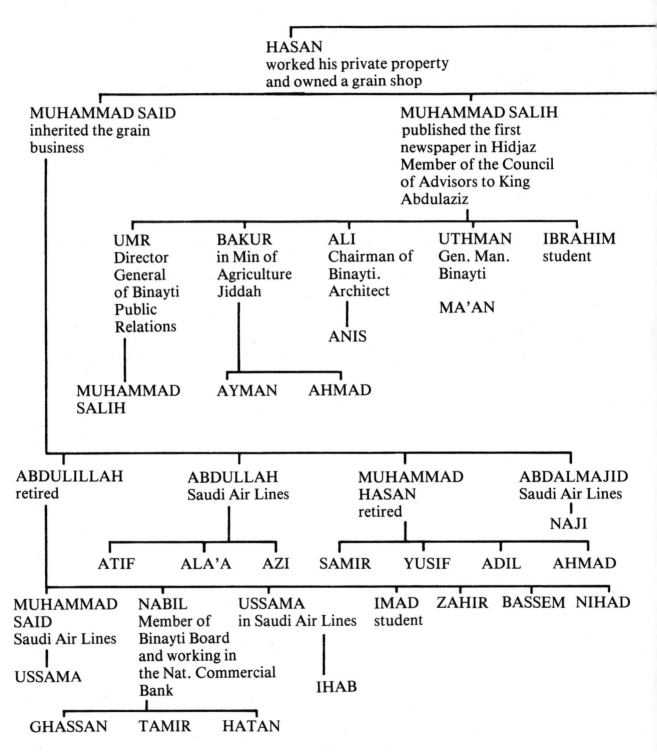

HASAN
worked his private property and owned a grain shop

MUHAMMAD SAID
inherited the grain business

MUHAMMAD SALIH
published the first newspaper in Hidjaz Member of the Council of Advisors to King Abdulaziz

UMR
Director General of Binayti Public Relations

BAKUR
in Min of Agriculture Jiddah

ALI
Chairman of Binayti. Architect

UTHMAN
Gen. Man. Binayti

MA'AN

IBRAHIM
student

ANIS

MUHAMMAD SALIH

AYMAN   AHMAD

ABDULILLAH
retired

ABDULLAH
Saudi Air Lines

MUHAMMAD HASAN
retired

ABDALMAJID
Saudi Air Lines

NAJI

ATIF   ALA'A   AZI   SAMIR   YUSIF   ADIL   AHMAD

MUHAMMAD SAID
Saudi Air Lines

USSAMA

NABIL
Member of Binayti Board and working in the Nat. Commercial Bank

USSAMA
in Saudi Air Lines

IMAD
student

ZAHIR   BASSEM   NIHAD

IHAB

GHASSAN   TAMIR   HATAN

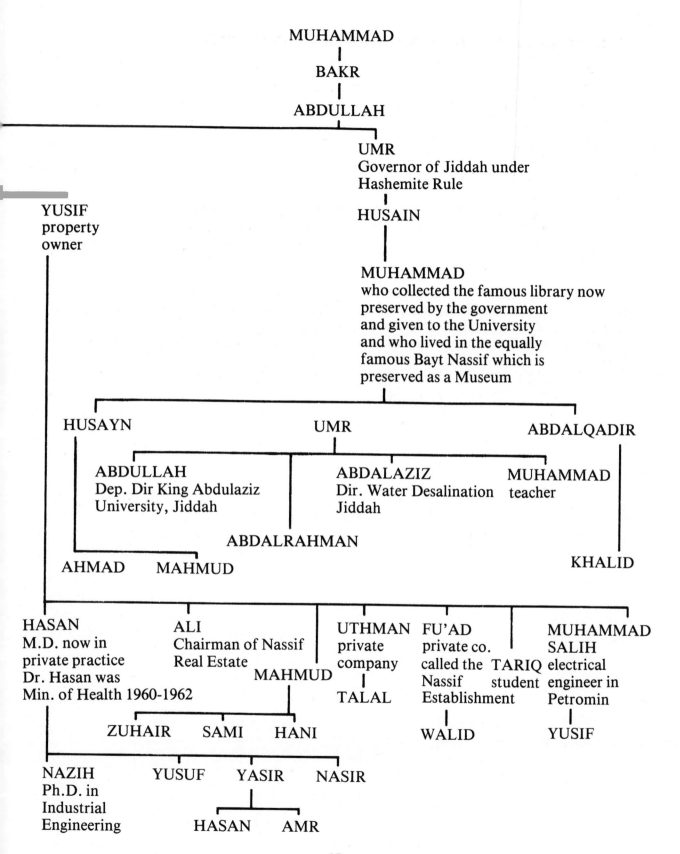

MUHAMMAD

BAKR

ABDULLAH

YUSIF
property
owner

UMR
Governor of Jiddah under
Hashemite Rule

HUSAIN

MUHAMMAD
who collected the famous library now
preserved by the government
and given to the University
and who lived in the equally
famous Bayt Nassif which is
preserved as a Museum

HUSAYN

UMR

ABDALQADIR

ABDULLAH
Dep. Dir King Abdulaziz
University, Jiddah

ABDALAZIZ
Dir. Water Desalination
Jiddah

MUHAMMAD
teacher

ABDALRAHMAN

KHALID

AHMAD   MAHMUD

HASAN
M.D. now in
private practice
Dr. Hasan was
Min. of Health 1960-1962

ALI
Chairman of Nassif
Real Estate

MAHMUD

UTHMAN
private
company

TALAL

FU'AD
private co.
called the   TARIQ
Nassif   student
Establishment

MUHAMMAD
SALIH
electrical
engineer in
Petromin

ZUHAIR   SAMI   HANI

WALID

YUSIF

NAZIH
Ph.D. in
Industrial
Engineering

YUSUF   YASIR   NASIR

HASAN   AMR

Abdullah Al Rashed Abunayyan Establishment

Address head office P.O. 321 Riyadh

Telephone 34769, 23359

Telex 20201 MOON SJ

Cable address ABUNAYAN

Subsidiary offices Jiddah P.O. Box 3960, tel. 36306

Proprietor Sh. Abdullah Al Rashed

Company History

 Sh. Abdullah gained his commercial experience trading for his father in foodstuffs and travelled to Syria, Bahrain and Kuwait. The present company was started in 1954 and specializes in agricultural machinery in which field most demand is for water pumps and diesel engines.

Business activity

 The company operates an exclusive agency for Puma Bamford of the UK and non-exclusive agencies for Burnett Atlanta International of UK, BKB Electric Co. of UK, GFA of Brussels, Redwood of Italy and Compressor Bernard and Luchard of France. In conjunction with Pump Guinard of France they are establishing a joint venture to manufacture pumps in the Kingdom.

Bankers Saudi British Bank, National Commercial Bank, Riyadh Bank, Saudi Hollandi Bank.

The Family of ABU NAYYAN

The family hails from the Dhurma area to the west of Riyadh.

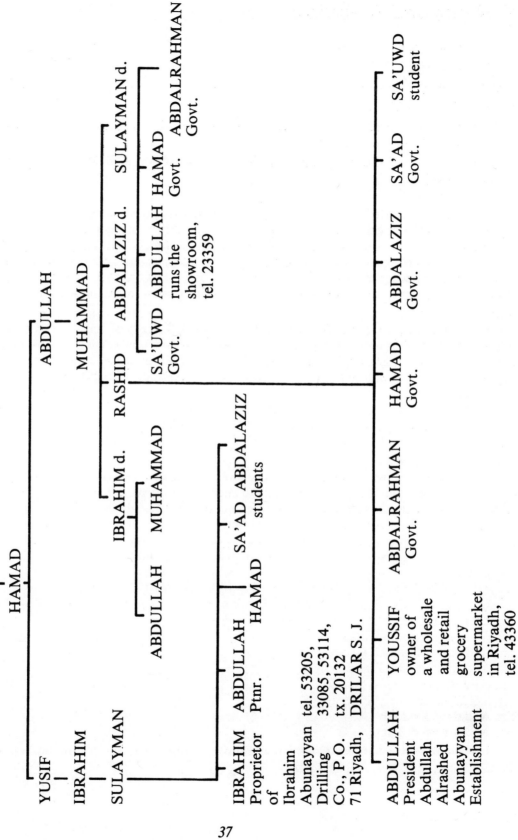

A Rajab and A Silsilah

Address head office P.O. 203 Jiddah
Telephone 25188, 25382
Telex 401180 ARNDAS S J
Cable address ARANDAS
Subsidiary offices Riyadh P.O. 2815, cable ARANDASCO, Dammam, cable ARANDASCO; also offices in Al Khobar and Mecca.

The company is a 50/50 partnership between Sh. Abdalaziz Abdullah Rajab and Sh. Abdullah Ibrahim Silsilah.

Company History
The company was started in 1945 as an import company supplying electrical and electronic equipment, consumer goods and household appliances. With foresight a projects department was established twenty-two years ago and presaged the company's present development. Today the company represents considerable overseas interests and operates on a broad front with particular specialisation in generating installations, street lighting, fittings, scientific and industrial equipment, cables, fire alarms, power stations and telecommunications.

Agencies
Philips of Holland, Kelvinator and Leonard, USA and UK, Kelly of Italy, H D Sheldon and Co. of New York—household appliances, Fox Bompani and Technogas of Italy—household appliances, British Lightning Preventer of UK, Société Commerciale Toute Electrique of France, Manhattan Commercial Corporation, American Export Group Inc., Union Carbide and McGraw Edison of the USA, Horst von Valtier and MWM (Motoren) Werke of West Germany, Elin Union Electrical Equipment of Austria, Cable Export and Apex of Italy, Erni and Co. of Switzerland, Petit Jean et Co. of France and Semafori Controlli Automazione of Italy.

Associated Companies
1. Saudi Trading Co. for consumer products and contracting. This company is wholly owned by the partnership and trades in fertilizers and chemicals operating in Jiddah.
2. Rajab and Tayeb Co. in Riyadh. A partnership between Rajab and Silsilah and Ahmed Tayeb working as electrical and mechanical contractors.
3. Saudi Air Conditioning Co. in Jiddah and Riyadh specialising in installation and maintenance; this company is a partnership between Rajab and Silsilah and various other partners.
4. Arabian Mechanical and Electrical Contracting Co. (AMECCO) in Riyadh.
5. Sagr Insurance Co. Saudi Arabia Ltd. This is a joint venture company with Hong Kong Middle East Holdings Ltd. The partners in Saudi Arabia are:
Sh. Abdullah Ibrahim Silsilah
Sh. Abdalaziz Abdullah Rajab
Sh. Abdalra'ouf Abu Zinada (q.v.)
Sh. Zaid Muhammad Al Sudairi
Sh. Saad Muhammad Al Mo'ajil (q.v.)
Sh. Abdalatif Banajah
Sh. Abdalrahman Turki

Bankers Arab Bank, National Commercial Bank, Riyadh Bank, Saudi Hollandi Bank, Saudi Britani Bank, First National City Bank.

The Family of SILSILAH

A family of Mecca.

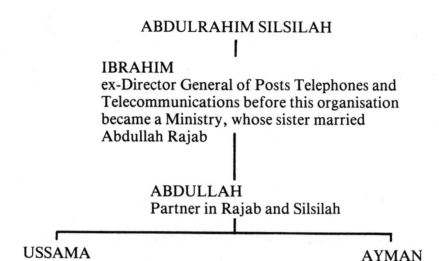

ABDULRAHIM SILSILAH

IBRAHIM
ex-Director General of Posts Telephones and
Telecommunications before this organisation
became a Ministry, whose sister married
Abdullah Rajab

ABDULLAH
Partner in Rajab and Silsilah

USSAMA   AYMAN

The Family of RAJAB.

A family of Jiddah.

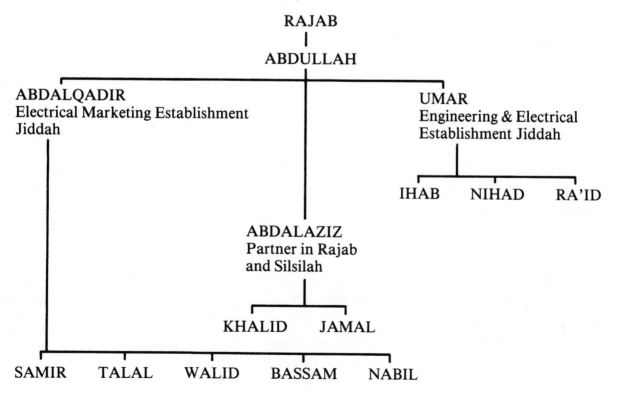

RAJAB

ABDULLAH

ABDALQADIR
Electrical Marketing Establishment
Jiddah

UMAR
Engineering & Electrical
Establishment Jiddah

IHAB   NIHAD   RA'ID

ABDALAZIZ
Partner in Rajab
and Silsilah

KHALID   JAMAL

SAMIR   TALAL   WALID   BASSAM   NABIL

S A Ashoor

Head office P.O. 1989 Jiddah
Telephone 28245
Cables RELSERVE

The publishing house of S A Ashoor is famous as the birthplace of the Saudi Economic Survey which is an indispensable adjunct to the business world of the Kingdom. The magazine was founded in February 1967 and has been produced weekly ever since. It is a reliable source of business statistics and reflects important economic views, containing marketing surveys and reproducing Government legislation when this is relevant to commerce. The Survey is distributed throughout Europe, the USA, Canada, Japan and Korea.

The Family of ASHOOR

A family of Mecca.

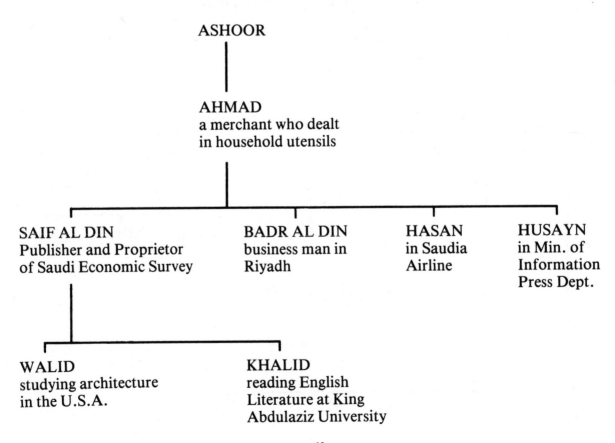

ASHOOR

AHMAD
a merchant who dealt
in household utensils

SAIF AL DIN
Publisher and Proprietor
of Saudi Economic Survey

BADR AL DIN
business man in
Riyadh

HASAN
in Saudia
Airline

HUSAYN
in Min. of
Information
Press Dept.

WALID
studying architecture
in the U.S.A.

KHALID
reading English
Literature at King
Abdulaziz University

Saddik and Mohamed Attar Co.

Address head office P.O. 439 Jiddah

Telephone 23244, 23437

Telex 401074 SJ

Board Members
Chairman Sh. Umr Attar who with Sh. Said Saddik owns 50% of the company. The remaining 50% is shared between the other members of the board:
Sh. Abdalrahim Mahmoud Attar
Sh. Mohamed Mahmoud Attar
Sh. Said Saddik Attar (Executive Director)
Sh. Saddik Umr (M.D. in Riyadh)
Sh. Sami Mahmoud (Executive Director)

Business Activity
Saddik and Mohamed Attar are General Service and Handling Agents for British Airways, S.A.S., Rock Airways, Kuwait Airways, Quantas, and Cyprus Air; and Handling Agents for Lufthansa, Korean Airlines, Olympic, and Air India and are thus the largest travel agents in the Kingdom.

They also operate a Shipping Department and their Commercial Department holds the Rolex agency and represents Diebold of the USA in the security systems and safes field. The company has invested extensively in real estate and is developing industrial interest. To date the principle activity in this field is the establishment of a formica factory.

Sh. Saddik Umr Attar and Sh. Hasan Umr Attar are 50/50 partners in a limited liability partnership called Al Attar Trading and Contracting Customs Clearing Public Services and Public Transport Company which is presently operating in the jewellery, watches and gifts field. The company is situated in Khalid bin Walid Street, Jiddah, and was registered in May 1979.

Bankers Saudi Faransi Bank.

Mansur Attar Fakhri Co. (MAFCO)

Address head office P.O. 2486 Jiddah

Telephone 45512

Telex 401593 FAKHRY SJ

Cable address COMMERCIAL

Chairman H.R.H. Prince Talal bin Mansur bin Abdalaziz al Sauwd

Board Members
Said Fakhri
Sami Mahmoud Attar
Abdalrahim Mahmoud Attar
Muhammad Mahmoud Attar

The company was founded to enter the construction field but also has a joint venture subsidiary called MAFCO, Gulf United Freight Systems, with an American company based in San Francisco. This subsidiary specializes in door to door delivery of goods, freight forwarding and packing. They act as agents for Medfurn at Heathrow. This is a branch of Medsales (UK) Ltd, Elseley House 24 Gt. Tichfield St., London, S.W.1., tel 01 580 9432. Medfurn in Jiddah are at P.O. 2951, tel. 55857, tx. 401082 SINDIC SJ.

In addition to these activities MAFCO Trade deals in cement, wood, sugar and other commodities in conjunction with Tennants Bank in London.

Bankers City Bank, National Commercial Bank.

The Family of ATTAR

They are descendants of the Caliph Abu Bakr who was the first successor to the Prophet Muhammad.

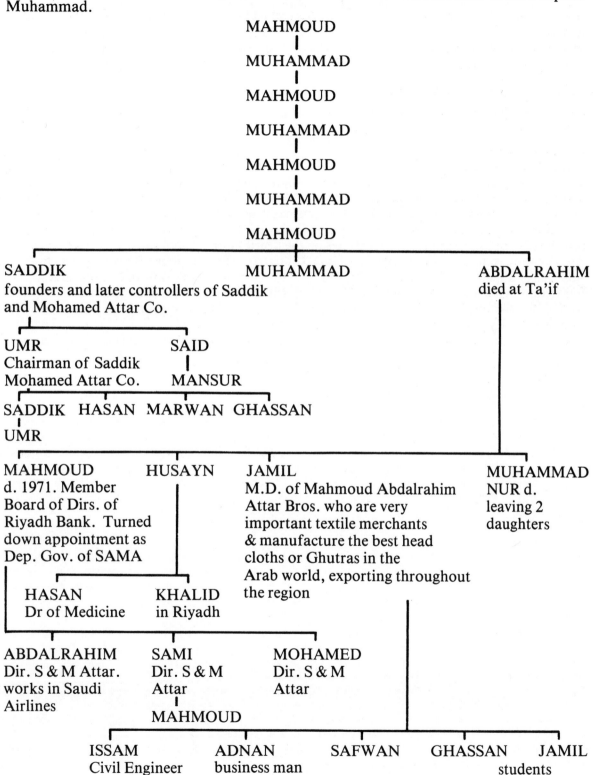

MAHMOUD

MUHAMMAD

MAHMOUD

MUHAMMAD

MAHMOUD

MUHAMMAD

MAHMOUD

SADDIK
founders and later controllers of Saddik and Mohamed Attar Co.

MUHAMMAD

ABDALRAHIM
died at Ta'if

UMR
Chairman of Saddik Mohamed Attar Co.

SAID

MANSUR

SADDIK   HASAN   MARWAN   GHASSAN

UMR

MAHMOUD
d. 1971. Member Board of Dirs. of Riyadh Bank. Turned down appointment as Dep. Gov. of SAMA

HUSAYN

JAMIL
M.D. of Mahmoud Abdalrahim Attar Bros. who are very important textile merchants & manufacture the best head cloths or Ghutras in the Arab world, exporting throughout the region

MUHAMMAD
NUR d. leaving 2 daughters

HASAN
Dr of Medicine

KHALID
in Riyadh

ABDALRAHIM
Dir. S & M Attar. works in Saudi Airlines

SAMI
Dir. S & M Attar

MOHAMED
Dir. S & M Attar

MAHMOUD

ISSAM
Civil Engineer

ADNAN
business man

SAFWAN

GHASSAN

JAMIL

students

43

International Publications Agencies

Address head office Said Salah Building, 28th Street Al Khobar; for airmail, P.O. 70 Dhahran Airport.

Telephone 41784, 46767

Telex 671229 SALAH SJ

Cable address SALAH AL KHOBAR

Subsidiary offices Jiddah, Beirut, Al Khobar, Singapore, Dubai

Proprietor Said H. Salah

Company History
Said Salah commenced operations in Jiddah in 1957 and in the following year established his business in the Eastern Province in Al Khobar. Initially he represented almost all newspapers and magazines of note and supplied the whole of Aramco. However he has relinquished most of this huge number of agencies and the business has developed into a noted publishing house in its own right and has invested in real estate. Today the I.P.A. publishes books and brochures in its own name and concentrates on the distribution of books and art work. Their latest venture is the construction of a new bookshop to be called Supreme Bookshop which will occupy a space of 1500 square metres and will thus almost certainly be one of the largest bookshops in the world. The Supreme Bookshop will display technical and social works in Arabic, English and French as well as children's books. I.P.A. also owns a large warehouse from which they re-export to Kuwait, Bahrain, the U.A.E. and Beirut and they are happy to extend credit facilities for the right projects. I.P.A. is on top of an expanding market and a most go-ahead and modern concern.

Turnover 15 million Saudi riyals

Bankers Arab Bank

The Family of AL SALAH

Originating in the Palestine Sanjac of the Ottoman Empire.

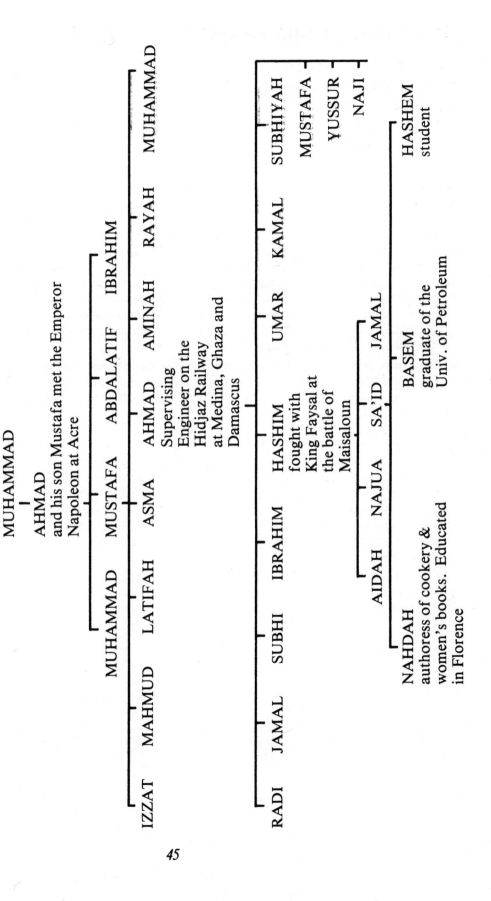

SAID BEY AL SALAH
a landowner in Lebanon, Syria and Palestine
honoured by the Ottoman Sultan of the day

MUHAMMAD

AHMAD
and his son Mustafa met the Emperor
Napoleon at Acre

MUSTAFA

ASMA — ABDALATIF — IBRAHIM

AHMAD
Supervising
Engineer on the
Hidjaz Railway
at Medina, Ghaza and
Damascus

AMINAH — RAYAH — MUHAMMAD

IZZAT — MAHMUD — LATIFAH — MUHAMMAD

RADI — JAMAL — SUBHI — IBRAHIM

HASHIM
fought with
King Faysal at
the battle of
Maisaloun

UMAR — KAMAL — SUBHIYAH — MUSTAFA — YUSSUR — NAJI

AIDAH — NAJUA — SA'ID — JAMAL

BASEM
graduate of the
Univ. of Petroleum

HASHEM
student

NAHDAH
authoress of cookery &
women's books. Educated
in Florence

45

Dr Solaiman Faqih Hospital

Address head office P.O. 2537 Jiddah

Telephone 61451, 61452/3/4

Telex 401433 FAQIH SJ

Cable address FAQIH

Proprietor Dr Solaiman Faqih

Board members
Dr Abdalmajid Hajar, Dr Jabir

Activities
The hospital was founded in 1976 and has a prominent position amongst the private hospitals in Jiddah. Dr Solaiman used to be in the Government Health Service and held positions as Director of the Giad and Maternity Hospitals in Mecca, and later he was transferred to Jiddah as General Director of the Western Region. He held this post for four years and then when a regulation appeared making it impossible to work both for the Government and in practice he resigned from administrative medicine and in conjunction with Goldfinch of the UK designed the present hospital. To begin with there was an enormous financial problem but a personal appeal by Dr Solaiman to H.M. King Faisal led to the Government arranging loans of up to half the cost for private hospitals.

Building took three years and installation had to be done three times to achieve the perfection seen today. Dr Solaiman recruits all the staff himself and has travelled the world in search of people. The present hospital is luxurious but in fact cheaper than many hotels. The combination of high standards of medical care, beautiful wards and cheap treatment leads to the hospital's 125 beds being full most of the time. The eight storeys contain three classes of room having their own washing facilities and television as well as comfortable facilities for visitors; all parts of the hospital are reached by lifts and gleaming marble corridors. The medical facilities can hardly be equalled anywhere and combine kitchens in the basement and a central sterile supply department. Facilities for out patients and internal medicine, paediatricians, obstetrics, gynaecology, ear nose and throat, cardiology and a dental clinic, physiotherapy, pathology, laboratory and a comprehensive pharmacy are all placed on the ground floor. The hospital operates its own X-ray department and a range of the most up-to-date operating theatres.

The future of private medicine seems assured in the Kingdom though the Government has recently put a ban on the erection of private hospitals of this sort as there are now enough of them to serve the present community.

The Family of FAQIH

An old family of Mecca descending from religious teachers as their name implies.

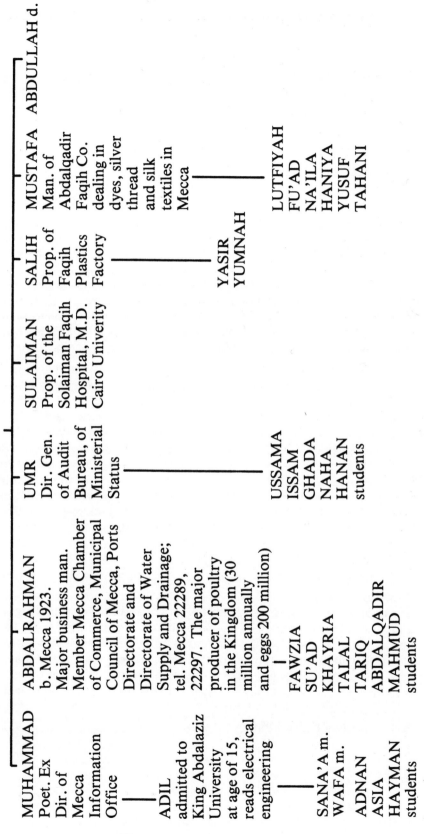

MUHAMMAD AL FAQIH

ABDULQADIR d. started a business which is carried on today by his son Mustafa

MUHAMMAD — Poet. Ex Dir. of Mecca Information Office
- ADIL — admitted to King Abdalaziz University at age of 15, reads electrical engineering
- SANA'A m. WAFA m. ADNAN ASIA HAYMAN students

ABDALRAHMAN — b. Mecca 1923. Major business man. Member Mecca Chamber of Commerce, Municipal Council of Mecca, Ports Directorate and Directorate of Water Supply and Drainage; tel. Mecca 22289, 22297. The major producer of poultry in the Kingdom (30 million annually and eggs 200 million)
- FAWZIA SU'AD KHAYRIA TALAL TARIQ ABDALQADIR MAHMUD students

UMR — Dir. Gen. of Audit Bureau, of Ministerial Status
- USSAMA ISSAM GHADA NAHA HANAN students

SULAIMAN — Prop. of the Solaiman Faqih Hospital, M.D. Cairo Univerity

SALIH — Prop. of Faqih Plastics Factory
- YASIR YUMNAH

MUSTAFA — Man. of Abdalqadir Faqih Co. dealing in dyes, silver thread and silk textiles in Mecca
- LUTFIYAH FU'AD NA'ILA HANIYA YUSUF TAHANI

ABDULLAH d.

Ahmad Mohamed Saleh Baeshen and Company

Address head office P.O. 18 Jiddah

Telephone 32964, 31471

Telex 401664 FRIEND SJ

Cable address AMEEN

Proprietor Partnership

Board Members
Su'ad Bint Ahmad Baeshen
Ahmad Abubaker Baeshen

Company History
The company was established in 1887.
The family moved to Jiddah from Hadramawt around 1790 because the father of Abdullah left his garden in Robat, Wadi Du'an, to a mosque he had built. This meant that his children had to earn their own living. Ali bin Abdullah began by importing rice, white flour and goods from India. He had a half share in a sailing dhow with one Muhammad Jawhar whose family has become extinct. In those days the dhows made two voyages each year and there were three main fleets in Jiddah, one sailing to Bombay and Calicut, one to Malabar and one to Basra for dates and barley. Ali prospered and built a compound for his own family in 1849 and another twenty years later in 1869. He died when he was ninety four years old.

Sh. Ahmad Muhammad Salih Baeshen, whose daughter and her husband are today the proprietors of the company that bears his name, is now seventy seven years of age and the main pillar of commercial history in Jiddah with a life span bridging the old and the new. In addition to the offices mentioned in the family tree he has sat in the Commercial Court and was a Member of the Board of Jiddah Municipality from 1933-1969. He remembers seeing Lawrence in Jiddah during the First World War and was a member of the delegation that welcomed King Abdalaziz when the city opened its gates after the Sharif Ali had fled.
Sh. Ahmad remembers the generosity and friendliness of the great king and recalls how he used to stay in Jiddah for the three Hajj months every year and how all the senior citizens were expected to lunch and dine with him every day. If someone was absent the King always enquired the reason and solved the problems of the day as they arose whilst chatting and joking with his guests. ʼSh. Ahmad also remembers with great amusement how the senior citizens of Jiddah once formed a committee to ban football because they considered it a waste of time and the younger generation should be found something more profitable to do.

Business Activity
The name of Baeshen is really famous for tea and they are the Kings of Tea in Saudi Arabia and throughout the region. The company imports and wholesales foodstuffs, ghee, coffee beans, sugar, evaporated and condensed milk, rice, wheat, butter, jams, marmalade, sweets, biscuits, fruit juice and tinned fruit. They also deal in soap and matches as well as polythene bags and textiles, gifts and general merchandise and are always keen to consider new commodities. However they rightly insist that these should be priced CIF Jiddah and any offer must be accompanied by samples.

Bankers Saudi Faransi Bank

The Family of BAESHEN

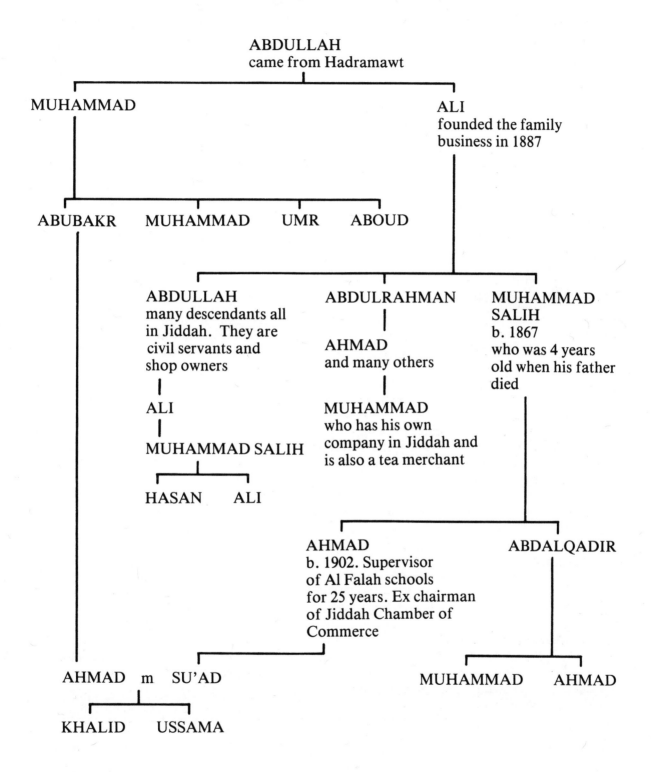

ABDULLAH
came from Hadramawt

MUHAMMAD

ALI
founded the family
business in 1887

ABUBAKR **MUHAMMAD** **UMR** **ABOUD**

ABDULLAH
many descendants all
in Jiddah. They are
civil servants and
shop owners

ALI

MUHAMMAD SALIH

HASAN **ALI**

ABDULRAHMAN

AHMAD
and many others

MUHAMMAD
who has his own
company in Jiddah and
is also a tea merchant

**MUHAMMAD
SALIH**
b. 1867
who was 4 years
old when his father
died

AHMAD
b. 1902. Supervisor
of Al Falah schools
for 25 years. Ex chairman
of Jiddah Chamber of
Commerce

ABDALQADIR

AHMAD m **SU'AD**

MUHAMMAD **AHMAD**

KHALID **USSAMA**

Al Sayed Abdullah Muhammad Baroom Company

Address head office P.O. 1346 Jiddah

Telephone 22366

Telex 401165 BAROOM SJ

Cable address PORTLAND JIDDAH

Subsidiary offices
Riyadh, Sitteen St., tel. 63873
Bahrain, tx. 9106 TRARAB BN
Cairo, tel. 934845, tx. 2421 BAROOM
London, tel. 01 486 2466, tx. 24458 BAROOM LDN
(6 Portman Towers, George St., London W 1)
New York, tel. 212 751 0566, tx. 236496 TUDR UR
Houston, tel. 713 795 5102-3, tx. 79 1125 USA

Proprietor and Chairman
Sayed Abdullah Muhammad Baroom

Vice Chairman
Sayed Ahmad Muhammad Baroom

Company History
The company was founded in 1955 and established agents throughout the Kingdom. Today they are one of the largest stockists of building materials in Saudi Arabia with an annual sales volume of nearly five hundred million riyals. The main company above now represents many international companies and is organised into three main divisions.
1. Baroom Shipping and Barges Division
which controls a fleet of fifteen barges and three motor vessels as well as operating as Shipping Agents.
2. Baroom Cranes and Transport Division
which owns some fifty tractors and trailers and fifteen cranes of capacities varying from twelve to a hundred and twenty tons.
3. Baroom Real Estate Division
which manages the considerable holdings in land and developed properties owned by the company, which last amount to about a hundred and fifty buildings and villas throughout the Kingdom.

In addition to the above Al Sayed Abdullah Muhammad Baroom has interests in the following other companies
1. Bilmat Saudi Arabia Establishment
This company is wholly owned by Sayed Abdullah Muhammad Baroom and is active in the construction business where it is presently involved in a 250 million riyal contract for the Presidency of Youth Welfare.
2. Saudi Steel Re-inforcement Ltd
Sayed Abdullah owns 75% of this joint venture and Helical Bar of the UK hold the remaining 25%. The company was established in 1978 with a capital of three million Saudi riyals and produces cut and bent steel to specification.
3. Jiddah Cement Company Ltd
Sayed Abdullah's company is a major shareholder in this enterprise which operates one of the largest floating terminals in the Middle East.

4. Saudi Construction Company

The headquarters of this company are in Riyadh and Sayed Abdullah Mohammad Baroom owns a 25% share of it.

5. Trans Arabian Bahrain and Trans Capital New York

The Baroom company is a founding member and holds the controlling interest in both these companies.

6. Red Sea Insurance Ltd of Hong Kong

Red Sea Development Company of Jiddah

Where the Baroom company are founding members and shareholders.

7. Nova Park AG

Al Sayed Abdullah Muhammad is a member of the Board of Directors and a main shareholder in this Zurich based international hotel chain group.

8. The Saudi National Maritime Transportation Company

Baroom is a founding member and holds 5515 shares.

9. Saudi Swiss Outworker Services

A majority shareholder and founding member, Al Sayed Abdullah Muhammad Baroom operates general maintenance services through this company throughout Saudi Arabia.

Bankers Saudi British Bank, National Commercial Bank, Bank Melli of Iran, Saudi Cario Bank.

The Family of BAROOM

A family of Sada (Sayyids, descendants of the Prophet Muhammad) who, though originating in the Holy City of Mecca more recently immigrated to Jiddah from the Wadi Du'an in Hadramawt.

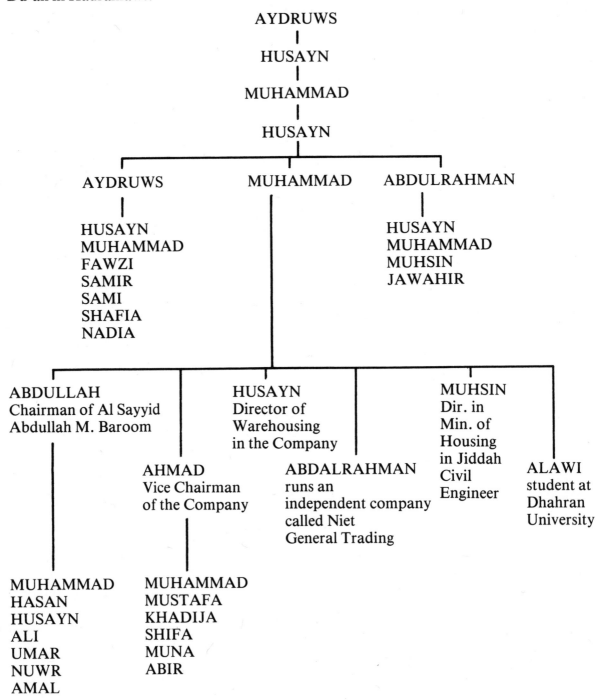

AYDRUWS
|
HUSAYN
|
MUHAMMAD
|
HUSAYN

AYDRUWS — MUHAMMAD — ABDULRAHMAN

HUSAYN
MUHAMMAD
FAWZI
SAMIR
SAMI
SHAFIA
NADIA

HUSAYN
MUHAMMAD
MUHSIN
JAWAHIR

ABDULLAH
Chairman of Al Sayyid
Abdullah M. Baroom

HUSAYN
Director of
Warehousing
in the Company

MUHSIN
Dir. in
Min. of
Housing
in Jiddah
Civil
Engineer

AHMAD
Vice Chairman
of the Company

ABDALRAHMAN
runs an
independent company
called Niet
General Trading

ALAWI
student at
Dhahran
University

MUHAMMAD
HASAN
HUSAYN
ALI
UMAR
NUWR
AMAL

MUHAMMAD
MUSTAFA
KHADIJA
SHIFA
MUNA
ABIR

Abdalatif Jamil Establishment

Address head office P.O. 248 Jiddah

Telephone 56119, 56151, 56154

Telex 401139 YOUSEF SJ

Cable address YOUSEF

Subsidiary offices

Jiddah Branch Office, tel. 72025, 72026, 73301, tx. 401139 YOUSEF SJ

Riyadh, tel. 65234, 64896/7, 61999, 64898, tx. 201237 YOUSEF SJ

Ta'if, tel. 20682, tx. 451021

Dammam, tel. 26657, 26920, 31318, 31658, 21004, tx. 601076

Al Khobar, tel. 47645, 47392

Mecca, tel. 20664

Hofuf, tel. 25160, tx. 661008

Jiddah Central Parts Dept, tel. 57285

London office: Jamil Organisation Ltd., 99 Bishopsgate London E.C.2M3XD, tel. 01 588 4239/4230

Proprietor Sh. Abdalatif Jamil

Board

Chairman Sh. Abdalatif Jamil

President Sh. Yusif Jamil

Deputy President Sh. Mohamed Jamil

Administration Director Khalid Habash

Marketing Director Shakir Nabulsi

Finance Director Colin Parker

Parts and Services Director Dennis Richmond

Company History

Sh. Abdalatif Jamil, who though over seventy is still energetically overseeing his company's activities, began as a clerk in Jiddah Customs. However, in about 1938 he resigned and with a joint capital of 8,000 riyals he and his friend Ali Dafa went into business as partners. With the advent of the Second World War importing became almost impossible and apart from the distribution of aid from the USA and UK, Jiddah merchants were reduced to getting what goods they could from passing ships. Eventually this trade, long winked at by the Saudi Government, became legal. After the war the partnership concentrated on spare parts for American cars and developed into an association between Sh. Abdulatif and his brothers. This lasted until 1952 by which time they had established the first petrol station and the largest mechanical workshops in the Kingdom and were agents for Pirelli Tyres, Oldham Batteries, spare parts and Plutolite of the USA. In 1952 Sh. Abdalatif went into business by himself and acquired the Vittiwinkle paints agency from Holland and dealt in various goods from the UK and serviced Government tenders. At this time he was to build the largest petrol station in the Kingdom. In 1954 he held the Borgward Isabella agency but relinquished it after a year; he then acquired a sub-dealership from Chrysler. It was in 1955 that he imported the first Toyota. This was a Landcruiser and his first customer was H.R.H. Prince Khalid ibn Abdalaziz al Sa'ud who is now the King of Saudi Arabia.

Agencies

Toyota of Japan, represented throughout their range including fork lift trucks.

Kubota of Japan, agricultural equipment, generators and tractors.

MAN of Munich, West Germany, trucks.

Other interests include ownership of Jamil Housing Projects in Jiddah and Riyadh, each comprising 150 villas, shipowning and shipping agency. Under construction is a freighter for 4,000 cars. This is being built in Japan.

Bankers National Commercial Bank, Citibank, Arab Bank, Saudi Cairo Bank, Saudi British Bank, Riyadh Bank, Leitz Bank, First National City Bank of Chicago, BBME London and Geneva, Chase Manhattan, American Express, Bank of America, and Manufacturers Hanover Trust Company.

The Family of JAMIL

A family whose origins go to the Saadi of Palestine in the early part of the nineteenth century.

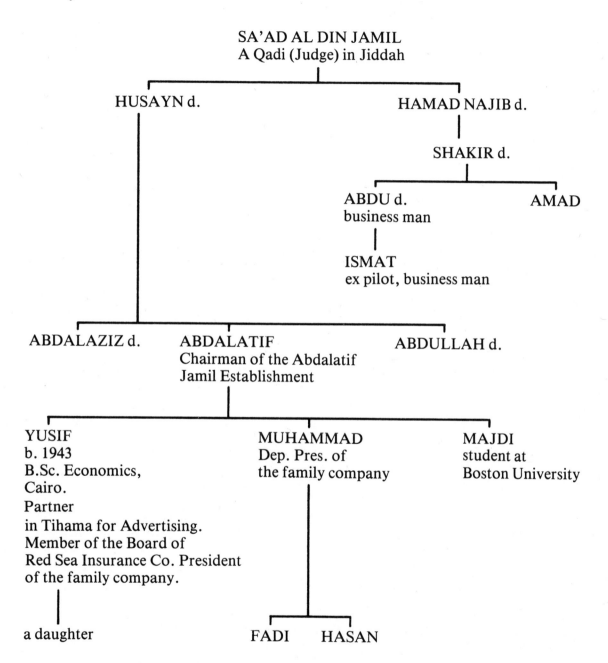

SA'AD AL DIN JAMIL
A Qadi (Judge) in Jiddah

HUSAYN d.

HAMAD NAJIB d.

SHAKIR d.

ABDU d.
business man

AMAD

ISMAT
ex pilot, business man

ABDALAZIZ d.

ABDALATIF
Chairman of the Abdalatif
Jamil Establishment

ABDULLAH d.

YUSIF
b. 1943
B.Sc. Economics,
Cairo.
Partner
in Tihama for Advertising.
Member of the Board of
Red Sea Insurance Co. President
of the family company.

MUHAMMAD
Dep. Pres. of
the family company

MAJDI
student at
Boston University

a daughter

FADI   HASAN

Al Esayi Trading Corporation

Address P.O. 1342 Jiddah

Telephone 78444, 78662, 72201

Telex 401063 ESAYCO SJ

Cable AL ESAYCO

Proprietors The company is a partnership between Sh. Ali Abdullah Al Esayi 50% and Sh. Omar Qasim Al Esayi 50%.

Activity
The company was founded in 1961 and is engaged in operating the following agencies:
Chrysler cars and trucks.
Mitsubishi cars, trucks, and excavators.
Tokyu, cranes.
Newplan of West Germany, buses. Arrangements have been made to supply SATCO, the partly Government owned Saudi Arabian Transport Company.

Bankers National Commercial Bank, Al Jazira Bank, Citibank.

The partners have other commercial interests apart from this company.

Sh. Ali Abdullah Al Esayi
Canada Dry Factory, Nitto Tyres, textiles, Concord tyres, Armstrong Tyres, Tongshin of Korea (tyres), Ureidestin of Holland (tyres), CEAT of Italy (tyres), General (air conditioners).

Sh. Omar Qasim Al Esayi industrial interests
A founder of Saudi Arabian Carpets Factory, Saudi Ceramic in Riyadh, the Yanbo Cement Co., the Saudi Vegetable Oil and Ghee Co., MARWA advertising (q.v.), The Canada Dry Factory in Riyadh and Dammam which is a joint venture with Bugshan Bros. called the Arabian Beverage Corporation.

Investments
1. The Yemen
The Yemen Marketing and Trading Co. which is a partnership. He is a shareholder in the Yemen Ghee and Soap Co., the National Company for Plastic and Sponge Ltd, ARWA for Mineral Water and ARWA for Aluminium.
2. Lebanon
Broadway Centre, Omar Al Esayi and Partners, Beirut, The Astral Centre, Beirut.
3. France
A building at 65 Avenue Dlena, Paris.
4. United Kingdom
Jiddah International Trading Services, 49 Park Lane, London W 1, tel. 01 499 7546, tx. 266038 JIT G.

Other interests include partnership in the Maternity and Children's Hospital, Jiddah, and as a founder of the Red Sea Insurance Company. Both partners also have very valuable Real Estate Holdings.

Other Companies
1. Omaco, Omar Al Esayi Trading and General Contracting which is wholly owned.
2. Omar Saudi Trading Corporation which is owned 50/50 with Muhammad bin Shayhoon and is engaged in tyres and batteries.
3. Omar Al Esayi for clothes and textiles which is wholesale.

4. Omar Al Esayi for engineering and architectural contracting (q.v.).
5. Al Esayi Saif Noman (q.v.).
6. The Saudi French Company which is a joint venture with Jean Lefebure and Bugshan Bros and H.R.H. Prince Sa'ud bin Na'if bin Abdalaziz Al Sa'ud. This company is engaged in road construction in Yemen.
7. National Trading Construction and Development Company which is engaged in general construction and the operation of commercial agencies.
P.O. 2926 Jiddah, tel. 52304, Riyadh branch 36304. Apart from Sh. Omar Al Esayi the other members of the Board of Directors are: Chairman Sh. Salim Ahmad Buqshan, Sh. Sulaiman Abdalaziz Rajhi, Sh. Khalid bin Salim bin Mahfouz, Sh. Ali Abdullah Buqshan, Sh. Salih Abdalaziz Al Rajhi, Sh. Mohammed Salim bin Mahfouz.

Marwah

Address head office P.O. 3029 Jiddah

Telephone 57908, 676100, 693500

Telex 400321 MARWAN SJ

Cable address MARWALAN

Subsidiary offices
Riyadh, tel. 4780842
Dammam P.O. 4618, tel. 28796, tx. 670028 WATEUA SJ

The company is owned by the following partners who all have equal shares. Those with an asterisk are members of the controlling board.

Sh. Ahmad Salah Jamjoom, E A Juffali and Bros. where *Sh. Ali is the representative amongst Marwah partners, Sh. Abdulaziz Abdullah Al Salim, Sh. Mohammad Al Abdulrahman, Sh. Mohammed Al Abdulrahman Al Firaih, Sh. Mohammed Al Abdalaziz Al Hamidi, Sh. Mariee Abdullah Buqshan, Sh. Umran Muhammad Al Umran, Sh. Ahmad Hamad Al Hoshan, Sh. Fahad Al Abdullah Al Solaiman, Saudi Economic and Development Company, *Sh. Hamza Muhammad Bogari, Sh. Ahmad Abdalwahab Abdalwasa, Rajab and Silsilah, Sh. Omar Qasim Al Esayi, *Sh. Ayad Amin Madan, Sh. Abdullah Mohamed Al Hoqail, Sh. Mutlaq Al Abdullah Al Mutlaq, *Sh. Ahmad Mohammad Mahmud Ahmad, Sh. Abdalaziz Abdullah Hanafi, *Sh. Mohammad Salahuddin Hussain Omar who is the Managing Director.

Marwah was licensed in February 1979 and is the successor of Mecca Advertising. It has been established with a paid up capital of four million riyals and operates a complete in-house advertising service comprising creative work, photography, typesetting and the making of litho film. Their intention is to incorporate a printing press and the manufacture of neon signs.

Bankers National Commercial Bank, Riyadh Bank

Omar K Al Esayi for Engineering and Architectural Contracting

Address head office P.O. 2837 Jiddah

Telephone 22698, 25408

Telex 401547 SAIF SJ

Cable address OMAR AL ESAYI

Proprietor
Sh. Omar K Al Esayi
General Manager Sh. Saif Noman Said
Asst. General Manager Said Ahmad Noman

Company History
The company is an old and well established business in the contracting field. In 1976 a company was formed called Saif Noman Said and Partners which operates two plants producing Hollowcore as a joint venture with Holloware and J.R.C. of the UK. The plants are in Jiddah and Riyadh. This company is a partnership between Sh. Omar Esayi, Sh. Saif Noman Said, Sh. Mohammad Salim Mahfouz and Sh. Khalid Salim Mahfouz. A third part of this group is called the Saif Noman Said For Trade Establishment (P.O. 4544, tel. 22698, 25408, tx. 401547 SAIF SJ). This company specializes in the provision of building materials. The fourth member of the group is Al Esayi Saif Noman Company which is a joint venture with Douglas of Birmingham UK and is a contracting and civil engineering concern.

Bankers National Commercial Bank

The Family of AL ESAYI

The family originates in Upper Yafa from the Bani Malik though the present members have been citizens of the Kingdom for over a quarter of a century, and first began business in Jiddah 35 years ago. The two branches of the family represented by the partners in the Al Esayi Trading Corporation are related as cousins.

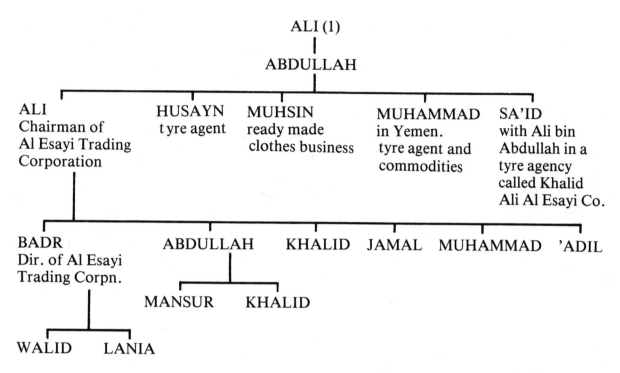

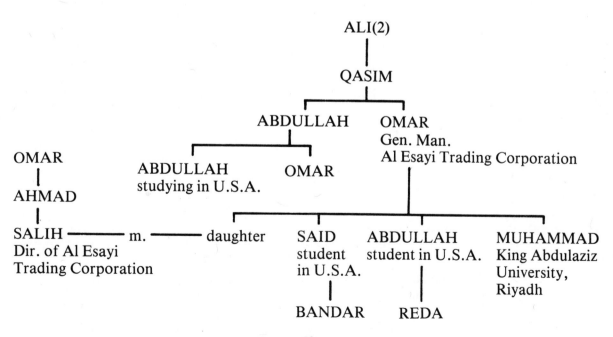

The Family of SAIF NOMAN SAID

The family originates from Hujariya near Ta'iz in Yemen.

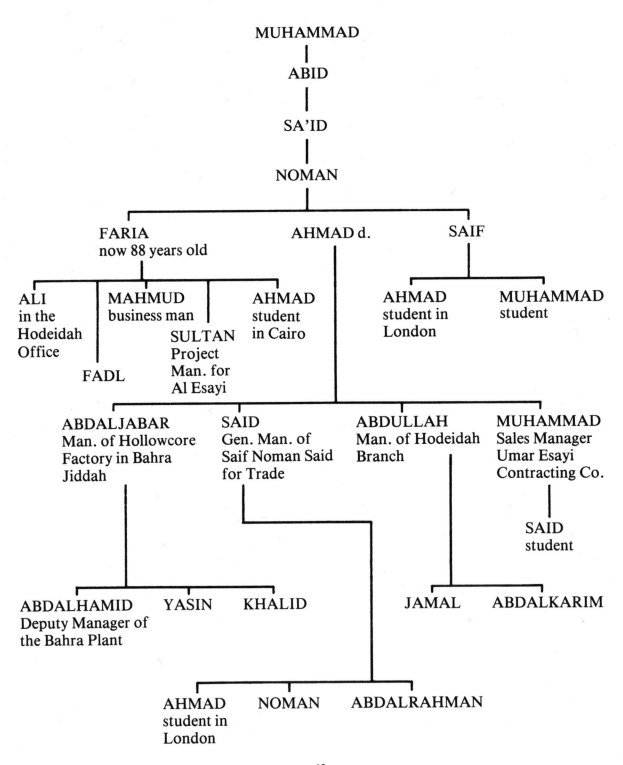

Abdullah Abbar and Ahmad Zainy

Address head office P.O. 461 Jiddah

Telephone 50143, 50296, 57354, 57353

Telex 401062 MOTASIM SJ

Cable address MOATASIM

Subsidiary offices
30 New Bond Street, London W 1, 01 493 8853, tx. 28583 MUTSIM, Riyadh, Dammam Al Kharj, Al Qatif, Buraidah, Dhahran, Hofuf, Jizan, Jubail, Mecca, Medina, Ras al Khafji, Tabuk, Ta'if, Yanbo.

Proprietor
The partnership between Sh. Abdullah Abbar and Sh. Ahmad Zainy.

The company is one of the largest trading companies in the Kingdom. Since the date of its foundation nearly forty years ago the company has been subject to enormous expansion from its original areas of interest which were in the fields of household and electrical appliances as well as foodstuffs. Today Abbar and Zainy are engaged in manufacturing, shipping, transport, construction and services to the oil industry. Their activities are currently subject to rationalisation and fall under the following company heads:

1. Abbar and Zainy
Acts as agent for over 400 overseas companies and deals as trader in food and other consumer goods, as wholesalers in catering, provisions, ship chandling, electrical, mechanical and agricultural equipment and electrical appliances.
2. Abbar and Zainy Catering
3. Abbar and Zainy Cold Stores
In addition to refrigerated stores they also operate their own reefer ships.
4. Abbar and Zainy Computers
Acting as representatives for Digital USA.
5. Abbar and Zainy MAK Maschinenbau
An Agency with a Krupp subsidiary for diesel engines.
6. Abbar and Zainy Sodexho Catering Co. Ltd.
A J/V with the famous French Company
7. Abbar and Zainy Star Groceries
Food retail and other goods.
8. Abbar and Zainy US Beef
Imports the finest American beef by air.
9. Arab International Gas and Transportation Ltd.
This company operates from a London office at 38 Dover Street (491 3389) and controls the brokerage of international transportation of liquid petroleum gas and petrochemicals.
10. Chiyoda Petrostar Co. Ltd.
A joint venture involved in petrochemical and refinery engineering construction and related activities with Chiyoda Chemical Engineering and Construction Co. Ltd. of Japan.
11. Ice Cream and Dairy Products Cortina Ltd.
Dairy Products.
12. Industry services, maintenance of gas turbines, gas/oil pumping equipment, electrical power generators where they represent Westinghouse Electric Corporation of the USA and Switzerland.
13. National Tahina and Tin Co.
Manufacture of local confectionery and cans.

14. Ogem Saudi Arabian Construction Co. Ltd.
A joint venture with Ogem BV of the Netherlands.
15. Patents International Affiliates (Saudi Arabia) Ltd.
Exhibition consultants.
16. Petrostar Co. Ltd.
This company owns tankers and operates bunkering of marine and aviation fuels as well as the marketing and transhipment of refined products.
17. Saudi Aviation Services Co. (SASCO)
Airport services operating buses for all airlines except Saudia and executive services.
18. Saudi Meat Factory
Meat Importation and Processing
19. Saudi Multina Gas and Transportation Co. Ltd.
Joint venture with Marine Service GmbH and Co. of West Germany for the marine transportation of LPG and LNG.
20. Star Navigation Co. Ltd.
Shipping agents, marine services and port management where they are currently running the temporary port at Yanbo.
21. Saudi Security and Technical Services Co. Ltd.
Dealing in insurance brokerage as a joint venture with Sedgwick Forbes Middle East Ltd. of the Bahamas.
22. United Arab Agencies (UNITAR)
Dealing as agents, trading and wholesaling commodities, indenting transport and services.
23. United Arab Agencies Construction Division
Construction and Engineering in the field of urban development.
24. Wadi Fatima Layer Project
Produces thirty five million eggs a year.

The Family of ZAINY

An old family of the Hidjaz, Wadi Fatima.

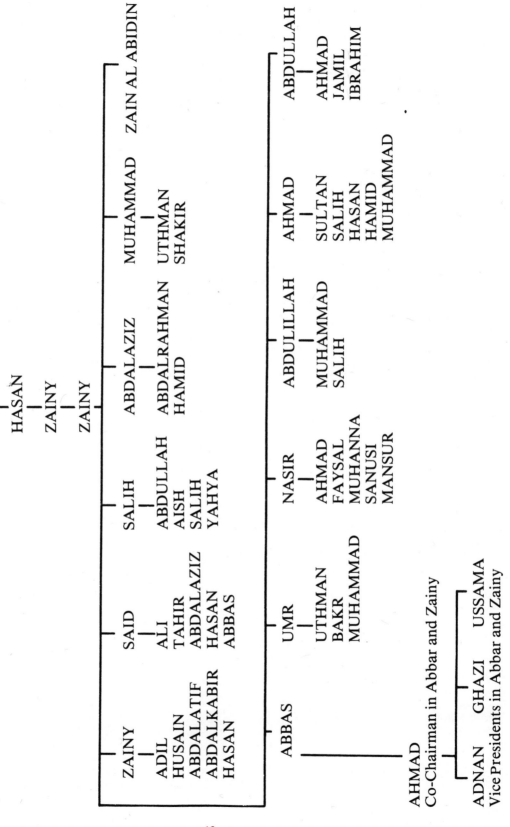

Mahmoud Salih Abbar Co.

Address head office P.O. 481 Jiddah

Telephone 50143, 50296, 57354, 57353

Telex 401790 ABARJO SJ

Cable address ABBAR

Subsidiary offices Mecca, Medina, Yanbo, Riyadh

Board of Directors
Chairman Sh. Mahmoud Salih Al Abbar
Dir. and Ch. Executive Sh. Khalid Ahmad Al Abbar
Director Sh. Ahmad Mahmoud Al Abbar
Director Sh. Abdullah Mahmoud Al Abbar
Director Sh. Reda Mahmoud Al Abbar

Company History
Began 22 years ago. Founded in Jiddah by M S Abbar.

Business Activity
The company operates over the whole field of electrical matters. These activities cover trading, especially in household appliances and central air conditioning machinery, maintenance and installation. They represent White Westinghouse and their technical capabilities extend to turbine installation. The company, called ABBAR for short, is a leader in their area and their energetic use of management skills enhances their wide experience which has been accumulated over many years. They are particularly well known in all areas of refrigeration including refrigerated transport, cold-stores and rooms. They are shareholders in the Saudi British Bank.

Bankers Saudi Faransi, Jazira Bank, First National City, National Commercial Bank, Saudi Cairo Bank.

The Family of ABBAR

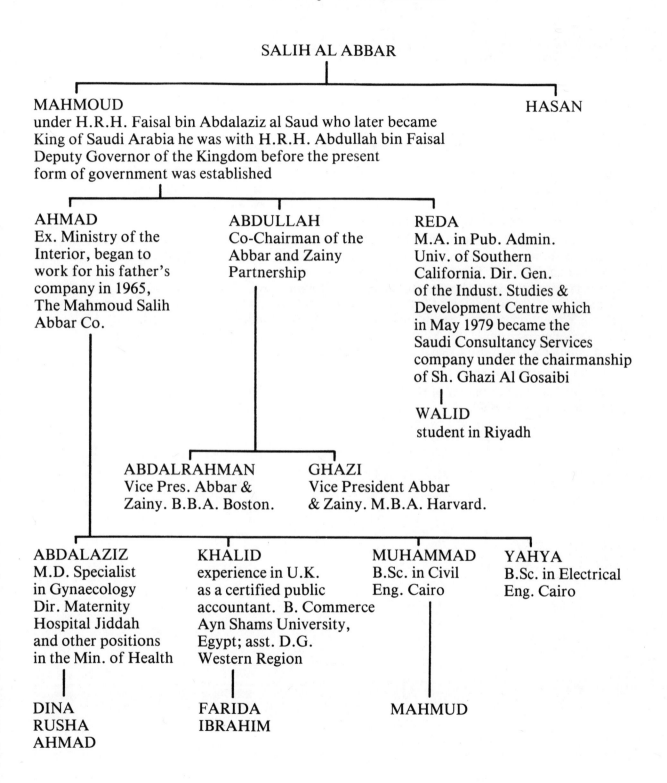

SALIH AL ABBAR

MAHMOUD
under H.R.H. Faisal bin Abdalaziz al Saud who later became
King of Saudi Arabia he was with H.R.H. Abdullah bin Faisal
Deputy Governor of the Kingdom before the present
form of government was established

HASAN

AHMAD
Ex. Ministry of the
Interior, began to
work for his father's
company in 1965,
The Mahmoud Salih
Abbar Co.

ABDULLAH
Co-Chairman of the
Abbar and Zainy
Partnership

REDA
M.A. in Pub. Admin.
Univ. of Southern
California. Dir. Gen.
of the Indust. Studies &
Development Centre which
in May 1979 became the
Saudi Consultancy Services
company under the chairmanship
of Sh. Ghazi Al Gosaibi

WALID
student in Riyadh

ABDALRAHMAN
Vice Pres. Abbar &
Zainy. B.B.A. Boston.

GHAZI
Vice President Abbar
& Zainy. M.B.A. Harvard.

ABDALAZIZ
M.D. Specialist
in Gynaecology
Dir. Maternity
Hospital Jiddah
and other positions
in the Min. of Health

KHALID
experience in U.K.
as a certified public
accountant. B. Commerce
Ayn Shams University,
Egypt; asst. D.G.
Western Region

MUHAMMAD
B.Sc. in Civil
Eng. Cairo

YAHYA
B.Sc. in Electrical
Eng. Cairo

DINA
RUSHA
AHMAD

FARIDA
IBRAHIM

MAHMUD

Eastern Corporation for Trading Contracting and Industry

Address head office P.O. 792 Riyadh

Telephone 23473, 23475

Telex 201089 ETCORP SJ

Cable address ETCORPE

Subsidiary office Dammam P.O. 375, tel. 26441, tx. 601565 ECHSSA SJ

Proprietors
Sh. Muhammad bin Abdalrahman Al Fraih 50%
Sh. Muhammad bin Abdalaziz Al Dughaithar Al Hasan 50%

Sh. Muhammad Al Fraih is the President of the Chamber of Commerce in Riyadh and a partner in the Saudi Ceramic Company. He is also a member of the board of the Saudi Hollandi Bank, the Saudi Banque of Paris, MABCO, the Nissah Co, al Alamiya Insurance Company and the Lightweight Concrete Company.

The Eastern Corporation of which Sh. Muhammad Al Fraih is Managing Director was started in 1966 and is divided into two main divisions: a construction division and a commercial division. This last contains a considerable travel section. The company represents the following interests: Hawker Siddeley Power Engineering, Hawker Siddeley Electric Export Ltd., Brush Switchgear Ltd., Brush Electrical Machines, Brush Power Equipment, Brush Transformers Ltd., Brush Fusegear Ltd., Hawker Siddeley Power Transformers Ltd., South Wales Switchgear, Yorkshire Electric Transformers Co. Ltd., Crow Hamilton and Co. Ltd., all in the UK. Also Cremar of Italy and Waste Management of the USA.

Turnover 30 million Saudi riyals

Bankers National Commercial Bank, Riyadh Bank, Saudi Hollandi Bank, Saudi Faransi Bank, First National City Bank.

The Family of AL FRAIH

Originate by descent from Tamim and came to Riyadh some forty years ago from Anaiza.

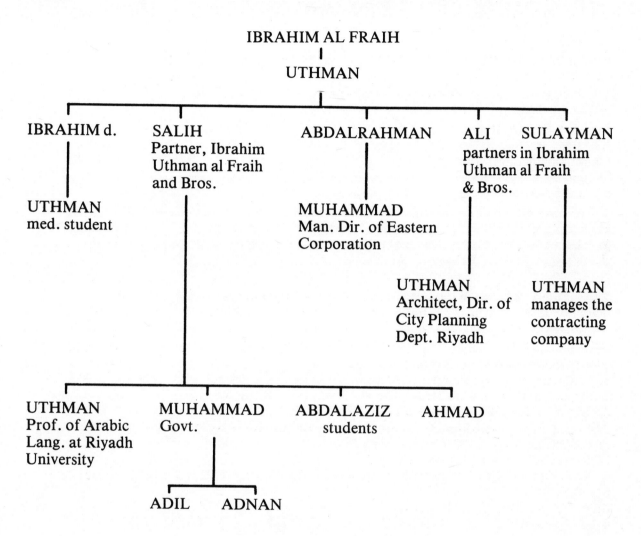

IBRAHIM AL FRAIH

UTHMAN

IBRAHIM d.

SALIH
Partner, Ibrahim
Uthman al Fraih
and Bros.

ABDALRAHMAN

ALI   SULAYMAN
partners in Ibrahim
Uthman al Fraih
& Bros.

UTHMAN
med. student

MUHAMMAD
Man. Dir. of Eastern
Corporation

UTHMAN
Architect, Dir. of
City Planning
Dept. Riyadh

UTHMAN
manages the
contracting
company

UTHMAN
Prof. of Arabic
Lang. at Riyadh
University

MUHAMMAD
Govt.

ABDALAZIZ
students

AHMAD

ADIL   ADNAN

Abdalmuhsin Abdullah Al Mutlaq and Bros.

Address head office P.O. 153 Al Khobar

Telephone 43254, 41077, 44360, 44253

Telex 670015 MUTLAQ S J

Subsidiary offices
Riyadh P.O. 1321, tel. 28800, tx. 201179 MUTLAQ S J
Jiddah P.O. 4645, tel. 55236

The operation is controlled by the holding company, Al Mutlaq Brothers.

Board of Directors
President Sh. Abdalmuhsin A Al Mutlaq
Vice President Sh. Mutlaq A Al Mutlaq
Sh. Muhammad A Al Mutlaq
Sh. Sulaiman A Al Mutlaq
Na'aman A Hantouli

The company was formed some thirty years ago in Al Khobar by the two men who are now President and Vice President of what has become the holding company. Sh. Abdalmuhsin is a member of the Board of the Dammam Chamber of Commerce and Sh. Mutlaq a member of the Board of Riyadh Chamber of Commerce.

Business Activity
The various companies in the Group cover a wide field of interests which include the manufacture of and trading in furniture, building construction, furnishing and contracting. The supply of steel buildings, industrial engineering services, the manufacture of automobile radiators, electrical engineering, real estate and the representation of foreign companies.

The Al Mutlaq Group of Companies
1. Al Mutlaq Furniture Company, which trades in furniture, Riyadh P.O. 1321, tel. 28800, 28100, tx. 201179 MUTLAQ S J
Man. Dir. Sh. Mutlaq A Al Mutlaq
2. Al Mutlaq Furniture Manufacturing Company, Industrial Zone, Dammam P.O. 710, tel. 27808, 28640, tx. 601492 MUTLAQ S J
Man. Dir. Sh. Abdalmuhsin A Al Mutlaq
3. Al Mutlaq Bossert Construction Company Ltd, Riyadh P.O. 1321, tel. 64127, tx. 201179 MUTLAQ S J
Man. Dir. Sh. Mutlaq A Al Mutlaq
4. Al Mutlaq Real Estate, Al Khobar P.O. 153, tel. 41226, tx. 670015 MUTLAQ S J
Man. Dir. Sh. Muhammad A Al Mutlaq
5. SISCO (Saudi Industrial Service Company), Dhahran Airport P.O. 319, tel. 44252, tx. 671311 MUTLAQ S J
Man. Dir. Sh. Muhammad A Al Mutlaq
Supply of warehouses and oil industry servicing.
6. SAPAT (Saudi Pan-Arab Technologists), Dhahran Airport P.O. 429, tel. 43075, tx. 671265 MUTLAQ S J
Man. Dir. Mr Ray Landen
Engineering and power station supply.
7. Al Mutlaq Design Decorating and Furnishing Company, Riyadh P.O. 1321, tel. 28192, tx. 201179 MUTLAQ S J
Man. Dir. Sh. Mutlaq A Al Mutlaq

The Family of AL MUTLAQ

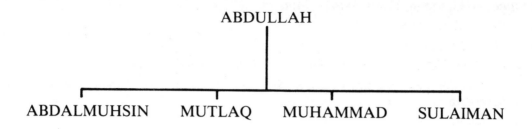

ABDULLAH

ABDALMUHSIN   MUTLAQ   MUHAMMAD   SULAIMAN

8. Lugano Office (Giovi SA), Riva A Caccia 1, 6900 Lugano, Switzerland, tel. 091 546341/2, tx. 73992 GIOVICH
Swiss liaison office.
9. Al Mutlaq Brothers (UK) Ltd, 7 Old Park Lane, London W1Y 3LJ, England,
tel. 01 499 5894/5, tx. 299123 MUTLAQ G.
British liaison office.

The offices in Switzerland and the UK service the Saudi companies and also offer the services of the Group to business men visiting Saudi Arabia.

Al Haramain Company

Address head office P.O. 2233 Jiddah

Telephone 54415, 58896, 51169, 53147, 50196

Telex 401404 ZIRWAH SJ

Cable address AL ZARWA

Subsidiary offices Riyadh, tel. 64737, Ta'if P.O. 940, tel. 25610, 65604

Proprietor The Company is a partnership between Sh. Abdalrahman Muhammad Al Howaish and Sh. Salih Ibrahim Zamil

Company History

The company was founded in 1958 and registered in 1962 and is a leader in the contracting and construction field. Their main activity is the building and maintenance of roads in which area they operate several contracts in Turbah, Dalam, Aqiq and Afif. However their main importance is their participation as main contractors with Sh. Muhammad Aboud Al Amoudi and Letco in the major project of 'New Jiddah'. At the present time they are involved in the first phase which is the construction of 870 villas. Haramain also operates a Technical Trading Division, tel. 51192, telex as above, which holds an agency for Friedrich air conditioners which the company imports from the USA and sells and maintains in the Western Province. They are also agents for Diakin air conditioners from Japan. This division replaces YINC. Haramain also operate a real estate office, tel. 51169.

Partnerships

1. Insulation Factory making polystyrene in partnership with Sh. Abdalrahman Sayyigh
2. Metal Work Factory making metal water tanks, trailers and tippers in partnership with Sh. Ali Thunayan.
3. Saudi Metal which is engaged in the provision of spare parts for heavy equipment. In partnership with Sh. Abdullah Miman.
4. The Jiddah Shopping Centre in partnership with Sh. Hasan Mahmud Arif.

The Family of HOWAISH

Emanating from Anaiza in Najd.

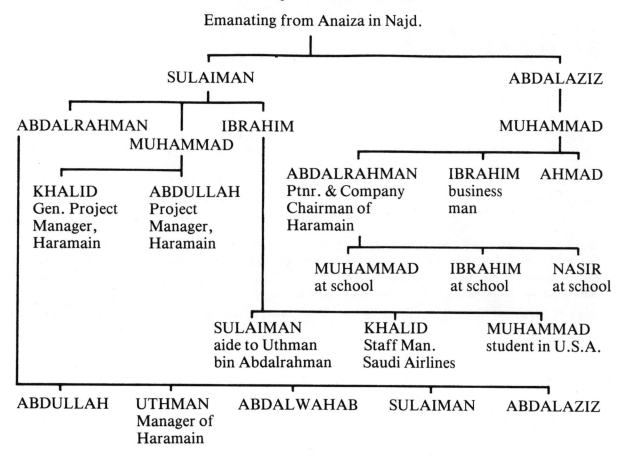

The Family of ZAMIL

This branch of the Zamil family is called the Al Mansur and emanates from Anaiza.

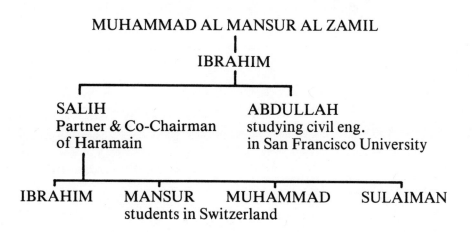

Khazindar Distributing Establishment

Head office P.O. 157 Jiddah

Telephone 74093, 71869

Subsidiary offices
Riyadh, tel. 24502, 24853, tx. 201319 SJ
Al Khobar, tel. 41746 P.O. 1036
Also branches in Mecca, Ta'if, Khamis Mushait, Yanbo, Medina, Tabuk and Buraidah.

The present company was formed in 1958 but grew out of the now defunct Dabbus Stores which owned the company from 1952. Khazindar are the most comprehensive distributors of books, newspapers and periodicals in the Kingdom. This they accomplish both directly through their modern and attractive shops in the main cities and through a very wide net of sub agents who cover the whole of the Kingdom. They act as sole agents for a wide range of material from English, Arab, French, American, German and Italian sources acting as distributors for the following:
Hatchette Gotch, Comag, Hatchette International, World Wide Media, Luchelle, International Herald Tribune, Time, OUP, Newsweek, International Communications, Burda, Bush Hansa, Agencie Internazionale Italiana, Rizzoli Editori, Rasconi Editori, Correra della Sera, Transworld, C.B.S., Feffer Symonds, Dell.

Bankers National Commercial Bank, Saudi Cairo Bank, Saudi Faransi Bank, Al Jazira Bank.

The Family of KHAZINDAR

Originating in Saudi Arabia the family name derives from two Turkish words meaning Guardian of the Treasury and probably dates to the Turkish administration in the Hidjaz or to the Sherifian administration which continued the use of Turkish nomenclature in official designations.

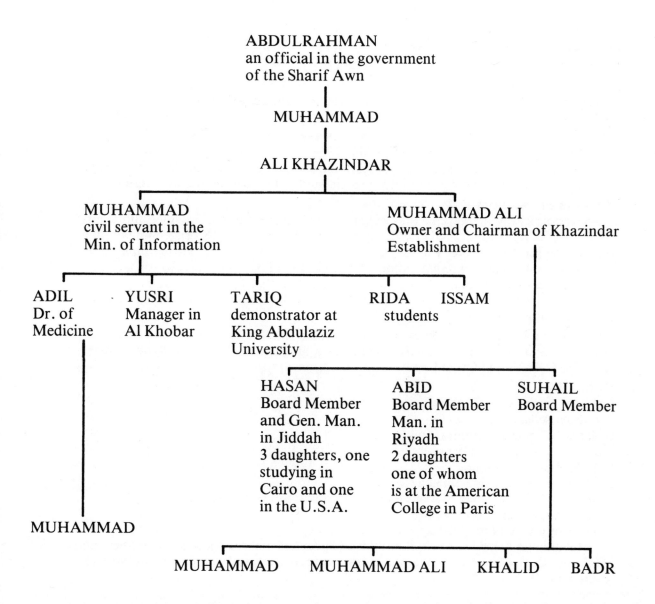

Saudi Arabian Markets

Head office P.O. 65 Jiddah

Telephone 23140, 23603

Cable MARKETS

Telex 401067 MARKET SJ

Branches
Riyadh P.O. 48, tel. 27860, 27820, tx. 201271 MARKET SJ
Al Khobar P.O. 246, tel. 41913, 42257, tx. 670065 MARKET SJ

Proprietor Sh. Muhammad Ashmawi and family

Company History
Saudi Arabian Markets, or SAM as it is called by everyone, was founded by Sh. Ahmad Ashmawi in 1947. His son, Sh. Muhammad, entered the business after schooling at Victoria College in Egypt. In 1960 he took over first as secretary general and then as general manager. On his father's death he became chairman in 1961.

Sh. Muhammad has been immensely successful in securing contracts and in diversifying an originally agency oriented business into financial and technological areas of interest.

Activities and Agencies
SAM represents and markets the following products. In the Western Province, lubricants for Shell, cars for Rolls Royce, Alfa Romeo and Aston Martin, Dexion Storage Systems, diesel engines and generator sets of R.A. Lister in the Western Province and Mosler International security systems. They represent Simplex Time Recorder Ltd and G.A. Harvey Office Furniture Ltd, Lansing Bagnall Fork Lift Trucks of UK, Lista Furniture and Trojan of the USA for motor boats and yachts, Foseco Minsep Co. chemical building products, Kalamazoo Ltd and Shinko chain-link fencing.

The company acts as General Sales Agents for Sudan Airways in the Western Province, Overseas National Airways and Air Canada. They are handling agents for Syrian Arab Airways, Gulf Air and Cargo Lux.

Partnerships
SAM are partners in the following companies:
Peninsula Aviation Services Co.
Granada Trading and Contracting
Jehan Contracting and Decoration
First Arabian Corporation
Hispanarabian Tankers Shipping Co.
Taylorplan Saudi Arabian Markets (with Taylorplan the UK Catering company)
Tihama Advertising Corporation
Cairo Establishment for Trading and Contracting
Sh. Muhammad Ashmawi is also chairman and proprietor of the National Investment and Marketing Company which specializes in real estate, real estate development and project investment.

The Family of ASHMAWI

Descending from early Arabian immigrants to Egypt the family originates in the Abu Sa'id of Hama'il.

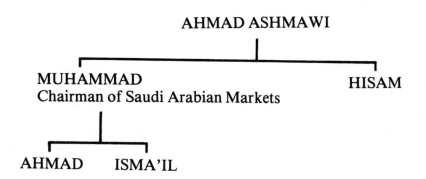

Al Rashid Company

Address head office P.O. 610 Riyadh

Telephone 22261, 20109

Telex 201260 RAMEZ SJ

Cable address RAMEZ

Subsidiary offices Jiddah, Dhahran, Jubail and Tabuk

Proprietor Sh. Yacoub Yusif Al Rashid

Activities

Sh. Yacoub began business in 1966 and specializes in the area of mechanical, electrical and industrial engineering. He represents many Western companies and is extremely alert to commercial possibilities whilst being a little reticent as to the details of his precise interests. He acts for Hawker Siddeley, Trans America and John Brown Turbines. He has a partnership with MOCOL for fibre glass pipes, where his company owns 65%, and another with Felton of West Germany.

Turnover 600 million U.S. dollars

Bankers Arab Bank, First National City

The Family of AL RASHIYD

Originally from the immediate environs of Riyadh they spread throughout Najd and are Al Dughaithar of Anaiza. Rashiyd bin Ibrahim, his son and his grandson Yusif were traders in horses to India.

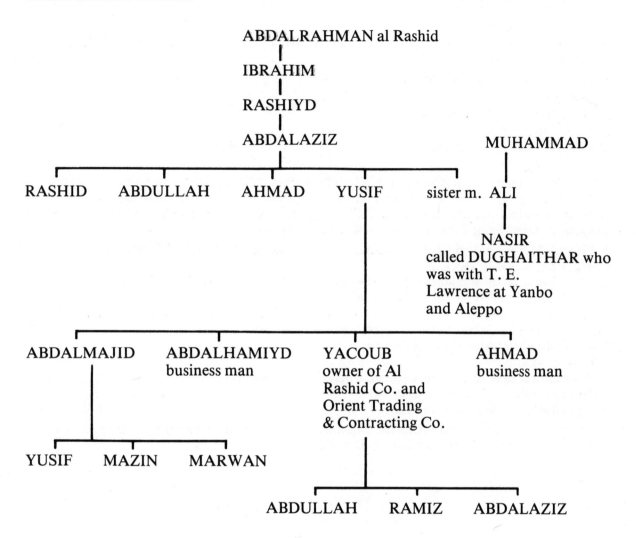

Abdulaziz and M A Al Jomaih Co.

Address head office P.O. 132 Riyadh

Telephone 35033, 35217, 35118, 35224

Telex 201023 JOMAIH S J

Cable address AL JOMAIH

Subsidiary offices Jiddah P.O. 467, tel. 23706, tx. 401147 JOMAIH SJ; Dammam P.O. 224, tel. 23740, tx. 601054 JOMAIH SJ

Proprietor Sh. Muhammad Abdullah Al Jomaih

Board Members
Abdalrahman Abdalaziz, Vice President
Muhammad Abdalaziz, Vice President
Hamad Abdalaziz, Vice President

Company History
The business was started in Shaqara near Riyadh in about 1928. Initially the family concerned itself with the grocery trade and general trading. They moved to Riyadh thirty years ago to form and build the present very considerable company with its wide spread of interest and they are actively considering expansion into new spheres of operation.

1. General Motor Cars: in Riyadh—Buick, Pontiac, Cadillac, GMC Opel; in Dammam—Buick, Pontiac, GMC Opel; in Jiddah—Chevrolet
2. Shell Products: oil and lubricants in Riyadh and Dammam (cf. Saudi Arabian Markets)
3. Yokohama Tyres: throughout the Kingdom
4. Heavy equipment: Fiat Allis—dozers, loaders, graders and excavators; Galion—cranes; AEG—road rollers, asphalt pavers; Leroi—air compressors
5. Generating sets: Aifo Man MTU
6. Fork lifts: TCM
7. Agricultural equipment: Fiat Trattori, Claas, Perkins, Ransome
8. Fire apparatus and fire extinguishers
9. Foodstuffs in Jiddah and Dammam

They are representatives and agents for international heavy industry companies and owners of Pepsi Cola, Miranda, Teem and Carbon Dioxide factories.

The Family of JUMAIH

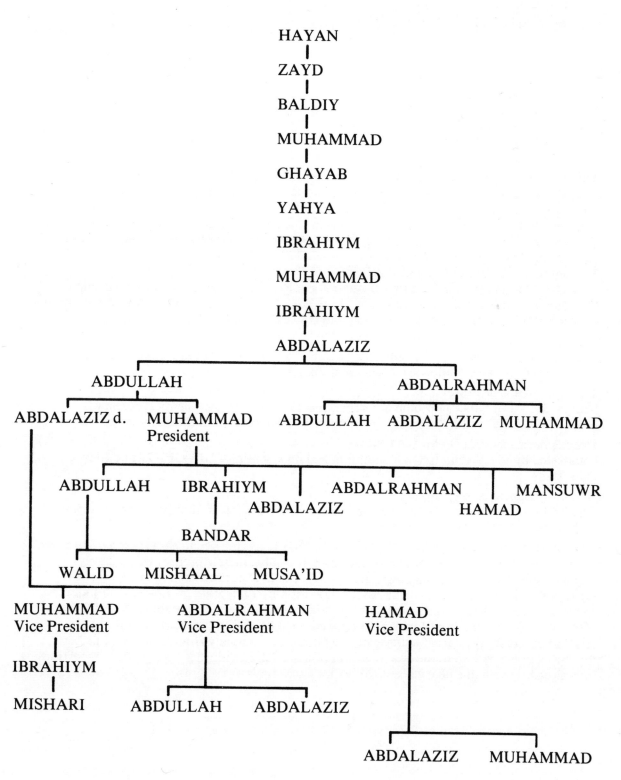

HAYAN

ZAYD

BALDIY

MUHAMMAD

GHAYAB

YAHYA

IBRAHIYM

MUHAMMAD

IBRAHIYM

ABDALAZIZ

ABDULLAH — ABDALRAHMAN

ABDALAZIZ d. — MUHAMMAD President — ABDULLAH — ABDALAZIZ — MUHAMMAD

ABDULLAH — IBRAHIYM — ABDALAZIZ — ABDALRAHMAN — HAMAD — MANSUWR

BANDAR

WALID — MISHAAL — MUSA'ID

MUHAMMAD Vice President — ABDALRAHMAN Vice President — HAMAD Vice President

IBRAHIYM

MISHARI — ABDULLAH — ABDALAZIZ

ABDALAZIZ — MUHAMMAD

79

Jamjoom Agencies

Address P.O. 2127 Jiddah
Telephone 23190, 23195
Telex 401169 JAMJOOM SJ

Board
Chairman Dr Abdalatif Salah Jamjoom
Sh. Husayn Salah Jamjoom
Sh. Ahmad Salah Jamjoom
Sh. Hamza Salah Jamjoom
Sh. Yusuf Salah Jamjoom

Company History
The Jamjoom family settled in Jiddah about a hundred and fifty years ago when Abdalaziz came for the Hajj and stayed, founding his business on the pilgrimage trade. Early misfortune was overcome when Abdalraouf and Muhammad Salah took over and a prospering business allowed the family to take an interest in charitable foundation and education. At this time the family business centred around foodstuffs, timber, and kerosene. Today the family is engaged in the following companies:

Muhammad Nur Salah Jamjoom and Bros.
which handles finance, administration, shipping and real estate under the chairmanship of Sh. Muhammad Nur who is also director of the Badwa Trading Company. A General Trading Division handles agencies for Parker Pens and Uncle Ben's Rice.

Jamjoom Construction Co.
A partnership with Babich, the Jamjooms holding 70%. This company deals in partitions, aluminium doors and windows, building materials and steel products.

Jamjoom Medicine Stores
Run by Sh. Yusuf Salah Jamjoom and represents the Pfizer Pharmaceutical Agency, Continental of Belgium, Hausmann of Switzerland, Allergan EUE Products of the USA.

Depot Pharmaceutical Du Moyen Orient
Controlled by Dr Abdalatif Salah Jamjoom and representing CIBA GEIGY and Merek Darmstadt.

Jamjoom Vehicles and Equipment
Headed by Sh. Ahmad Salah, agents for Peugeot, Hino trucks, Kleber tyres and motoring accessories.

The Jamjooms act as agents for Sakai vibration rollers, Japan: Benati shovels and excavators, Italy; Selma electric and motor lifts, Canada; Whiteman concrete pumps, USA; Davey Compressors, USA; and Dyna power generators, USA. Distribution in the Central and Eastern Provinces is handled by the Anbah Trading Co. Like other groups the Jamjooms are participating in industrialisation and whilst the construction of an assembly plant with Hino Motors and Toyo Menka of Japan has not lived up to its earlier expectations, they have established a dairy products factory with the Foremost Company from America. Further diversification may lead to the establishment of a local drug industry utilizing the connections they already have in the pharmaceutical field.

CAC

Head office P.O. 6285 Jiddah
Telephone 74288, 77098, 73825
Telex 401365 MONEER SJ, 401169 JAMJOOM SJ

CAC is an architectural and design firm with a growing reputation and a fine record of achievement.

Partners
Sh. Osman Salah Jamjoom
Sh. Ja'afar Salah Jamjoom

The Family of JAMJOOM

A notable and successful Jiddah family originating in Egypt.

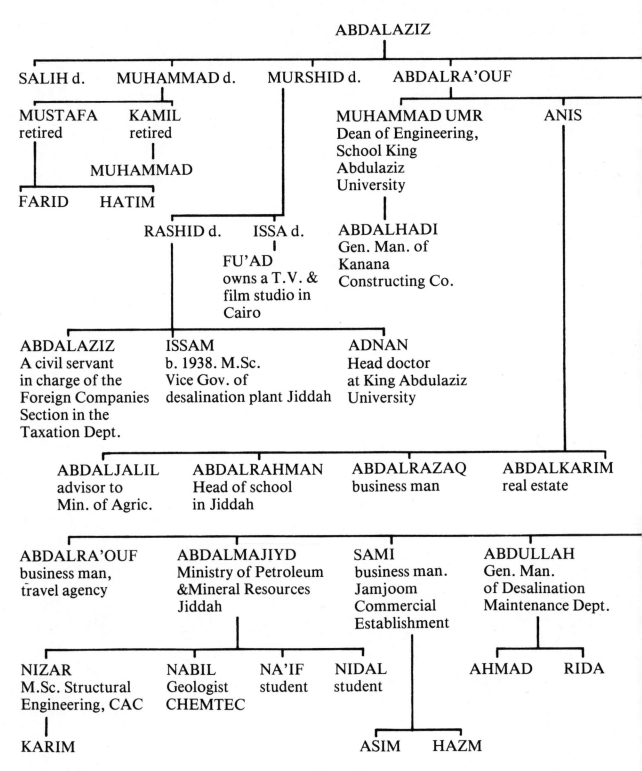

ABDALAZIZ

- **SALIH** d.
- **MUHAMMAD** d.
- **MURSHID** d.
- **ABDALRA'OUF**

MUSTAFA retired

KAMIL retired

MUHAMMAD

FARID   **HATIM**

MUHAMMAD UMR
Dean of Engineering,
School King
Abdulaziz
University

ANIS

RASHID d.   **ISSA** d.

FU'AD
owns a T.V. &
film studio in
Cairo

ABDALHADI
Gen. Man. of
Kanana
Constructing Co.

ABDALAZIZ
A civil servant
in charge of the
Foreign Companies
Section in the
Taxation Dept.

ISSAM
b. 1938. M.Sc.
Vice Gov. of
desalination plant Jiddah

ADNAN
Head doctor
at King Abdulaziz
University

ABDALJALIL
advisor to
Min. of Agric.

ABDALRAHMAN
Head of school
in Jiddah

ABDALRAZAQ
business man

ABDALKARIM
real estate

ABDALRA'OUF
business man,
travel agency

ABDALMAJIYD
Ministry of Petroleum
&Mineral Resources
Jiddah

SAMI
business man.
Jamjoom
Commercial
Establishment

ABDULLAH
Gen. Man.
of Desalination
Maintenance Dept.

NIZAR
M.Sc. Structural
Engineering, CAC

NABIL
Geologist
CHEMTEC

NA'IF
student

NIDAL
student

AHMAD   **RIDA**

KARIM

ASIM   **HAZM**

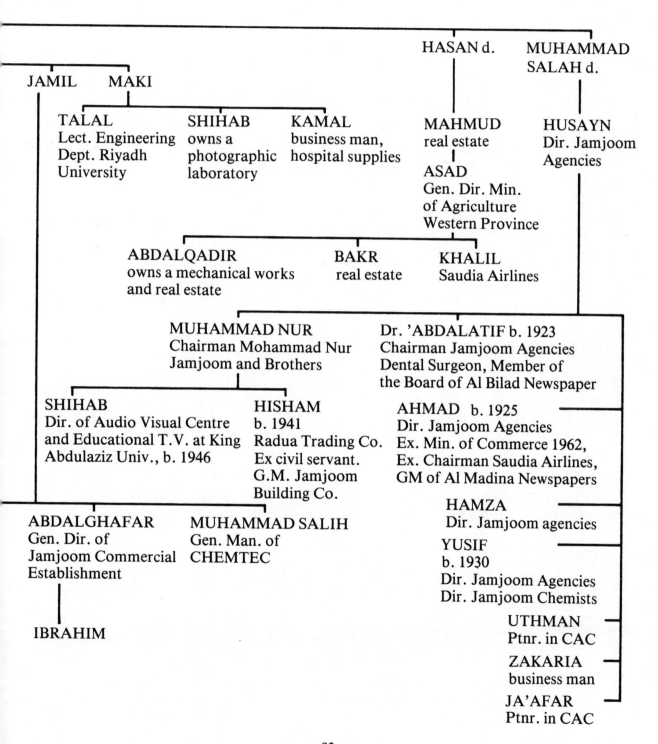

HASAN d.   MUHAMMAD
                        SALAH d.

JAMIL   MAKI

TALAL   SHIHAB   KAMAL   MAHMUD   HUSAYN
Lect. Engineering   owns a   business man,   real estate   Dir. Jamjoom
Dept. Riyadh   photographic   hospital supplies   Agencies
University   laboratory   ASAD
                                                       Gen. Dir. Min.
                                                       of Agriculture
                                                       Western Province

            ABDALQADIR   BAKR   KHALIL
            owns a mechanical works   real estate   Saudia Airlines
            and real estate

            MUHAMMAD NUR   Dr. 'ABDALATIF b. 1923
            Chairman Mohammad Nur   Chairman Jamjoom Agencies
            Jamjoom and Brothers   Dental Surgeon, Member of
                                          the Board of Al Bilad Newspaper

SHIHAB   HISHAM   AHMAD b. 1925
Dir. of Audio Visual Centre b. 1941   Dir. Jamjoom Agencies
and Educational T.V. at King Radua Trading Co. Ex. Min. of Commerce 1962,
Abdulaziz Univ., b. 1946   Ex civil servant.   Ex. Chairman Saudia Airlines,
                             G.M. Jamjoom   GM of Al Madina Newspapers
                             Building Co.
                                                 HAMZA
                                                 Dir. Jamjoom agencies

ABDALGHAFAR   MUHAMMAD SALIH   YUSIF
Gen. Dir. of   Gen. Man. of   b. 1930
Jamjoom Commercial   CHEMTEC   Dir. Jamjoom Agencies
Establishment   Dir. Jamjoom Chemists

                                              UTHMAN
                                              Ptnr. in CAC
IBRAHIM
                                              ZAKARIA
                                              business man

                                              JA'AFAR
                                              Ptnr. in CAC

Abdalaziz and Sa'ad Al Mo'ajil

Address head office P.O. 207 Riyadh
Telephone 27357, 28053
Telex 201203 MOAJIL SJ
Cable address MOAJILCO

Board Members A collective company
Sh. Abdalaziz bin Muhammad Al Mo'ajil 50%
Sh. Sa'ad bin Muhammad Al Mo'ajil 50%

Subsidiary offices
Al Mo'ajil Furniture, tel. 20687   Tayar Electric, tel. 39271   Real Estate Office, tel. 27357

Company History
The two brothers began their business careers when they moved from Hawtat Sudair to Jubail in 1935. To begin with they imported foodstuffs and textiles from Iraq and Kuwait but at first they suffered many losses due to bedouin raids and prospered only when peace was restored by King Abdalaziz al Sa'uwd. In 1950 they established the office in Qatif. Today Abdalaziz acts as President of the company in Riyadh and his brother, Sa'ad, as President in Dammam.

The Riyadh Business
Handles the furniture business which deals in contract, office and domestic furniture as well as carpeting, electrical installation and real estate.

Agencies
ACEC of Belgium for transformers and high/low voltage switch gear.
Crowse Hinds of the USA for airport lighting, area lighting, materials and industrial fittings.

Bankers City Bank, Saudi British Bank, Al Bank al Saudi al Hollandi

Abdalaziz and Sa'ad Al Mo'ajil

Address head office P.O. 53 Dammam
Telephone 21254, 21256, 22756
Telex 601055 MOAJIL SJ
Cable address AL MOAJIL

Proprietor The Collective Company

Board Members in Dammam
President Sh. Sa'ad bin Muhammad al Mo'ajil
Sh. Fahad bin Sa'ad
Sh. Khalid bin Sa'ad
Sh. Muhammad bin Sa'ad
Mr. Wahid

Activities
1. Stockists and importers of rice and sugar to the extent of half the national needs. This involves the company storing a permanent stock of 50,000 tons of sugar and an annual importation of 90,000 tons and 100,000 tons of rice.
2. Suppliers to ARAMCO and other oil companies.
3. Building materials, cement, steel, and lumber.
4. Industrial equipment, pipes, casing and chemicals.
5. Factories for the manufacture of polypropylene, cement products and wooden pallettes.

Agencies
Mitsubishi cement for over 25 years and for whom they import 40,000 tons a year.
Rheem Manufacturing Co. of the USA, gas and electric water heaters.
Yale Locks, UK, Italy, West Germany and the USA.

The company is founder member and shareholder in the Saudi British Bank and the Jazira Bank. At the moment they are expanding into overseas banking interests.

Turnover on trading account for rice and sugar amounts to 116 million Saudi riyals.

The Family of MO'AJIL

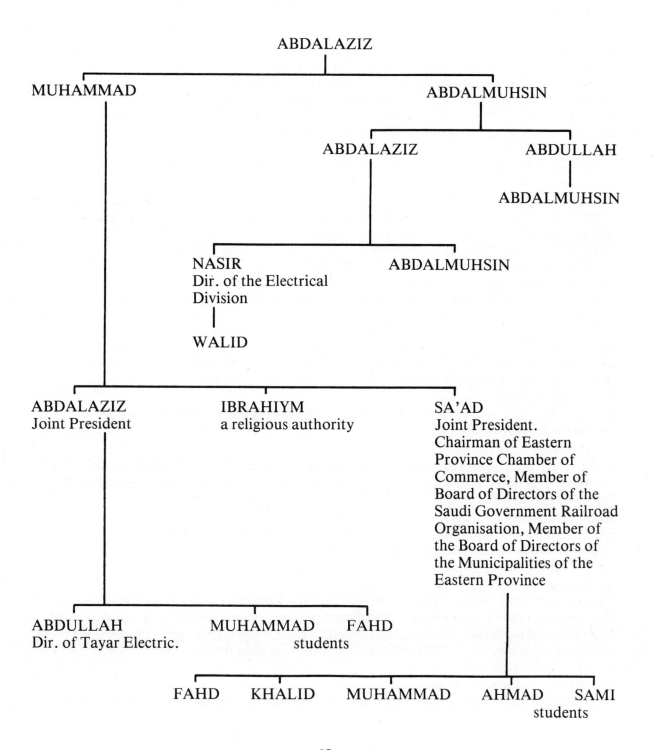

Ali and Fahd Shobokshi Group

Head office P.O. 5470 Jiddah

Telephone 58208, 58209

Telex 401008 GAC SJ

Cables GAC

Subsidiary offices
Riyadh P.O. 3511, tel. 61713, 60372, tx. 201314 EWM SJ
Dammam P.O. 1058 Dhahran Airport, tel. 31184, tx. 670074 EWM SJ
Al Aroussa Furniture Factory P.O. 4515 Jiddah, tel. 23061, 33621, tx. 401525 OIA SJ
Saudi International Consulting Centre P.O. 5470 Jiddah, tel. 26868, 33318, tx. 401008 GAC SJ
Shobokshi Commercial Enterprises 173 Syngrou Avenue, Athens, Greece, tel. 9341119,
tx. 219747 SHEP GR
Shobokshi Maritime P.O. 5470 Jiddah, tel. 23312, 24170, tx. 401746 SHOMAR SJ

Activities
The Shobokshi group is a company founded on enterprise and energy and represents the new
commercial concern in Saudi Arabia where the latest in modern technique has been applied
with great success. The two brothers themselves are a success story almost without equal.
The Shobokshi group acts as a holding company for the following interests which have
developed since founding the original company in 1953.

General Agencies Corporation GAC
The group's civil engineering division, building bridges, roads and housing as well as
desalination plants and water and sewage treatment plants on a turnkey basis. GAC also
operates as the group's trading arm. Starting in 1971 by importing paper in roll and sheet it
has diversified into cement, gypsum and steel as well as sanitary ware, electrical appliances
and household goods. New developments have branched into the foodstuffs field, ready-made
clothing, fruit juice and mineral water.

Shobokshi Industrial Complex
Produces aggregate, asphalt, concrete kerbstones and hollow blocks. Most of the output is
used in the group's own projects.

Electric Work and Maintenance
EWM is the electrical engineering division of the group and is a leader in the field of power
generation, HT and LT distribution systems, street and traffic lighting systems and industrial
and domestic electrification. The head office of this division is in Riyadh.

Agencies include:
Klein, Schanzin and Becker (KSB), Motoren Fabrik Hatz KG West Germany
Philips Telecommunicatie Industrie BV of Holland
Thorn Lighting UK

Al Aroussa
This company is a subsidiary of the group and operates a furniture factory equipped with the
most modern automated equipment. The company also imports furniture from abroad as well
as carpets, wallpapers and curtain fabrics through Orient International Agencies, another
subsidiary company. Al Aroussa and a sister company Al Ariss have their own showrooms
throughout the Kingdom.

Shobokshi Commercial Enterprises
This Athens based company is a subsidiary of the Shobokshi group and its activity is mainly

in the tours field. The company operates Government agency franchises in Greece and undertakes guided tours in the Aegean as well as a chartered yacht service.

Shobokshi Maritime

A further division of the Shobokshi group which has several important shipping agencies and provides stevedoring, clearing and forwarding services for door to door delivery. The company also acts as charter agent, broker, chandler and banker's agent.

Automotive division

A branch of the Shobokshi Group which acts as the sole distributor within the Kingdom for the Hyundai Company of the popular Pony range of Korean cars and trucks. The company provides a complete after-sales service from its own workshops.

The Group has further diversified into the area of management services, an operation carried out by the Saudi International Consulting Centre (SICC); into catering through the medium of Shobak which carries out a full range of catering services to hospitals, schools, labour camps and airlines. A specialisation from this activity has developed into the comprehensive Shobokshi Aviation Division which provides maintenance services to private aircraft operators as well as Shobal which is a partnership with Sh. Salih Kamel (q.v.) and Brothers for hotels based in London.

Sh. Ali Shobokshi holds the following commercial posts:
President of Orient International Agencies
Chairman of the OKAZ for Printing and Publishing Company
Chairman of OKAZ Organisation for Press and Publication
Founder of the Saudi International Consulting Centre
Chairman of the MISR Group for Investment and Development
Founder and Managing Director of Tihama for Advertising, Public Relations and Marketing Studies (q.v.)
Sh. Fahd Shobokshi holds the following commercial posts:
Member of the Board of the Red Sea Insurance Company
Co-Founder of Tihama
President of the General Agencies Corporation
President of the Electrical Work and Maintenance Company
Managing Director of OKAZ for Distribution
Managing Director of Saudi EXPO
Managing Director of Saudi AD
Member of the Board of the Egyptian Islamic Faisal Bank
Member of the Board of the Saudi Corporation for Catering and Tourism

Tihama
Board of Directors
His Royal Highness, Prince Saud bin Fahd bin Abdulaziz Al Sa'ud is the Chairman of the Board of Directors.
Sh. Ali Hussein Shobokshi, Authorized Member of the Board of Directors.
Sh. Mohammed Saed Tayyeb, Director General.
Sh. Ahmed Al Abdullah Al Suleiman, Member.
Sh. Salem Mohammed bin Laden, Member.
Sh. Saleh Abdullah Kamil, Member.
Sh. Yousef Abdullatif Jamil, Member.
Sh. Mohamed Ibrahim Al Issa.

Headquarters Jiddah (Ministry of Foreign Affairs Square) P.O. Box 5455, tel. 40000 (20 lines), cable TIHAMCO, Jiddah, tx. 401205 TIHAMA SJ.

Mecca Branch Alzahir Rei Alkohl, P.O. Box 1074, tel. 36206, 32709, cable TIHAMCO Mecca

Riyadh Branch King Faisal Street, Azizyah Bldg, P.O. Box 4681, tel. 33482, 32979, cable TIHAMCO Riyadh, tx. 20305 TIHAMA R S J, Advertising Dept. Airport St., tel. 65121, 62775.

Dammam Branch Prince Mohammed Street (in front of the Post Office Al Zamil Bldg., 4th Floor, Apt. 13 and 16), tel. 20243, 20434, P.O. Box 2666, cable TIHAMCO Dammam

Outdoor Adv. Jiddah (Albughdadiyah) Hassan Bin Thabet Street, tel. 29952, 20668

At the beginning of 1975 Tihama started work after having been legally established as a limited company in Jiddah with a fully paid capital of SR 2,450,000.00. Within two years Tihama progressed to the point where its capital needed to be increased to SR 10,045,000.00. Its activities are a follows:

Advertising
Design and construction of signs, road signboards and advertising panels
Preparation of advertising gifts and samples
Exhibitions
Arranging for participation in international exhibitions
Preparation of designs and implementation of all printing work for catalogues bulletins,
    reports, directories etc.
Production of slides and documentary films
In addition to these activities, Tihama has been granted exclusivity for advertising in the major sports stadia in Riyadh, Jiddah and Dammam
Within the advertising field Tihama has obtained advertising exclusivity for the following
    Saudi dailies and weeklies:
    Okaz, daily newspaper, issued in Jiddah
    Alriyadh, daily newspaper, issued in Riyadh
    Al Bilad, daily newspaper, issued in Mecca
    Al Yamama, weekly magazine
    Iqraa weekly magazine
In addition Tihama is presently extending its advertising activities beyond the Kingdom through newspapers, magazines (dailies and weeklies), radio and TV stations and films. To achieve this, Tihama has cooperative relationships with leading advertising agencies around the world. For instance Tihama represents the Financial Times in the Kingdom.

Public Relations
The Public Relations Division has a staff of experienced specialists who are there to serve efficiently both Government agencies and establishments as well as local and international companies in all areas of public relations. The department also provides advice to Tihama's clients with respect to mass communication plans.

Marketing Research
Government Agencies, as well as local and international companies, require precise and accurate data to help them in making the right decision to further their progress. The Marketing Research Department was established in order to provide clients with the following services: consumer and audience research, research into motivation, production and services, sales, distribution, pricing, advertising and communication, public opinion and feasibility studies.

The Family of SHOBOKSHI

The family have been resident in Jiddah for many years and tradition states that they originally are from Egypt.

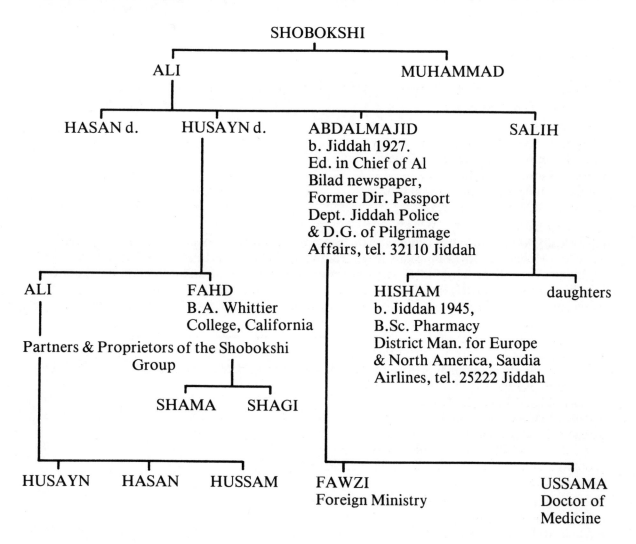

SHOBOKSHI

ALI   MUHAMMAD

HASAN d.   HUSAYN d.   ABDALMAJID
b. Jiddah 1927.
Ed. in Chief of Al
Bilad newspaper,
Former Dir. Passport
Dept. Jiddah Police
& D.G. of Pilgrimage
Affairs, tel. 32110 Jiddah   SALIH

ALI   FAHD
B.A. Whittier
College, California   HISHAM
b. Jiddah 1945,
B.Sc. Pharmacy
District Man. for Europe
& North America, Saudia
Airlines, tel. 25222 Jiddah   daughters

Partners & Proprietors of the Shobokshi Group

SHAMA   SHAGI

HUSAYN   HASAN   HUSSAM   FAWZI
Foreign Ministry   USSAMA
Doctor of
Medicine

Said M O Binzagr and Partners Co.

Address head office P.O. 54 Jiddah

Telephone 23529, 23769, 23188

Telex 401131 IKBAL SJ

Cable address IKBAL

Subsidiary offices
Riyadh P.O. 392, tel. 20802, 20803, tx. 201702, IKBAL SJ
Al Khobar P.O. 96, tel. 41430, 41431, tx, 670021 IKBAL SJ

Proprietor The Partnership

Board Members
Chairman, Said M O Binzagr
Chief Executive, Wahib Said Binzagr
Director Faisal Said Binzagr
Director Muhammad Obaid Said Binzagr
Director Abdullah Said Binzagr

Company History
Historically what is nowadays known as the Binzagr Group began over a hundred years ago when Sh. Mohamed Obaid Binzagr started trading in Jiddah. It is thus one of the oldest companies in the Kingdom. In 1825 a partnership was formed called Shinkar and Binzagr Co. It is this company which is the direct ancestor of the present enterprise in which sound modern management is combined with a desire for innovation to provide one of the most successful and skilled selling organisations in the Saudi market. The company's activities in the marketing field include the following services: importation, modern central and regional warehousing, selling, direct distribution, advertising and merchandising. The company is organised into three regional offices and ten local branches. The range of products is arranged in divisions as follows:
Household and Toiletries Division
Food and Drinks Division
Tobacco Products Division
Agriculture and Chemical Products Division
Industrial and Automotive Products Division
Consumer Durables Division

The Binzagr Group holds the following other commercial interests:
1. Wholly owned companies
Binzagr Match Factory in partnership with A. H. Herring of Germany.
Binzagr Saudi Shipping Ltd. with Barber International of Norway.
Saudi Express Services with Palm Line of UK for customs clearance and freight forwarding.
Advance Services with Advance Linen Services Ltd. of the UK for cleaning services.
2. Foreign Joint Ventures
Binzagr Lever Ltd with Unilever Commonwealth Holding Ltd of UK for soaps and toiletries
    manufacture.
Binzagr Coro Group with Coro A S of Denmark for soft drink manufacture.
Trans Arabia Ltd with S.J. Investments CI Ltd of the Channel Islands for trucking.
Binzagr Pauling Ltd with Pauling Middle East Ltd of UK for contracting.
Cicatrade Ltd with the Cica Group of Brazil for export from Brazil.
Saudi Danish Technical Installation Ltd with Monberg and Thorsen of Denmark for mechanical and electrical contracting.

3. Minority Interests in the following:

Al Alamiya Insurance Co Ltd UK with Sun Alliance Ltd UK for insurance.

Saudi Ghee Industry Ltd with Saudi partners for oil and fat refining.

Wilkinson Sword Middle East Ltd with Wilkinson Sword UK and the Egyptian Government for the manufacture of razor blades.

The Souqs Co Ltd with Southland of USA and Saudi partners for supermarkets and convenience stores.

Utility companies with Saudi partners for electricity.

Saudi British Bank with the British Bank of the Middle East.

Saudi Investment Banking Corporation (q.v.) with Chase Manhattan.

4. Other Binzagr Companies

Wahib Saudi Arabia Binzagr and Brothers for property investment, representation of foreign companies and the assisting of them in Saudi Arabia.

International Agencies Ltd Saudi Arabia for office equipment, furniture and security equipment. Managed by East Asiatic Co Ltd of Denmark.

ARMSA Arabian Resource Management SA Switzerland for new business development, consulting services and marketing.

ARMSA Arabian Resource Management Saudi Arabia, as above.

PLYMS NV for international investment, managed by ARMSA.

Saudibras Investimentos for investment property.

Agropecuaria E Representacoes Ltda, Brazil, for investment.

Binzagr International Trading Co. Managed by ARMSA for specialised trading in Saudi Arabia, USA and Europe.

Binzagr Services Ltd UK commercial and marketing services.

Bankers (Saudi Arabia) Al Bank al Saudi al Hollandi, The Saudi British Bank, Al Bank al Saudi al Faransi, Citibank, National Commercial Bank, Riyadh Bank, Saudi Investment Banking Corporation, BBME, Saudi International Bank.

The Family of BINZAGR

The family has been an important part of the commercial life of Jiddah for over a century and a street behind the National Commercial Bank is named after them. Originally they came from the north of the Wadi Hadramawt coming from Ajlaniya village in Sa'yar country, and are of Kinda stock. Sh. Wahib is probably the only Saudi citizen who assists the playing of cricket and both he and his brother Abdullah presented the Binzagr Cup for the Saudi Cricket League Tournament in Jiddah in honour of the One Flame Match Co. The Binzagr Company has its own team too, which has played matches in the Sudan as well as all over the Kingdom of Saudi Arabia.

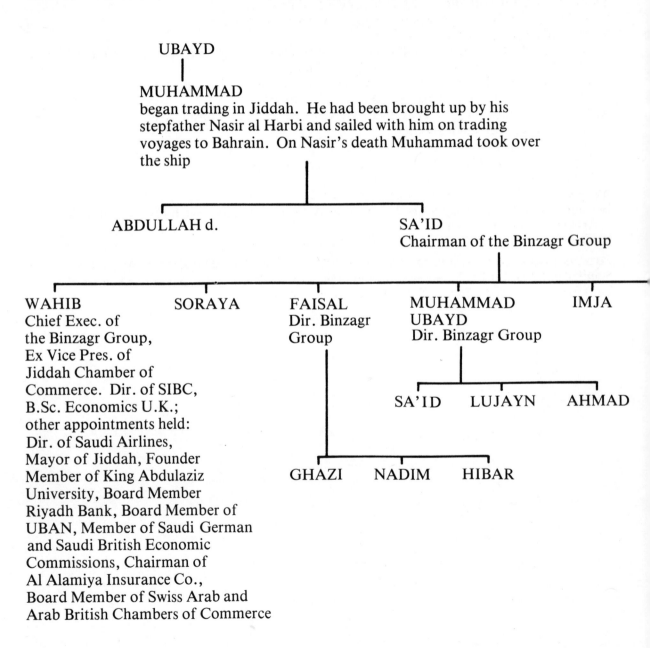

UBAYD

MUHAMMAD
began trading in Jiddah. He had been brought up by his stepfather Nasir al Harbi and sailed with him on trading voyages to Bahrain. On Nasir's death Muhammad took over the ship

ABDULLAH d.

SA'ID
Chairman of the Binzagr Group

WAHIB
Chief Exec. of the Binzagr Group, Ex Vice Pres. of Jiddah Chamber of Commerce. Dir. of SIBC, B.Sc. Economics U.K.; other appointments held: Dir. of Saudi Airlines, Mayor of Jiddah, Founder Member of King Abdulaziz University, Board Member Riyadh Bank, Board Member of UBAN, Member of Saudi German and Saudi British Economic Commissions, Chairman of Al Alamiya Insurance Co., Board Member of Swiss Arab and Arab British Chambers of Commerce

SORAYA

FAISAL
Dir. Binzagr Group

MUHAMMAD UBAYD
Dir. Binzagr Group

IMJA

SA'ID   LUJAYN   AHMAD

GHAZI   NADIM   HIBAR

Both the Binzagr Family and the Bin Mahfoudh (q.v.) emanate from the Sa'yar of Hadramawt and both are very successful. It may be apposite to note that this tribe had a fearsome reputation for raiding in the old days and were feared throughout the area of the Empty Quarter, being called the wolves of the desert by Philby. However, today they are even more successful at a more peaceful form of commerce.

SAFIYA	ABDULLAH	SU'AD	OFFAT
an artist of great reputation and talent, a number of whose works have been published in book form	Dir. Binzagr Group		a graduate of Wellesley. M.A. Columbia University and reading for a Ph.D. at Oxford

Introduction to the El Khereiji Family Businesses

In the generation following that of the founders of the first El Khereiji Company (see family tree), the seniority had passed to Abdullah bin Abdalkarim who continued in Medina for a short while and then moved to Jiddah where he formed a company with Sulaiman bin Abdalaziz called the Abdullah and Sulaiman El Khereiji Company. Having visited the USA and Europe, Abdullah and Sulaiman began to import and introduce new products to the Saudi market like refrigerators and ceiling fans. They sent Abdalkarim bin Abdalaziz to study in England and Yusuf bin Abdullah to the States at this time. On their return the boys were absorbed into the business, Abdalkarim taking over the family interests in Dammam and Yusuf those in Riyadh. At a later stage Yusuf left the El Khereiji Company and became independent founding DITCO and Abdullah bin Abdalaziz took over the family interests in Riyadh. After three years he too felt the need for independence and Abdulmuhsin took his place in the capital.

The motivation for independence has been strong in the family and the third and fourth generations have amply emulated the family tradition.

The El Khereiji businesses thus present the following picture today:
Sulaiman bin Abdalaziz formed a company for his sons called The United Brothers Company
Yusuf bin Abdullah formed DITCO and TPCC
Yusuf, Ibrahim and the other sons of Abdullah bin Abdalkarim formed the International Centre
Abdalkarim bin Abdalaziz formed El Khereiji Trading and Electricity
Abdullah bin Abdalaziz formed the El Khereiji Corporation
Ibrahim Abdullah formed the Al Gazira Corporation
Sulaiman bin Abdullah established an architect's practice

The original partnership between Abdullah and Sulaiman has become absorbed and developed by the Khalid Abdulrahman Trading Corporation.

The El Khereiji Corporation

Address head office P.O. 3971 Riyadh

Telephone 4780925

Telex 201747 KHEREIJI SJ

Cable address KHEREIJI

Proprietor Sh. Abdullah bin Abdalaziz El Khereiji who is a Member of Lloyds

Board Members
Chairman Sh. Ali bin Abdalaziz El Khereiji
Sh. Abdullah bin Abdalaziz El Khereiji
Syd. Khalil M. Saraf
Syd. Michel Karam

Business Activity
El Khereiji Hotel P.O. 1075, tel. 39919
Rajhi Building Batha Street, Riyadh
Lana Printing Press
Nada Laundry
Airport Services, Riyadh, Dhahran, Medina & Jiddah
Insurance, representing General Accident of UK and INA

Joint Ventures
1. El Khereiji with Wahib of Lebanon for electrical contracting
2. El Khereiji with Foulsham, Meldrum and Burrows of Australia for architectural planning
3. Pan Arabian Insurance in the Bahamas. This is 51% Khereiji and 49% Gen. Accident and INA

Turnover 100 million Saudi riyals

Bankers Riyadh Bank, Arab Bank, National Commercial Bank, BCCI of London, Morgan Guaranty of New York

El Khereiji Trading and Electronics

Address head office P.O. 25 Dammam

Telephone 22985, 22555, 24442

Telex 601022 KHEREIJI SJ

Cable address EL KHEREIJI

Subsidiary Offices
Jiddah tel. 47756
Riyadh tel. 20890
Qatif tel. 51773

Proprietor Sh. Abdalkarim bin Abdalaziz El Khereiji

Board Members
Chairman Sh. Abdalkarim bin Abdalaziz El Khereiji
Founding partner of Al Jazira Bank and subscriber to The Saudi Faransi Bank, The Saudi Hollandi Bank, The Saudi Cairo Bank, Member of Lloyds, the Municipal Council of Dammam and the Dammam Chamber of Commerce and founding member of Al Yowm Newspaper.
Mr. Taysir Zayton
Mr. Jishi

Business Activity
This company which has some interests in common with the El Khereiji Corporation concerns itself with insurance, electronic and electrical equipment, general trading, household appliances and investment in real estate.

Agencies
Insurance of North America, INA
General Accident of the UK
Hotpoint of UK
Racal Milgo Ltd of UK (Electronics)
'Green Cards' for insurance and carnet service to vehicles leaving the Kingdom

Partnerships
El Khereiji and Al Kohaimi (KKMC) for machinery
El Khereiji and Wahab (electrical)
The El Khereiji Hotel in Riyadh
Pan Arab Insurance (joint venture)
Khereiji ABV Construction Co (a joint venture with a Swedish company)

Bankers Arab Bank, National Commercial Bank, Saudi Investment Corporation.

Development International Trade Company Ltd (DITCO)

Address head office P.O. 5030 Jiddah

Telephone 55459

Telex 401112 SJ

Board Members
Chairman Sh. Yusif Abdullah El Khereiji
Director Sh. Ibrahim Abdullah El Khereiji
Director Sh. Abdalghani Abdullah El Khereiji
Man. Dir. Mr Peter Tsitseklis

Company History
The company was formed in 1965 and made a very marked impression in the contracting field following expansion into this area in 1973. Projects undertaken are a measure of their competence and the scale of the company's operations.

1. Development of Yanbo Port, involving dredging of 8.5 million cu. metres, pouring 55,000 cu. metres of concrete and 230,000 cu. metres of rock filling as well as road services and warehousing.
   value: over a billion riyals.
2. Routine maintenance of the Jiddah-Medina road including the branch Badr-Yanbo.
   value: 32 million riyals.
3. Preventative maintenance on the Jiddah-Medina road
   value: 31 million riyals.
4. Bridge at Tuwwal which is 180 m long.
   value: 10 million riyals.

DITCO specialises in pre-cast concrete and further projects to a value of three hundred and ninety million riyals have either been completed or are in hand.

Bankers City Bank, Al Bank al Saudi al Faransi.

Joint ventures
Saudi Dredging which is a joint venture between DITCO and HAM Co. of Holland and Dredging International of Belgium.

Other associated but independent companies
1. TPCC
Chairman Sh. Yusif Abdullah El Khereiji
Director and General Manager Sh. Ibrahim Abdullah El Khereiji
This company operates woodwork and concrete block factories and acts in a supportive role to the activities of the group.
2. International Centre for Commercial Contracting
P.O. Jiddah 2388, tel. 55670, 670108, tx. 400534 INCENT SJ
Chairman Sh. Yusif Abdullah El Khereiji
Gen. Manager Sh. Abdalghani Abdullah El Khereiji
Tech. Manager Sh. Sulayman Abdullah El Khereiji
Legal Adviser Sh. Muhammad Abdullah El Khereiji
The company, called IC, engages in building construction and commerce where it specialises in the provision of furniture for institutional purposes.
3. Saudi Metin Co.
Chairman Sh. Yusif Abdullah El Khereiji
Director Sh. Ibrahim Abdullah El Khereiji

Gen. Manager Mr R Gratwick
tel. 54750, 52822
4. Architectural Consultancy
P.O. 2388, tel. 670108, 674409, tx. 400534 INCENT SJ
Sh. Sulayman Abdullah El Khereiji

United Brothers Company

Address head office P.O. 6093 Jiddah

Telephone 23859, 41128, 41129

Telex 401177 UBC SJ

Cable address JESARA

Board Members
Chairman Sh. Sulayman bin Abdalaziz El Khereiji
President Sh. Abdulqader bin Sulaiman El Khereiji
Vice Pres. Sh. Muhammad bin Sulaiman El Khereiji
Vice Pres. Sh. Abdulaziz bin Sulaiman El Khereiji

Company History
The company was founded in 1976 and offers a complete auto package hinging around their agency for Renault Cars which is situated in pleasant modern offices in the Medina Road. United Brothers represent also Elf lubricants, Creusot Loire and Lescot car accessories of France. They cover the insurance field through Gras Savoye. They also have a specialized interest in the importation of medical equipment for which activity Sh. Abdalaziz's doctorate in medicine from Cairo gives the company great in-house expertise. The United Brothers also represent Korean interests in trade and commerce as well as construction.

In May 1979 the members of the Khereiji Family who form this business interest established a limited liability partnership called the KAAB Trading and Contracting Co. The company is engaged in economic development projects, building contracts and general trading. The partners are as follows:
Sh. Sulaiman Abdulaziz El Khereiji 42.5%
Sh. Abdalaziz Hamad Al Mabian 17.5%
Sh. Abdalqadir Sulaiman El Khereiji 10%
Sh. Muhammad Sulaiman El Khereiji 10%
Sh. Abdalaziz Sulaiman El Khereiji 10%
Badriah Sulaiman El Khereiji 10%

Bankers National Commercial Bank, Saudi Faransi Bank.

The Family of EL KHEREIJI

An old family of Najd directly related to Zamil.

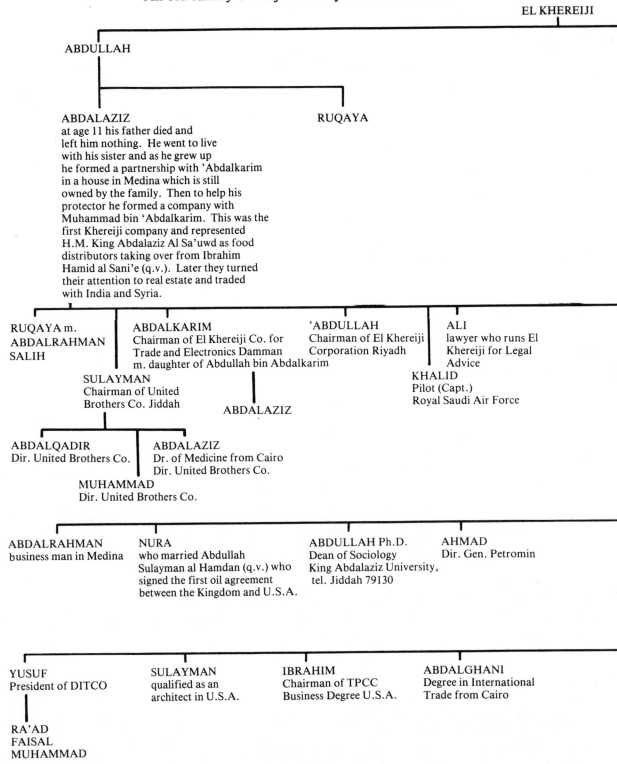

EL KHEREIJI

ABDULLAH

ABDALAZIZ
at age 11 his father died and
left him nothing. He went to live
with his sister and as he grew up
he formed a partnership with 'Abdalkarim
in a house in Medina which is still
owned by the family. Then to help his
protector he formed a company with
Muhammad bin 'Abdalkarim. This was the
first Khereiji company and represented
H.M. King Abdalaziz Al Sa'uwd as food
distributors taking over from Ibrahim
Hamid al Sani'e (q.v.). Later they turned
their attention to real estate and traded
with India and Syria.

RUQAYA

RUQAYA m.
ABDALRAHMAN
SALIH

ABDALKARIM
Chairman of El Khereiji Co. for
Trade and Electronics Damman
m. daughter of Abdullah bin Abdalkarim

SULAYMAN
Chairman of United
Brothers Co. Jiddah

ABDALAZIZ

'ABDULLAH
Chairman of El Khereiji
Corporation Riyadh

ALI
lawyer who runs El
Khereiji for Legal
Advice

KHALID
Pilot (Capt.)
Royal Saudi Air Force

ABDALQADIR
Dir. United Brothers Co.

ABDALAZIZ
Dr. of Medicine from Cairo
Dir. United Brothers Co.

MUHAMMAD
Dir. United Brothers Co.

ABDALRAHMAN
business man in Medina

NURA
who married Abdullah
Sulayman al Hamdan (q.v.) who
signed the first oil agreement
between the Kingdom and U.S.A.

ABDULLAH Ph.D.
Dean of Sociology
King Abdalaziz University,
tel. Jiddah 79130

AHMAD
Dir. Gen. Petromin

YUSUF
President of DITCO

SULAYMAN
qualified as an
architect in U.S.A.

IBRAHIM
Chairman of TPCC
Business Degree U.S.A.

ABDALGHANI
Degree in International
Trade from Cairo

RA'AD
FAISAL
MUHAMMAD

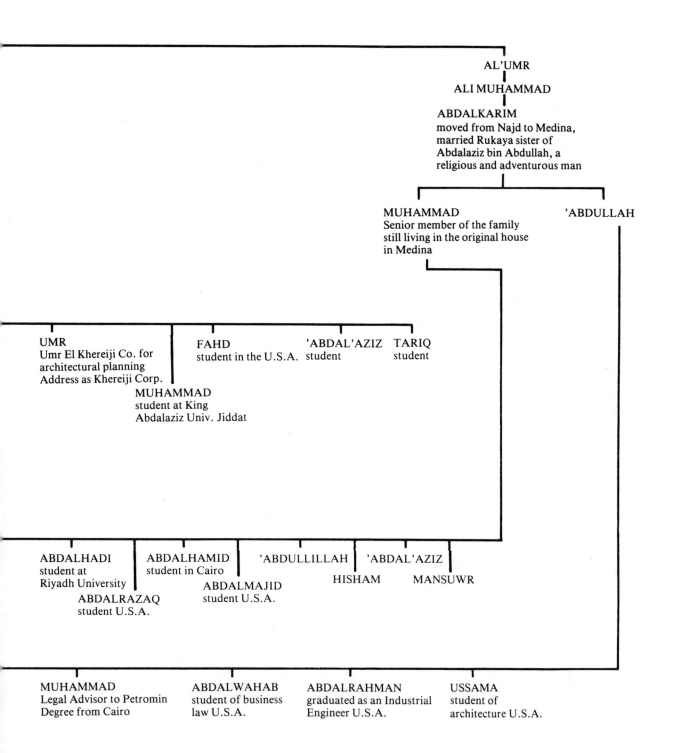

AL'UMR

ALI MUHAMMAD

ABDALKARIM
moved from Najd to Medina,
married Rukaya sister of
Abdalaziz bin Abdullah, a
religious and adventurous man

MUHAMMAD
Senior member of the family
still living in the original house
in Medina

'ABDULLAH

UMR
Umr El Khereiji Co. for
architectural planning
Address as Khereiji Corp.

MUHAMMAD
student at King
Abdalaziz Univ. Jiddat

FAHD
student in the U.S.A.

'ABDAL'AZIZ
student

TARIQ
student

ABDALHADI
student at
Riyadh University

ABDALRAZAQ
student U.S.A.

ABDALHAMID
student in Cairo

ABDALMAJID
student U.S.A.

'ABDULLILLAH

HISHAM

'ABDAL'AZIZ

MANSUWR

MUHAMMAD
Legal Advisor to Petromin
Degree from Cairo

ABDALWAHAB
student of business
law U.S.A.

ABDALRAHMAN
graduated as an Industrial
Engineer U.S.A.

USSAMA
student of
architecture U.S.A.

The Family of EL KHEREIJI (Branch)

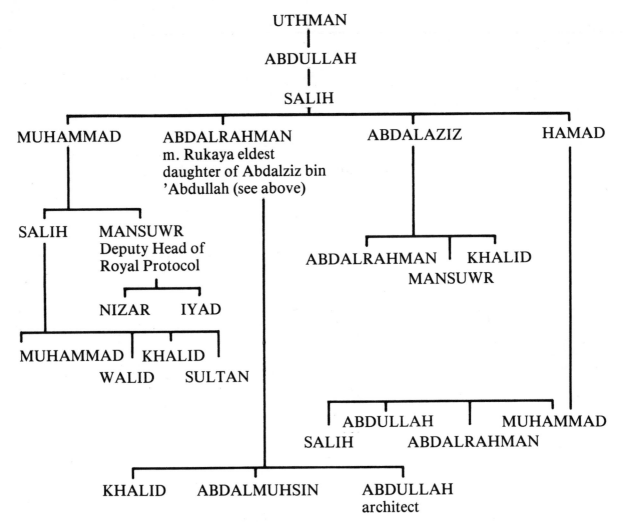

UTHMAN

ABDULLAH

SALIH

MUHAMMAD ABDALRAHMAN
m. Rukaya eldest
daughter of Abdalziz bin
'Abdullah (see above)

ABDALAZIZ HAMAD

SALIH MANSUWR
Deputy Head of
Royal Protocol

ABDALRAHMAN KHALID
MANSUWR

NIZAR IYAD

MUHAMMAD KHALID
WALID SULTAN

ABDULLAH MUHAMMAD
SALIH ABDALRAHMAN

KHALID ABDALMUHSIN ABDULLAH
architect

The Khalid Abdalrahman
Trading Corporation
P.O. 2813 Riyadh,
tel. 4654281, 4658782,
tx. 200583 KAKTCO S.J.
(Central Air Conditioning - Austria
Steel construction with Lonardi of Italy)

Khalifa Abdulrahman Al Gosaibi Contracting

Address head office P.O. 222 Dammam

Telephone 24450, 24430, 24780

Telex 601035

Cable address CONTRACTS

Proprietor Sh. Khalifa Abdulrahman Al Gosaibi

Board Members
Sh. Muhammad Khalifa Al Gosaibi
Sh. Sami Khalifa Al Gosaibi
Sh. Salah Khalifa Al Gosaibi

Activities
The central business of this branch of the family, which may develop into a holding company proper though it is now almost that in all but name, revolves around the Diving Service Khalifa Al Gosaibi in Al Khobar and Bahrain and the Khalifa Al Gosaibi Cold Store in Dammam. The company activities embrace fishing, camp catering, wholesale food and food storage, the production and manufacture of building materials and investment in real estate.

The following companies are represented by Khalifa Abdulrahman Al Gosaibi Contracting:
1. The Caracola Division of Dragados Constructors, Spain. High quality modular buildings for camps, schools, offices, hospitals and houses.
2. Burmeister and Wain, Denmark. Job-camp housing.
3. Guerdon Industries Inc., USA. Mobile homes, multi-storied town houses and planned communities.
4. Nippon Benkan Co. Ltd , Japan. Plumbing fittings.
5. Building Systems and Equipment Ltd, USA. Concrete forms and products.
6. Ishikawajima-Harima Heavy Industries Co. Ltd, Japan. Heavy industrial capability in rolling mills, chemical plants, sewerage treatment and air conditioning.
7. Sanki Engineering Co. Ltd, Japan. Port and cargo handling systems.
8. Mitsubishi Electric, Japan. All types of electrical equipment, switch gear, transformers and generators.
9. Callaway Carpets (a division of Millinken & Co.). Carpets and rugs.

Partnerships/Joint Ventures
The company owns the Construction Materials Company Ltd with 90% equity; Al Gosaibi Grandmet 50% and Al Gosaibi Rea 50%. They also have joint ventures with Atlas of Wales for cranes of light, medium or heavy sizes for lease or sub-contract, with Global Electrification Systems Inc. of the Philippines for the installation of transmission lines, power houses and generating stations, with Partek of Finland for pre-cast concrete components and Rea Galaxy of the Philippines for trucking and hauling. A joint venture is in process of finalisation with Mitsui Harbour and Urban Construction Corporation of Japan.

Ahmad Hamad Al Gosaibi Brothers

Address head office P.O. 106 Al Khobar

Telephone 42666, 42862

Telex
670123 ALGOSO SJ
601069 GACSHIP SJ
671335 SUICO SJ (insurance)

Cable address AHMAD AL GOSAIBI

Subsidiary offices Branches in Dammam, Ras Tanura, Al Khafji, Al Hasa, Riyadh and Jiddah.

Proprietor Collective Company in which the following are the partners:
Sh. Ahmad bin Hamad Al Gosaibi
Sh. Abdulaziz bin Hamad Al Gosaibi
Sh. Sulaiman bin Hamad Al Gosaibi

Company History
The business was founded by Sh. Hamad bin Ahmad in 1937 as a general trading concern which has developed into a modern business with wide and diversified interests. It owns the following companies:
Ahmad Hamad Al Gosaibi & Bros (Commission Agents), tel. 42666, 42862
Al Gosaibi Trading Company, tel. 42666, 42862
Al Gosaibi Real Estate
Al Gosaibi Service Station

In the manufacturing field they also own the National Bottling Co. (Pepsi Cola), tel. 43222, 43366; A H Al Gosaibi & Bros Co. Plant, tel. 43222, 43366; A H Al Gosaibi & Bros Ice Plant, tel. 42666. The company owns the Al Gosaibi Hotel in Al Khobar, tel. 42466, 46466, tx. 670008 GOSTEL SJ, P.O. 51 Dhahran Airport, and has a founding shareholding in the Saudi Hotel Services Co. Ltd in Riyadh (Riyadh Palace Hotel) and the Egyptian Saudi Hotel Co. (Ramada). Their wholly owned shipping interests are in Al Gosaibi Shipping Co., Dammam, tel. 23813, 23426, 23427; the Gulf Agency Co. (Saudi Arabia) Ltd, Dammam, tel. 23813, 23426; and International Offshore Services Corporation, Dammam, tel. 23818, 23426. In the transportation field they have two wholly owned companies, International Associated Cargo Carriers, Dammam, tel. 23813, 23426, 23427, and Yousuf Al Gosaibi Travel Agency, Al Khobar, tel. 41916, 41922.

Ahmad Hamad Al Gosaibi and Brothers are also founders and shareholders in the following companies:
Saudi Cement Company
Dhahran Electric Supply Co.
Hofuf Electric Supply Co.
El Khat Co. (Printing Press), tel. 42666, 22343
Saudi Glass Manufacturing Company, Dammam.
Saudi Company for Vegetable Oil and Ghee, Jiddah
Saudi Crowncaps Manufacturing Co. Ltd, Riyadh, tel. 36310
Al Gosaibi Maritime Services Co., Dammam, tel. 23813, 21095
Gulf Ro-Ro Services, Dammam, tel. 23813, 23426, 23427
International Air Cargo Corporation, tel. 23813, 23426, 23427
Gulf Marine Transport Co. KSC, Kuwait, tel. 449981
The Saudi British Bank

Al Jazira Contracting Company, Bahrain
Saudi United Insurance Co. Ltd Al Khobar, tel. 42863, 45866, 45716 in which they have 60%

Their joint venture enterprises are in the Oilfield Chemical Company (Saudi Arabia) Ltd, Dammam, with Essochem of Belgium, tel. 42666, the Continental Can of Saudi Arabia Ltd, Dammam, with the Continental Group Inc. of USA, tel. 42666, the Saudi National Pipe Co., Dammam, the Saudi Korean Stevedoring Co., tel. 23813, 28762, the International Trucking Express Co., Dammam, tel. 23813, 23426, 23427. These interests are rounded off with partnerships in the Swiss Reinsurance Co. of Switzerland, the Commercial Union Assurance Company of Great Britain and Baloise Insurance Company Ltd of Switzerland.

Bankers Arab Bank, Riyadh Bank, Saudi British Bank.

Al Amar Trading and Construction Establishment

Address head office P.O. 274 Dhahran Airport   *Telex* 601044 ARNDASS SJ

Telephone 24157 Dammam   *Cable address* AMARCO

Proprietor Sh. Ibrahim bin Hasan Al Gosaibi

Company History
Sh. Ibrahim founded his company in 1969. Specialising in construction, it has been responsible for the successful completion of many contracts. At the present time his company is anxious to expand its activities and is showing considerable interest in entering into a joint venture with a UK concern willing to start negotiations. It is in partnership with a French company, Girard Dot Co., for electrical contracting, fittings and maintenance.

Bankers Saudi Cairo Bank, Riyadh Bank, Arab Bank.

Al Gosaibi Trading and Contracting Company

Address head office P.O. 2784 Dammam

Telephone 27221

Telex 601382 GTCC SJ

Cable address HIACO

Subsidiary offices
Riyadh tel, 66284, 69899
Hasa tel. 25255, 24744, P.O. 367, cable GOSABCO
Jiddah agent - Nasir Al Adwan

A Collective Partnership
Ghazi Muhammad Muhammad Al Gosaibi (Riyadh Director)
Rashid Khalifa Abdalrahman Al Gosaibi (Dammam Director)
Adil Muhammad Muhammad Al Gosaibi

Company History
This young company which continues the family predilection for forming new and independent businesses was founded in 1974. It is a go-ahead concern concentrating on a narrow range of commodities and agency relationships. They import foodstuffs and tinned goods from Korea, Japan, Singapore, and Thailand and market California rice for Tewfiq the importer.

Agencies
Their agencies are thus a marketing relationship with Pacific International Rice Mills and directly with the Shin Heung Flourmills Co. Ltd. of Korea.

Bankers Saudi British Bank, Bank al Jazira, and the National Commercial Bank in Hasa.

BATCO

Address head office P.O. 613 Dammam

Telephone 44408

Telex 670185 BATCO SJ

Proprietor Sh. Khalifa bin Sa'ad Al Gosaibi

Company History

The foundation of Sh. Khalifa's company dates from 1968 when he entered the building and contracting field and also conducted business as a general trader. His activities are typical of his independently minded family. His company is extremely successful and one that is most attractive to the business man from Europe.

Partnership

A partnership has been formed, called Batco Kent, with an Irish company, and they operate in the field of electrical contracting and maintenance.

Turnover 2 million Saudi riyals (partnership)

Bankers Saudi Faransi Bank

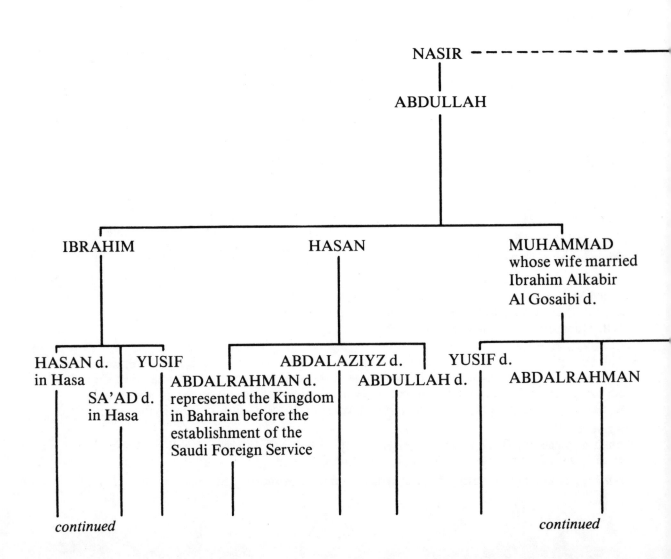

continued

continued

The Family of AL GOSAIBI

The family originates in Hofuf where they were involved in agriculture, trading through Bahrain to India with dates. There are family connections with Huraymlat and possibly Qasab.

The part of the family below, which is the most important, descend from two brothers (the second of whom married his elder brother's wife on his death). Agricultural produce led to diversification into trade in pearls and gold and the establishment of the wide range of family businesses seen today.

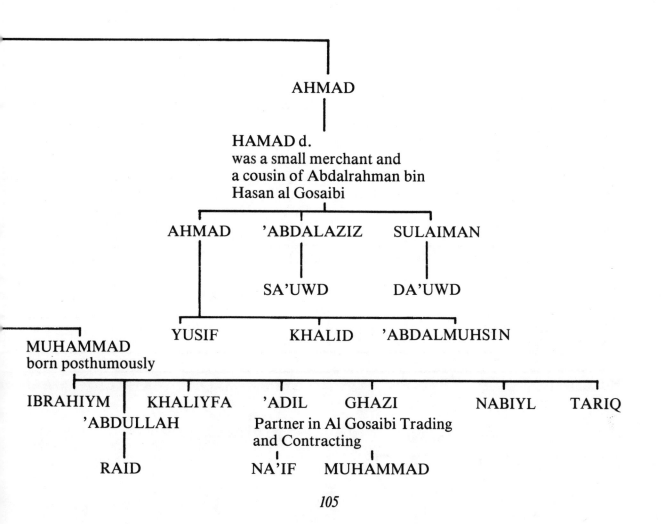

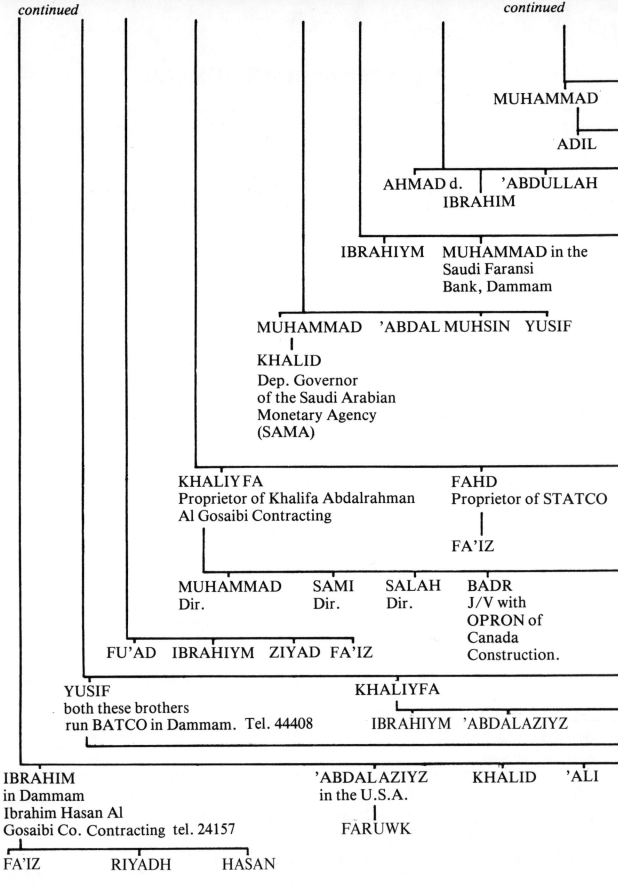

MUHAMMAD

ADIL

AHMAD d.   'ABDULLAH
IBRAHIM

IBRAHIYM   MUHAMMAD in the
Saudi Faransi
Bank, Dammam

MUHAMMAD   'ABDAL MUHSIN   YUSIF

KHALID
Dep. Governor
of the Saudi Arabian
Monetary Agency
(SAMA)

KHALIYFA   FAHD
Proprietor of Khalifa Abdalrahman   Proprietor of STATCO
Al Gosaibi Contracting

FA'IZ

MUHAMMAD   SAMI   SALAH   BADR
Dir.   Dir.   Dir.   J/V with
OPRON of
Canada
Construction.

FU'AD   IBRAHIYM   ZIYAD   FA'IZ

YUSIF   KHALIYFA
both these brothers
run BATCO in Dammam. Tel. 44408   IBRAHIYM   'ABDALAZIYZ

IBRAHIM   'ABDALAZIYZ   KHALID   'ALI
in Dammam   in the U.S.A.
Ibrahim Hasan Al
Gosaibi Co. Contracting tel. 24157   FARUWK

FA'IZ   RIYADH   HASAN

106

FAYSAL   FU'AD

GHAZI   ADNAN

MUHAMMAD   MAHMUWD   FAWZI   'UMAR   SAUWD   KHALID   USSAMA

'ABDALAZIYZ   KHALID

GHAZI
Minister of Industry and
Electricity. Ph.D. London.
b. 1940 Poet.

MUSTAFA

KHALID

IBRAHIYM
The Ibrahim Al Ghosaibi Co.
Qatar
General Trading

NABIYL d.

FARIS

SAMIR   WALIYD

AZIYZ

RASHID
Partner in Al
Gosaibi Trading
& Contracting Co.

KHALID   'ABDALAZIYZ d.

'ABDALWAHAB

MUHAMMAD

ADIL

WALIYD   SA'AD

SA'AD

SA'AD

BADR

HASAN

FU'AD   FA'IZ   ADIL

Binladen Brothers for Contracting and Industry

Head office P.O. 2734 Jiddah

Telephone 29088, 29333, 28487

Cables LADENCO

Telex 401044 BINLDN SJ, 401071 BINBRS SJ

Subsidiary offices
Riyadh P.O. 105, tel. 61427, 61428, tx. 201104 BINRIAD SJ
Dammam P.O. 58, tel. 24070
Amman P.O. 5181, tel. 41620, tx. 1207 JURHTL J.O., 1267 JURHTL J O
Dubai P.O. 1555, tel.. 21516, 27726, 27632, tx. BINLADEN DB
Cairo 19 Arab League Building, tel. 708634, 707252
Beirut P.O. 113-5013, tel. 346662, tx. 21692 RAYCO LE
London Suite 2, 140 Park Lane W1, tel. 01 493 0522/3, tx. 299971 BINLON G, 269885
    SALLAN G
Houston Texas Suite 1109, Fannin Bank Building, tel. (713) 795 0004, tx. 774552 BINBROS
    HOUS, 775858 EXECJET HOUS

The company acts as the main holder of joint family interests in the famous commercial empire founded by Sh. Muhammad. The company is administered by a Board of Directors under the Chairmanship of Sh. Salem Mohammad Binladen and was founded in 1972.

Board Members
Sh. Hassan Mohammad Binladen
Sh. Bakr Mohammad Binladen
Sh. Ghalib Mohammad Binladen
Sh. Thabit Mohammad Binladen
Sh. Omar Mohammad Binladen
Sh. Mahrous Mohammad Binladen

Company History
In all Sh. Muhammad had some fifty four sons and many work in the family business whilst others have formed their own companies either as well or independently. The story of Sh. Mohammad's journey from Hadramawt and his rebuilding of Mecca, which job he obtained having built a ramp to enable King Abdalaziz to get his car into his palace is one of the most romantic success stories in the history of Saudi Arabian business. However the romance of the company and its present controllers should not be confused with the sturdy business acumen which holds the group so successfully together and which has led them to develop and diversify into the very self sufficient organisation we see today.

In addition to the above Binladen Brothers have a substantial stake in Al Fadl Binladen J & P for pre-fabrication and a joint venture with Hunting Surveys Ltd. of the UK. These enormous resources demonstrate clearly the capabilities of the Binladen Brothers Group and they are rounded off by a Trading Division which imports structural steel elements and acts as exclusive agents for Heras Hekwerk of Holland for fencing materials, Alphacoustic of France for quality suspended ceilings and Pander Projects of Holland for standard and luxury contract furniture.

The Family of BINLADEN

A family with origins in Hadramawt.

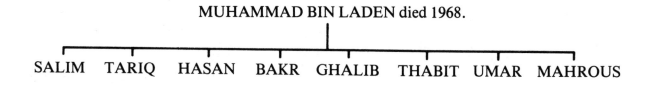

MUHAMMAD BIN LADEN died 1968.

SALIM   TARIQ   HASAN   BAKR   GHALIB   THABIT   UMAR   MAHROUS

Addresses of Subsidiaries, Joint Ventures and Partnerships
Binladen Kaiser P.O. 2734 Jiddah, tel 51512, tx. 401071 BINBRS, 401044 BINLDN
Al Mihdar Binladen P.O. 4445 Jiddah, tel. 74791, 73403
Binladen Saxons Co. P.O. 3143 Jiddah, tel. 36873, 35705, tx. 401071, 401044, P.O. 54 Al
    Khobar, tel. 41933
Binladen Telecommunications Co. P.O. 6045 Jiddah, tel. 52041, 55186, tx. 401071 BINBRS
Binladen Trading P.O. 2742 Jiddah, tel. 34543, tx. 401071, 401044
Ready Mix Saudi P.O. 5948 Jiddah, tel. 55161/2/3, tx. c/o Binladen Brothers
Saudi Traffic Safety P.O. 105 Riyadh, tel. 33676, tx. 201104 BINRIAD

BINLADEN BROTHERS

AL MIHDAR BINLADEN DEVELOPMENT COMPANY (MBDC)
Offers a consultancy service to companies seeking entry into the Saudi Arabian market. They also study and implement joint venture arrangements for the parent company

BINLADEN KAISER LOSINGER
BKL is engaged in all aspects of Real Estate Development. Founded in 1975

BINLADEN TELECOMMUNICATIONS CO.
BTC represents Bell of Canada and coordinates the group members to implement the largest government schemes in this field

BINLADEN BROS. BRICK FACTORY
Situated near Medina this wholly owned factory produces 10 million hollow bricks a year in addition to solid bricks and decorative concrete blocks

BINLADEN AVIATION
BA is a semi-autonomous division operating some seven turbo prop aircraft in support of company operations. Excess capacity is offered to other private operations as well as technical services

BINLADEN KAISER
Binladen Bros. has a majority holding in BK which is one of the world's biggest engineering and construction companies. BK designs and constructs plants for aluminium, steel and cement, as well as mineral processing

BINLADEN EMCO
engaged in the provision of pre-stressed reinforced pre-cast concrete systems used in high rise residential blocks, mosques commercial centres, offices, hotels hospitals and sports stadia

SAUDI TRAFFIC SAFETY
In partnership with PRISMO Universal this company is the largest highway marking company in the world

BINLADEN BROTHERS ALUMINIUM

The factory manufactures aluminium doors and windows under licence from Crittall Windows Ltd. of the U.K. It has a capacity of 85,000 square metres a year.

READY MIX CONCRETE

Binladen Brothers are a major shareholder in Ready Mix Saudi Ltd. a joint venture with Redland Ready Mix of U.K.

SCAFFOLDING FABRICATION

Binladen Bros. has a controlling interest in the National Scaffolding Company, a Saudi company in partnership with Tower al Futeim scaffolding of the U.K.

BINLADEN BROTHERS AGGREGATE

The largest aggregate producer in the Middle East with a huge capacity and full transport and technical facilities.

DOORS AND PARTITIONS

In a joint venture with Bruynzeel of Holland, Binland Bros. produce wooden doors, partitions and kitchen units.

PERLITE SUPPLY

The Saudi Perlite company is controlled by Binladen Brothers and is actively engaged in marketing this superb insulation material.

BINLADEN SAXONS ELECTRO-MECHANICAL COMPANY

BSEM is a joint venture with Saxons Climate Condition Company and is one of the most experienced electro-mechanical companies in the Middle East. They are exclusive agents for Trane of U.S.A., Keep Rite window units, Remington floor units, Baltimore air coils, Powers regulators and Kone Westinghouse elevators.

Ahmad and Muhammad Saleh Kaki

Address head office P.O. 208 Riyadh, tel. 28880, 37455, P.O. 1224 Jiddah, tel. 31555

Telex 201313 AMSKRH SJ

Cable address WATANI

Subsidiary offices
P.O. 263 Dammam, tel. 21176
P.O. 234 Mecca tel, 21697
P.O. 53 Medina tel. 24448
P.O. 49 Ta'if tel. 21665

Proprietor The Board

Board Members
Joint President Sh. Muhammad Saleh Kaki
Joint President Sh. Ahmad Saleh Kaki
Members of the Board of Directors of the National Commercial Bank
Vice Presidents: Sh. Ghiath Muhammad, Sh. Abdulillah Muhammad, Sh. Muhammad Ahmad, and Sh. Abdalwahab Ahmad.

Company History
The company was established in 1945 in the city of Mecca and initially specialised in finance and foreign exchange, an activity expressed by their foundation of and continued interest (10%) in the National Commercial Bank. This led to expansion into the fields of merchandising, construction and contracting, an expansion which has continued successfully into the present day. A and M Saleh Kaki are a company whose history and present policies consist of a careful mixture of the cautious and the innovative.

Today the company is divided into six divisions:
1. The Engineering and Construction Division
Established 1950 this division produces revenues annually of some seventy million riyals.
2. The Industrial Division
comprises the group activities which involve manufacturing
a) Kaki Manufacturing Company; set up in 1961 this is primarily a textile and clothing factory which specializes in uniforms for the Saudi Arabian Armed Forces
b) Kaki Marble Factory; this was established in 1958 as a joint venture to meet rising demands in the construction field and imports high quality marbles into the Kingdom.
c) National Press Company; prints books and stationery for both the public and private market.
d) Aluminium Processing Company; a company which processes, cuts and assembles raw extruded aluminium into doors, windows and frames.
3. The Real Estate Division
This division manages the Kaki land and buildings throughout the Kingdom. These include the Kaki Hotel in Jiddah, P.O. 2559, tel. 48071/2/3, tx. 401739.
4. Technical Services Division
The most recent formation in the Kaki Group, this division handles the need for high technical services. At present efforts are concentrated in the fields of electronic security and detection systems, telecommunications, aircraft maintenance and operation, and the maintenance of facilities and engineering.

Of necessity this enormous and skillfully managed spread of commercial interest has necessitated the formation of many close relationships with foreign companies. A and M Saleh Kaki represent the following companies within the Kingdom:

Dynalectron USA, Wild Heerbrugg Ltd., Switzerland,
Ernst Leitz Wetzlar GmbH, West Germany,
Javelin Electronics, USA,
Albert Nestler KG, West Germany,
Kawasaki Heavy Industries, Japan,
Sheer Pride Ltd., UK,
Umberto Mascagni SPA, Italy,
Drevounia Foreign Trade Corporation, Czechoslovakia,
John Tann Ltd., England,
Homexpo Canada Ltd., Canada,
Traun SRL, Italy,
Leonardo D'Arienzo, Italy,
Photocan Surveys Ltd., Canada,
Plan Hpld, USA,
Varian AG, Switzerland,
Downs Surgical Ltd., England,
De Havilland Aircraft, Canada.

The Abdullah Muhammad Kaki and Muhammad Ahmad Kaki Company has formed a limited liability partnership with the Todesco Giovanni Establishment of Milan; the shares are 44% and 56% respectively. This new company called the United Todesco Constn. Company was formed in Spring, 1979.

Capital 330 million riyals

Bankers The National Commercial Bank, The Riyadh Bank.

5. The Investment Division
Formed to manage A & M Saleh Kaki investments which comprise shareholdings in the following Saudi Companies:
National Commercial Bank, Riyadh Gypsum Company, The Riyadh Bank, Riyadh Cement Company, Jeddah Cement Co., Arabian Navigation Company, Riyadh Electric Power Company, Dammam Electric Power Company, Jeddah Electric Power Company, Saudi Fertilizer Company, Jeddah Oil Refineries Company, and in the following overseas investments: Dubai Electric Power Company, Cement Company Dubai, Arab Hotels and Tourism Company Cairo, Alexandria Company for Navigation and Sea Operation Cairo, Cairo Investment and Development Company, Arabian Company for Wooden Products Cairo, Arab Company for Aluminium Industries Amman, Sheep and Chicken Co. Ltd Amman, Jordanian Chinaware Co., Amman, Glass Manufacturing Co. Jordan, Sharja Heavy Industries Company Sharjah.

6. The Commercial Division
This division is responsible for the supply of goods on a project retail and wholesale basis through Kaki warehouses, showrooms and stores. The areas of specialization include: office furniture, office supplies and equipment, technical and optical equipment, domestic electrical appliances.

The Family of KAKI

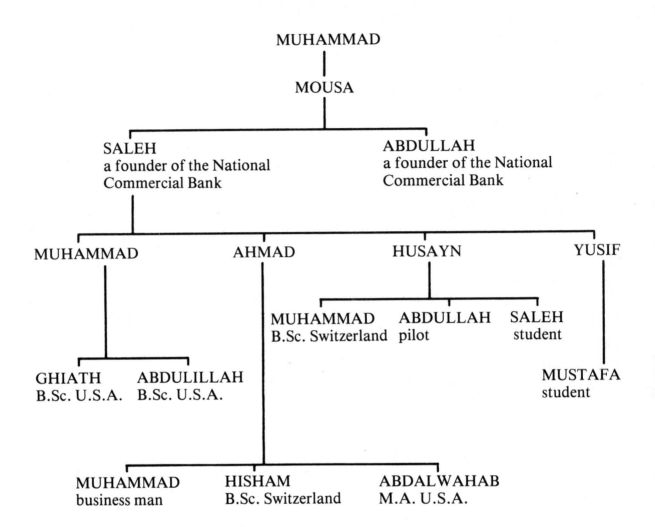

Ali Zaid Al Quraishi and Brothers

Address head office P.O. 339 Dammam

Telephone 21596, 21790

Telex 601058 AZAQ SJ

Proprietor The company is a partnership between the brothers who control AZAQ, the holding company, which is responsible for group planning financial control and development. In this way they direct the operations of the following members of the group:

1. AQOS which operates agencies for Craven A, Dunhill and Piccadilly as well as Land M Lark.
2. AQ Leisure Services operating further agencies for Dunhill and also Sansorite, Shaeffer, Ronson and Canon.
3. WESCOSA, which handles the distribution of electrical supply equipment as well as manufacture.
4. AQ Furniture Corporation. Responsible for retail and contract furnishing, office planning and design, and the distribution of Westinghouse Architectural Systems and Design.
5. Bowater Arabia, which handles contract furnishing for hotels and domestic housing and operates a complete design and installation system.
6. Teamwork. This is a 50/50 Partnership with Taylor Woodrow.
7. AQ Shipping Agencies which operates a complete service for shipping, clearing and forwarding.
8. AQ Investments. This company deals in financial investment property and new venture investment.

The Family of AL QURAISHI

The family has its origins in Bani Khalid of Ha'il.

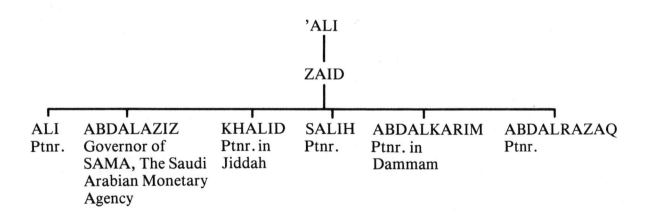

'ALI

ZAID

ALI	ABDALAZIZ	KHALID	SALIH	ABDALKARIM	ABDALRAZAQ
Ptnr.	Governor of SAMA, The Saudi Arabian Monetary Agency	Ptnr. in Jiddah	Ptnr.	Ptnr. in Dammam	Ptnr.

Saudi Research and Marketing Co.

Address head office P.O. 4556 Jiddah

Telephone 34962, 28708, 30213

Telex 401570 ARANEWS SJ

Cable address MARADNEWS

Subsidiary offices
Riyadh P.O. 478 tel, 38272, 30460, tx. 201660 MARAD
Al Khobar tel. 42991, 46616
Cairo tel. 818392
Beirut P.O. 8886, tel. 547090, tx. 20649
London tel. 01 353 4413, tx. 889272 ARABNEWS
Geneva tel. 211711, tx. 289005
Houston tel. (713) 961 0245, tx. 790209 ARABNEWS
Washington tel. (202) 638 7183, tx. 440568 SAUDI
Yokohama tel. (045) 573 6816, tx. 47896 UMULQURA

Ownership
The company is run as a partnership in which the executive partners are Syd. Hisham Ali
Hafiz and Syd. Muhammad Ali Hafiz. The remaining are sleeping partners. The business is
operated in two divisions.
1. The Publishing Division
This produces three papers, two daily and one weekly.
Arab News, 50,000 per day.
Sharqal Awsat, 64,000 per day in Saudi Arabia and 20,000 per day in London.
This paper is published in London and printed in Jiddah, London and Riyadh.
Saudi Business Weekly, 12,000 per week.
2. The Circulation Division
Which is responsible for the distribution of the company's own publications as well as others.
Advertising is handled by Tihama (q.v.). The company owns Central Press Photos of
London.

Bankers Saudi British Bank.

The Family of HAFIZ

The Hafiz Family is the oldest publishing family in the Kingdom and commenced operations in the City of Medina forty-five years ago. At that time they founded the National Daily Al Medina which was wholly owned by them. Today the family retain two shares in the paper having relinquished their total ownership fifteen years ago in response to the governments wish to spread ownership in this field. The family are of Bani Hashim descent and thus descendants of the Prophet Muhammed; because of this they should be addressed as Sayid rather than Shaykh.

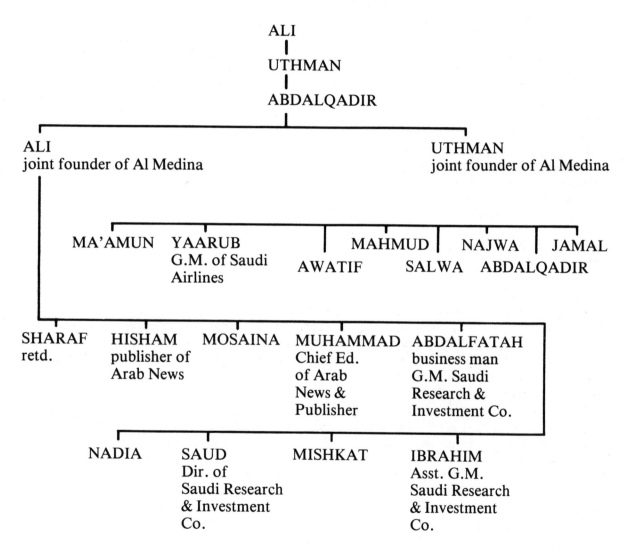

ALI
|
UTHMAN
|
ABDALQADIR

ALI
joint founder of Al Medina

UTHMAN
joint founder of Al Medina

MA'AMUN   YAARUB
G.M. of Saudi
Airlines

MAHMUD   NAJWA   JAMAL
AWATIF   SALWA   ABDALQADIR

SHARAF   HISHAM   MOSAINA   MUHAMMAD   ABDALFATAH
retd.   publisher of   Chief Ed.   business man
Arab News   of Arab   G.M. Saudi
News &   Research &
Publisher   Investment Co.

NADIA   SAUD   MISHKAT   IBRAHIM
Dir. of   Asst. G.M.
Saudi Research   Saudi Research
& Investment   & Investment
Co.   Co.

Samman Trading & Importing Co.

Address head office P.O. 4180 Jiddah

Telephone 692207, 690986

Telex 401907 SAMMAN SJ

Cable address NESYAN

Board Members
Sh. Adnan Taha Samman 40% Chairman
Sh. Tewfiq Taha Samman 30% Member
Sh. Muhammad Taha Samman 30% Dir. General

Activities
The company was established in 1976 as a corporation, becoming a limited company in 1977.
Sh. Adnan completed his period of public service in 1976 having finally held office as Executive
Vice Governor of the Saline Water Conversion Corporation before entering private business.
This company specializes in the import and marketing of the finest decorating materials,
project installation in this field, and furniture and decor studies to the highest and most
luxurious standards. The company acts as agent for the following:
Sommer of France; carpets and wall coverings.
Labiche of Canada and the US; carpets and wall coverings.
Boisseliers Durif Furniture.
Roman Deco and Decovea.
Laque d'Argent Marlin for lighting and wall coverings.
Vorwerk.
British Carpets and Forfar for carpets.
Bankers Saudi British Bank, Saudi Cairo Bank, Banque Liban Francaise, Paris.

Subsidiaries

1. Saudi Arabian Electronic Eqpt. Co.
P.O. 1874 Jiddah, tel. 46607, tx. 400167 SAEECO SJ
This company is a wholly owned joint venture between Sh. Adnan and Television Holdings
Inc. of Amsterdam. T.H.I. participate in the profits. The company was set up in 1977 and
specializes in maintenance contracts, sound systems, closed circuit T.V., repairs to electronic
equipment and audio visual systems.
Bankers Saudi British Bank.

2. Samman Trade and Industrial Investments Corporation
A company established in 1976 and wholly owned by Sh. Adnan and due to move to very
splendid new offices during the summer of 1979. The company studies and implements
industrial projects and has recently erected a plant for sulphuric acid and polyphosphates. It
will form joint ventures and specialise in petrochemical chemistry and mineral resources.
Bankers Saudi British Bank

(After September 1979 the company will have its own address but until that time it will
continue to operate from the premises of the Samman Trading and Importing Co.)

3. Samman Construction and Contracting Corporation
P.O. 5268, tel. 55029, 52338, tx. 401907 SAMMAN SJ also Riyadh tel. 821141. Established in
1977 the company is a joint venture with the Antler Corporation of the USA who participate
to the extent of 25% of the profits. The company is wholly owned by Sh. Adnan.
Though young the company has already completed some eighty million Saudi riyals worth of
contracts.
Bankers Saudi British Bank

The Family of SAMMAN

Descending from the Abdulsamad of the Wadi Muhrim between Ta'if and Al Hadal mountains they are Al Numur of the tribe of Thaqif. They acquired their present name because Abdullah and Da'uwd traded in the export of dates and Zamzam water from the Hidjaz to Syria. On the return journey they brought back foodstuffs and in particular ghee (Arabic samn). Some of the family settled in Syria and relations are to be found in Damascus to this day.

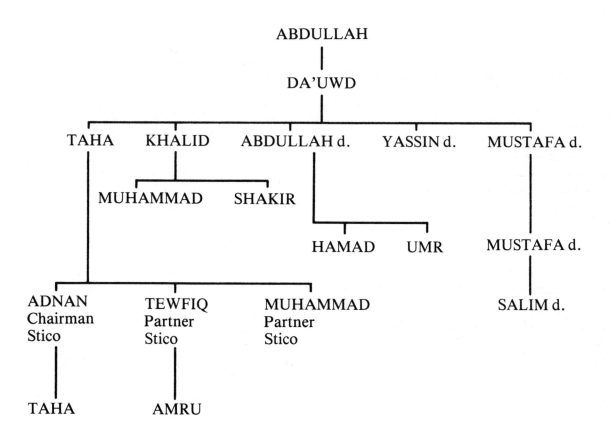

Alhuseini Corporation

Address P.O. 851 Jiddah

Telephone 44877, 45133, 27429, 38008

Telex 401163 HUSENI SJ

Company History

The business was founded by the late Syd. Muhammad Alhuseini who was a native of Medina. To begin with he operated in the commodity and textile fields starting in the early thirties. In 1947 an office was established in Karachi as most of the trading was with Pakistan at that date. In 1954 the head office was established in Jiddah and the import of building materials was developed. A Travel Office was set up in 1963 and in 1972 the Construction Division was founded to work in both the public and the private sectors. In 1977 expansion resulted in the establishment of an Automobile and Heavy Machinery Division.

Business Activities

Under the Chairmanship and direction of Syd. Abdulaziz the Corporation now operates in six divisions:
1. Trading Division
2. Travel Agency Division
3. Construction Division
4. Automobile and Heavy Machinery Division
5. Solar Energy Division
6. Freight Transportation and Handling Division

Agencies

Travel:Sales Agents for SDI, Saudi Arabian Airlines. General Sales Agents for Pakistan International Airlines, VARIG Brazilian Airlines, KM Air Malta Limited.

Automobile: The Corporation is the BMW concessionaire for the whole of the Kingdom of Saudi Arabia.

Partnerships/Joint Ventures

The Alhuseini Corporation holds 51% in the following enterprises:

Alhuseini-ADA Saudi Arabia Company Ltd.

The National Construction Saudi Arabia Company Ltd.

Alhuseini Macdonald Layton Company Ltd.

Boremaster Saudi Arabia Company Ltd.

The Family of HUSEINI

A very old and respected family descending from the son of the fourth Caliph, Ali, who was himself the son in law of the Prophet Muhammad.

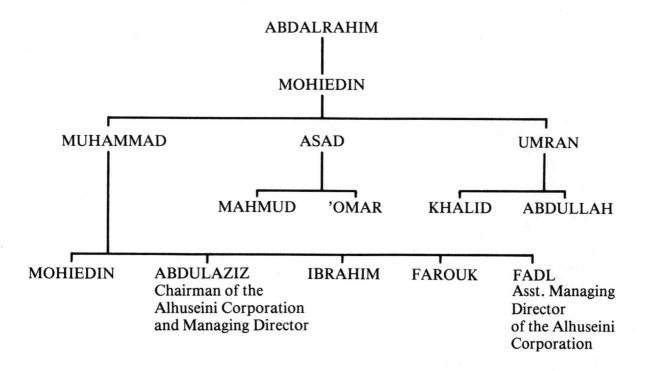

Aggad Investment Company

Address head office P.O. 2256 Riyadh

Telephone 24447, 22222

Telex 200276 AGGAD SJ

Cable address AGGAD

Proprietor
Umar A Aggad, a founder and Board Member of the Saudi British Bank

The Aggad Investment Company is a limited partnership which operates the interests of Omar Aggad in the following enterprises.

1. Engineering Projects and Products Company (EPPCO)
Head office P.O. 987 Riyadh, tel. 22222, tx. 201022 SJ, cables EPPCOL
Branches: Jiddah P.O. 1502, tel. 22222, Dammam P.O. 450, tel. 22222
Ownership: Sh. Ibrahim Juffali 60%
Sh. Ahmad Juffali, Chairman
Mr. Omar Aggad, Managing Director, 40%.
The Company is the major one in the telecommunications field with a turnover of 220 million riyals annually.
Bankers: Arab Bank and City Bank

2. Saudi Plastic Products Company Ltd. (SAPPCO)
Address: P.O. 2828 Riyadh, tel. 4041900, tx. 201025 SAPPCO SJ.
Sales office: Jiddah, tel. 28890
Ownership: the Partners
H.R.H. Prince Abdullah Al Faisal Al Sa'ud
Aggad Investment Company
Olayan Financing Company
Saleh and Abdalaziz Bahussain Company
Suliman Abdalmohsen Aba Nomay
Nasser Muhammad Alsaleh
Hassan Mishary Alhussein
Abbas Abdalfattah Aggad
The company, formed in 1969, manufactures PVC piping for all applications in sizes of 16 mm to 400 mm. SAPPCO also produces polystyrene insulation boards for industrial and domestic buildings, cold stores, air conditioned premises and refrigerated transport.

3. Arabian Plastic Manufacturing Company Ltd. (APLACO)
Address: P.O. 6193 Riyadh, tel. 4013424, tx. 201745 APLACO J, cables APLACO.
Ownership: Partnership.
Saudi Plastic Products Co. Ltd.
George Fischer Ltd. of Switzerland
Antone Anger of Austria
Chairman: Mr. Omar Aggad
APLACO was established in 1976 and produces and markets PVC fittings.

4. Arabian Technical Contracting Co. (ARTEC)
Address: P.O. 2987 Riyadh, tel. 4780584, 4789573, tx. 201372 ARTEC SJ.
Ownership: Partners Mr. Omar Aggad, Chairman, and Mr. Fahd Hammad
The company was formed in 1973 and operates in two divisions. The Contracting Division specializes in road construction and the Industrial Division in terrazo and cement tiles, supply and laying of asphalt and the supply of cement blocks and kerb stones.

5. Aluminium Products Co. Ltd (ALUPCO)
Address: P.O. 2080 Dammam, tel. 24934, 20789, tx. 601148 ALUPCO SJ, 601271 ALUPCO SJ, cables ALUPCO
The Company is controlled by a Board of Directors:
Mr. Omar Aggad, Chairman
Sh. Hashim S. Hashim, Man. Director
Sh. Suliman S. Olayan, Member

6. Health Water Bottling Co. Ltd. (NISSAH)
Address: P.O. 2948 Riyadh, tel. (office) 33300, (plant) 57512, tx. 201102 NISSAH SJ, cable HEALTHWATER
The company produces bottled water in its own bottles in capacities of half a litre and one and a half litres. The company distributes its own product both throughout the Kingdom and in the export field, though it does act through agents on occasion. Present expansion involves the erection of a fruit juice plant to implement the licences already held by the company.
Ownership: the Partners
Abdalrahman Al Murshid
Aggad Investment Co.
Olayan Saudi Holdings Co. Ltd.
Muhammad Abdalrahman Al Fraih (q.v.)
Hiram Charl Corm
H. E. Abdalrahman Al Shaikh
H. E. Naser Hamad Al Mangour
Muhammad Abdulrahman Al Hamidi
Sulaiman Abdulrahman Al Saleh
Mazen Ibrahim Al Angari
Ossama Omar Fageh
Ramzi Habib Sanbar

7. Steel Products Co. Ltd. (STEPCO)
Address: P.O. 4930 Riyadh, tel. 24447
Ownership: the Partners
Aggad Investment Co.
E. A. Juffali and Bros.
Korf Industry and Handel
Ibrahim Touq
The company was formed in 1976 and produces wiremesh for reinforcement.

8. Prefabricated Building Co. Ltd. (MABCO)
Address: P.O. 1549 Riyadh, tel. 39486, 30653, tx. 201364 MABCO SJ, cables PRECAST
MABCO was formed in 1975 and produces precast concrete elements for housing projects and other projects of a constructional or industrial nature.
Ownership: the Partners
H.R.H. Prince Fahd Ibn Salman Ibn Abdalaziz Al Sa'ud
H.R.H. Prince Abdalaziz Ibn Sattam Ibn Abdalaziz Al Sa'ud
Sh. Hassan Mishari Al Hussein
Al Aggad Investment Co.
Sh. Omar Abdulkader Faqih (q.v.)
Sh. Hamza Mohammed Boggarry
Sh. Mohammed Abdalrahman Al Fraih (q.v.)
Sh. Umran Mohammed Umran (q.v.)
Sh. Rashed Abdulrahman Al Rashed
Sh. Abdullah Abdalmuhsin Al Tuwaijri

Sh. Abdullah Ibrahim Al Hudaithi
Nefinnco B.V.
Partek B.V.

9. Saudi International Petroleum Carriers Ltd. (SIPCA)
Address: P.O. 5572 Riyadh, tel. 26940, tx. 201709 TEXACO SJ.
SIPCA was established in 1977 and is engaged in the transportation of petroleum and petroleum products and tanker chartering.
Ownership: the Partners
Aggad Investment Co.
Sh. Naser Al Saleh
Texaco Marine Investment Co.

10. Laminated Fabrics Manufacturing Co. Ltd (LAMINCO)
Address: P.O. 221 Riyadh, tel. 22818
This company was established in 1977 and produces thermo-plastic films, unsupported and thermoplastic coated sub-tracks.
Ownership:
Aggad Investment Co.
Sh. Mohammed Abdalrahman Al Fraih (q.v.)
Hassan Deeb Hamdan

11. Saudi Arabian Belgian Construction Co. (SABECO)
Address: P.O. 4929 Riyadh, tel. 68545, tx. 200142 SABECO SJ.
Established in 1977 SABECO operates in building and civil engineering construction.
Ownership: the Partners
Compagnie d'Enterprises (CFE) 40%
Sh. Hassan Mishari 14%
Omar Aggad 14%
Abdullah Baksh 10%
Omran Mohammed Omran 10%
Mahammed Charara 4%
Abdalmuhsin Abdalaziz Tuwaijri 4%
Abdalmuhsin Abdullah Tuwaijri 4%
Brussels Office c/o CFE 7, rue Belliaro, 1040 Bruxelles

12. Saudi SAC Contracting Co. Ltd (SAUDI SAC)
Address: P.O. 9376 Riyadh, tel. 67545
Saudi Sac was founded in 1978 and is engaged in contracting for electrical mechanical and sanitation projects. The company also runs and maintains electrical and mechanical machinery.
Ownership: the Partners
Aggad Investment Co.
Sh. Naser Al Saleh
Supplies and Contracts Holdings, Liberia.

13. Hygienic Paper Factory
Address: P.O. 3626 Riyadh, tel. 35102, tx. 202192 FINE SJ.
The company began in 1977 and manufactures a brand of face tissues called 'FINE'. A branch in Jiddah makes diapers, sanitary towels, toilet paper and napkins.
Ownership: the Partners
Aggad Investment Co.
Abdalaziz Shiha
Elia Nuqul

The Family of AGGAD

Originating in Bir Saba, Acre, Nablus and Jaffa.

The Juffali Group of Companies

Address head office P.O. 1049 Jiddah

Telephone 22222

Telex 401130 JUFFALI SJ

Cable address JUFFALICENT

Subsidiary offices

London, ENPRO Business Representatives Ltd, 7 Old Park Lane, W1, tel. 499 6620, 499 6629,
tx. 262707 ENPRO G

Beirut, P.O. 113 5327, tel. 353618, tx. 22136 EAJB LE

Zurich, ENPRO, Uraniastrasse 34, CH 8001, tel. 2113431, tx. 52859 ENPRO CH

Jiddah, P.O. 297, tel. 22222, tx. 401530 JUFFALI SJ

Riyadh, P.O. 86, tel. 22322, tx. 201049 JAFFALI SJ

Dammam, P.O. 24, tel. 23333, tx. 601025 EPPCO SJ

Jubail c/o P.O. 24 Dammam, tel. 51300, tx. 631280, 631281 JABEEN SJ

Offices of subsidiary and associated companies

EPPCO head office P.O. 987 Riyadh, tx. 201022 EPPCO SJ
   Jiddah P.O. 1502, tx. 401130 JUFFALI SJ
   Dammam P.O. 450, tx. 601025 EPPCO SJ

SEMCO Arabia Ltd, P.O. 215 Dhahran Airport

Saudi Electric Co. Ltd
   Ta'if P.O. 54
   Mecca P.O. 386
   Jiddah P.O. 1213

Saudi National Power Co., Jiddah P.O. 433

Medina Electric Power Co.
   Medina P.O. 128
   Jiddah P.O. 1049

Al Hasa Electric Co., Hofuf P.O. 32

Saudi Cement Co., Dammam P.O. 306, tx. 601068 CEMENT SJ

Fluor Arabia Ltd, Dammam P.O. 24

Petroserv, Dhahran Airport P.O. 215

Pool Arabia Ltd, Dhahran Airport P.O. 2568

Juffali Real Estate, Jiddah P.O. 1049, tx. 401130 JUFFALI SJ

National Insurance Co., Jiddah P.O. 5832, tx. 401130 JUFFALI SJ

E A Juffali & Brothers Central Parts Organisation, Jiddah P.O. 1049, tel. 77687, 77649,
   tx. 400246 JUFCPO SJ

E A Juffali & Brothers, E.D.P. Centre, Jiddah P.O. 1049, tel. 77687, 77649, tx. 400246
   JUFCPO SJ

E A Juffali & Brothers, Technical Training Centre, Jiddah P.O. 1049, tel. 72122, tx. 401130
   JUFFALI SJ

Diesel Electric, Jiddah P.O. 1049, tel. 22222, tx. 401130 JUFFALI SJ;
   branches: Jiddah P.O. 197, tel. 72122, tx. 401530 JUFFALI SJ;
   Riyadh P.O. 86, tel. 22622, 22125, tx. 201049 JUFFALI SJ;
   Dammam P.O. 24, tel. 22444, tx. 601025 EPPCO SJ

Company History

The activities of the Group began in 1948 and have contributed more than most to the
economic development of the Kingdom, characterised as they are by great energy, efficiency
and enthusiasm. The Juffali Group of Companies forms the largest association of industrial

and commercial enterprises in Saudi Arabia today. In size it is the equal of one of the three hundred largest industrial corporations in the world. The Group operates through some two dozen subsidiaries, affiliates and fully independent branches whose activities embrace the following: General Trading, Electric Power Utilities, Cement Production, Commercial Vehicle Assembly and Body Manufacture, Engineering Construction and Management Services for the petroleum industry; Oil Well Workover Services, Real Estate Development and Insurance.

Agencies held by E A Juffali and Brothers
American Lincoln USA, Adolf Mohr Maschinen Fabrik Germany, AC - DECCO (Gen Motors Corpn.) USA, Barber Greene Overseas USA, BICC Ltd, BICKEL K.G., E. Germany, Bunce (Ashbury) Ltd UK, Butler Manufacturing Co. USA, Clark International Marketing SA USA, Compagnie Francaise, BLAW-KNOX France, Comp Air Construction and Mining Ltd UK, Copperweld Steel International Co. USA, Daimler Benz AG Germany, DEMAG AG Germany, Demag Foerdertechnik Germany, Deutsch and Babcock AG Germany, the Ferrantz Engineering Co. Ltd UK, FMC Corporation USA, Frigor Denmark, GEC (Lamps and Lighting) Ltd UK, Gallion Mfg. Division USA, General Motors Overseas Distribution Corporation USA, GENT Chloride Ltd UK, H.U. Sheldon and Co. Inc. USA, Heidelberger Druckmaschinen AG Germany, IBM World Trade Corporation USA, Kelvinator International Corp. USA, Klimsch & Co. Germany, Landis and Gyr AG Switzerland, The Liner Concrete Machinery Co. Ltd UK, Linotype and Machinery Ltd UK, Litton Microwave Ovens USA, Massey Ferguson Ltd UK, Michelin et Cie France, The Perolin Co. Inc. USA, The Phoenix Engineering Co. Ltd UK, Peiner AG Germany, Triumph Adler Vertriebs GmbH Germany, Servis Domestic Appliances Ltd UK, Siemens AG Germany, Simon Engineering Dudley Ltd UK, Stahl 2 Co. Germany, Sunroz International Division USA, Sulzer Brothers Ltd Switzerland, Transformation Union AG Germany, Tyler Division (Clark International Marketing) USA, Volkswagenwerk AG Germany, Wallace and Tierman Ltd UK, Worthington Corporation USA, York International.

Agencies held by the Juffali Subsidiary Diesel Electric Company
Abacus Internation USA, Becker Autoradiowerk GmbH Germany, Robert Bosch GmbH Germany, Zahnradfabrik Friedrichschafen AG Germany.

Wholly Owned Subsidiaries
Engineering Projects and Products Co. Ltd. EPPCO
Riyadh P.O. 987, tel. 22222, tx. 201022 EPPCO SJ with branches in Jiddah and Dammam.

This company has installed all the exchange and subscriber systems in the Kingdom under Government contract and operates its own training centre as well as monitoring communications systems for development and its own research centre. The company is a partnership where Sh. Ibrahim Juffali holds 60% and Umar Aggad 40%. Sh. Ahmad Juffali is the Chairman.

Joint Ventures
Arabia Electric
Jiddah P.O. 4621, tel. 59521, tx. 401864 JUFSIE SJ
A joint venture with Siemens of Germany which designs, engineers and installs large scale electrical and electronic projects.
Branches in Riyadh (P.O. 86, tel. 22322, tx. 201049 JUFFALI SJ) and Dammam (P.O. 24, tel. 25364, tx. 601025 EPPCO SJ)

Arabian Chemical Co. Ltd.
Dammam P.O. 24, tel. 25364.
Branches in Jiddah (P.O. 1049, tel. 22222, tx. 40113 O JUFFALI SJ and Riyadh (P.O. 86, tel. 57138, tx. 201049 JUFFALI SJ) with DOW Chemicals USA.

Arabian Metal Industries Ltd.
Jiddah P.O. 5937, tel. 55035, 55243, tx. 401130 JUFFALI SJ.
With Carosserie Abillama of Lebanon the company produces special bodies for tippers,
trailers and water and fuel bowsers.

Beck Arabia
Dhahran Airport P.O. 378, tel. 42905, tx. 670152 BECK SJ
This company is a joint venture between E A JUFFALI Bros. and the Dallas based Heung C.
Beck Company. They provide management services for large scale civil construction projects
required by Saudi Arabia's Development Plans and the needs of the real estate development
division within the Juffali Group.

Fluor Arabia Ltd.
Dhahran Airport P.O. 360, tx. 601010 FLURAB SJ, with a branch in Riyadh (P.O. 86,
tel. 61967, tx. 200233 FLURY SJ) with the Fluor Corporation of USA and engaged in oil and
gas development in the Kingdom extending to equipment leasing, construction management
and training.

Juffali Sulzer Saudi Arabia Ltd.
Jiddah P.O. 5357, tel. 57434, tx. 401262 JSULZ SJ.
Branches in Riyadh (P.O. 86, tel. 66176, tx. 201049 JUFFALI SJ) and Dammam (P.O. 24,
tel. 31268, tx. 601025 EPPCO SJ). A joint venture company with Sulzer Brothers of
Switzerland, the leading air conditioning contractor in Europe.

Maintenance of Airconditioning and Refrigeration Co. (MARCO)
Jiddah P.O. 6290, tel. 58385, tx. 401826 MARCOL SJ.
Branches in Riyadh (P.O. 86, tel. 63383, tx. 201049 JUFFALI SJ) and Dammam (P.O. 7023,
tel. 25365, tx. 601025 EPPCO SJ). A company formed with York International which is a
division of Borg-Warner, the Kingdom's leading supplier of air conditioning equipment.

National Automobile Industry Co. Ltd.
Jiddah P.O. 5938, tel. 55035, 55333, tx. 400099 NAICAR SJ.
A joint venture with Daimler-Benz AG of Germany the company assembles commercial
vehicles in Saudi Arabia. Present production is nineteen vehicles a day and takes up 87% of
the Saudi Market. The company operates its own extremely well equipped training centre
which supplies its needs for skilled manpower.

Saudi Bahraini Cement Company
Dammam P.O. 2464, tel. 25362, tx. 601359 SBCDAM SJ.
A joint venture between the Saudi Cement Co. and the Government of Bahrain.

Saudi Building Systems
Jiddah P.O. 4980, tel. 58749, tx. 401130 JUFFALI SJ.   Branches Riyadh (P.O. 86, tel. 60230,
tx. 201049 JUFFALI SJ), Dammam (P.O. 24, tel. 45838, tx. 601025 EPPCO SJ).
A joint venture between E A Juffali and Batler International of the USA.

Steel Products Co. Ltd (STEPCO)
Riyadh P.O. 4930, tel. 22222, tx. 201022 EPPCO SJ.
Partners: E A Juffali Bros., Aggad Investment Co., Korf Industry and Handel, Ibrahim
Touq.
Produces meshes for reinforcement.

Associate Companies

Saudi Cement Company
Dammam P.O. 306, tel. 22480, tx. 601068 CEMENT SJ. The branch office in Jiddah is the
Technical Advisor's office (P.O. 1049, tel. 22222, tx. 401130 JUFFALI SJ). The company is
one of the largest cement manufacturers in the Middle East. The plant is situated in Hofuf and

produces over 4,500 tons a day using natural gas to fire the kilns. This company is a publicly owned company in which E A Juffali are the major shareholders and of which Sh. Ahmad Juffali is the Managing Director.

Medina Electric Company
Medina P.O. 128, tel. 21122, tx. 470014 KAHRBA SJ.
A public company in which EA Juffali are major shareholders. The chief engineer's office is in Jiddah (P.O. 1049, tel. 22222).

Aster S.P.A.
New Jiddah International Airport P.O. 5909, tel. 692700 ex 4015, tx. 401130 JUFFALI SJ.
A company formed to fulfill the air conditioning and mechanical sub-contract for the new international airport in Jiddah. This project is the largest ever undertaken in the Kingdom involving 12 chillers of 1000 tons each and this is only an initial specification. It is expected that this will be increased to a total of 52,000 tons.

National Electric Products Co. Ltd. NEPCO
Jiddah P.O. 6619, tel. 59404, tx. 400297 SJ.

National Insurance Co. SA
Jiddah P.O. 5832, tel. 30167, 36861, tx. 401791 NICOM SJ
Branches in Riyadh, P.O. 86, tel. 67548, tx. 201049 JUFFALI SJ
Dammam, P.O. 2312, tel. 25237, tx. 601025 EPPCO SJ
This company is incorporated in Luxembourg and E A Juffali Bros are major shareholders in partnership with the Munich Reinsurance Company. The company is engaged in all classes of non-life insurance, and specialises in engineering, fire and marine risks.

Orient Transport Company
Jiddah P.O. 6983, tel. 46745, tx. 401832 OTC SJ
Branches in Riyadh, P.O. 86, tel. 22322, tx. 201049 JUFFALI SJ for OTC
Dammam, P.O. 24, tel. 31359, tx. 601025 EPPCO SJ for OTC

Petroserv
Dhahran Airport P.O. 215, tel. 44994, tx. 670151 PETSER SJ
Provides supply and maintenance services to the petroleum industry.

Pool Arabia
Dhahran Airport P.O. 2568, tel. 44407, 43280, tx. 670154 POOLSA SJ with Pool International a subsidiary of the Lone Star Gas Company.

The Family of JUFFALI

The family tradition is that they descend from the great conqueror, Khalid ibn al Walid. They migrated from Anaiza in Qasim and the present commercial giant is based on an early association with G.E.C. The family name is said to derive from one of two beautiful horses owned by the mother of Abdullah bin Salih. These were named Fadl and Jaffal and both gave their names to famous families.

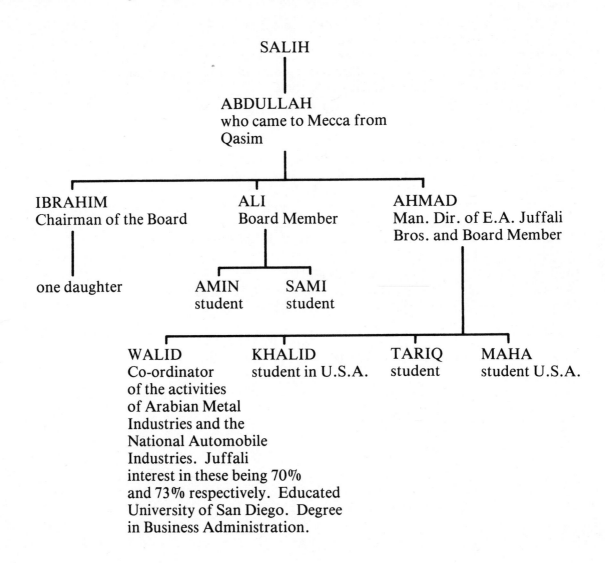

SALIH

ABDULLAH
who came to Mecca from
Qasim

IBRAHIM
Chairman of the Board

ALI
Board Member

AHMAD
Man. Dir. of E.A. Juffali
Bros. and Board Member

one daughter

AMIN
student

SAMI
student

WALID
Co-ordinator
of the activities
of Arabian Metal
Industries and the
National Automobile
Industries. Juffali
interest in these being 70%
and 73% respectively. Educated
University of San Diego. Degree
in Business Administration.

KHALID
student in U.S.A.

TARIQ
student

MAHA
student U.S.A.

Umran and Umran and Brothers

Address head office P.O. 550 Riyadh

Telephone 30059, 22758

Telex 201935 SASCOM SJ

Cable address VENSCO

Subsidiary offices
Jiddah P.O. 4319, tel. 51696
Dammam P.O. 1238
Riyadh, Khazzan St., tel. 85017

Proprietor Sh. Umran bin Muhammad and his brothers Abdalaziz and Abdalrahman.

The Company acts as a holding company for the family interests. Sh. Umran has a wide personal involvement in commercial affairs. He is the Managing Director of the Rashid and Al Umran Co., whose partners are his uncle (by marriage) Rashid Al Rashid (40%) and Sh. Umran and his brothers hold 20% each. Sh. Umran is also Managing Director of the Civil Works Co. in which the holdings are The Rashid and Al Umran Co. 60% and Tamimi and Fouad 40%, and Managing Director of the Arabian Industries Co. which is shared 70% by the Civil Works Co and 30% by others. This company is concerned with silica sand, bricks and a hydrated lime factory and will shortly manufacture white cement; it was established in 1977. Sh. Umran is a partner in Dirab Co. for quarrying and ready mixed asphalt, has 50% of Al Umran and Toug Co. with Sh. Ibrahim al Toug holding the other 50%. Sh. Ibrahim is second Chairman of the Riyadh Chamber of Commerce and General Manager of Messrs Juffali. Sh. Umran is a member of the board of the Saudi Faransi Bank, MABCO for pre-cast concrete, and SABICO the Saudi Belgian Company, the Saudi Public Transport Company and his interest in the Saudi Arabian Service Company is through the Rashid and Al Umran Co. which owns 70%, the remaining 30% being owned by Salih Mosaad.

The Al Rashid and Al Umran Company, the Civil Works Company and Arabian Industries share the offices and telephones of Umran and Umran and Brothers. Sh. Abdalaziz bin Muhammad uses the Riyadh subsidiary office and acts as deputy for Sh. Umran. The Al Umran and Al Toug Company is in King Faisal St., P.O. 2743, tel. 37356. SABICO is at Riyadh P.O. 987, tel. 68545 and tx. 20022.

Bankers American Express Bahrain, al Saudi al Faransi Bank, the National Commercial Bank.

The Family of UMRAN

Probably the oldest family in the capital, Riyadh.

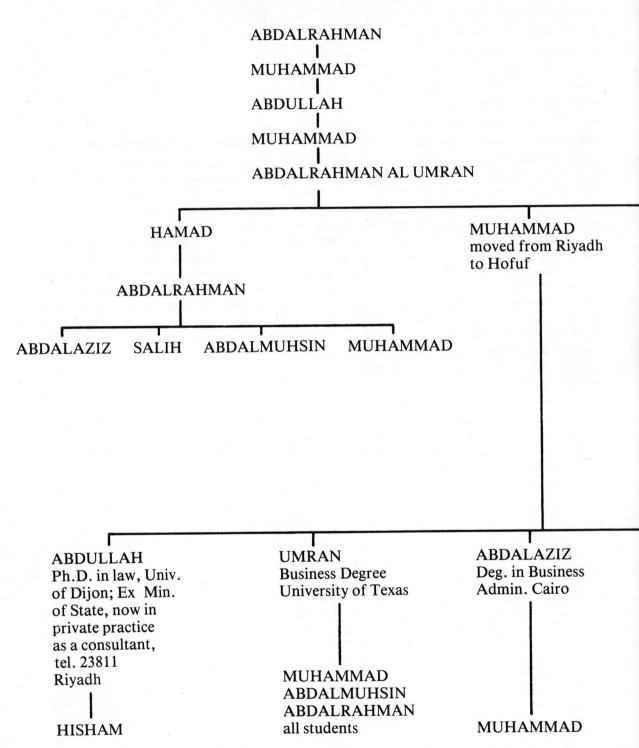

ABDALRAHMAN
|
MUHAMMAD
|
ABDULLAH
|
MUHAMMAD
|
ABDALRAHMAN AL UMRAN

HAMAD

MUHAMMAD
moved from Riyadh
to Hofuf

ABDALRAHMAN

ABDALAZIZ   SALIH   ABDALMUHSIN   MUHAMMAD

ABDULLAH
Ph.D. in law, Univ.
of Dijon; Ex Min.
of State, now in
private practice
as a consultant,
tel. 23811
Riyadh
|
HISHAM

UMRAN
Business Degree
University of Texas
|
MUHAMMAD
ABDALMUHSIN
ABDALRAHMAN
all students

ABDALAZIZ
Deg. in Business
Admin. Cairo
|
MUHAMMAD

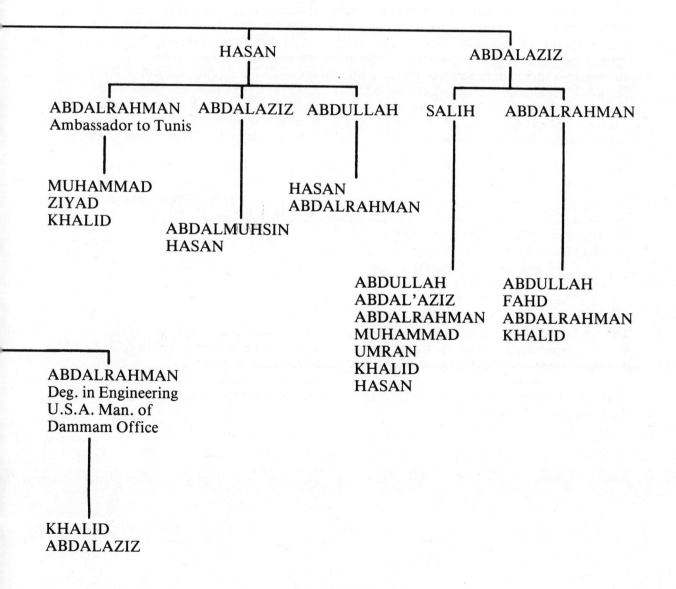

HASAN ABDALAZIZ

ABDALRAHMAN   ABDALAZIZ   ABDULLAH   SALIH   ABDALRAHMAN
Ambassador to Tunis

MUHAMMAD   HASAN
ZIYAD   ABDALRAHMAN
KHALID

         ABDALMUHSIN
         HASAN

                                    ABDULLAH   ABDULLAH
                                    ABDAL'AZIZ   FAHD
                                    ABDALRAHMAN   ABDALRAHMAN
                                    MUHAMMAD   KHALID
                                    UMRAN
                                    KHALID
                                    HASAN

ABDALRAHMAN
Deg. in Engineering
U.S.A. Man. of
Dammam Office

KHALID
ABDALAZIZ

SIACO Saudi International Corporation

Address head office P.O. 4571 Jiddah

Telephone 61691, 61692

Telex 401501 SITIFO SJ, 401096 GENERY SJ, 401806 TRANSCO SJ

Cable address KAZADYOU

Subsidiary offices
SITIFO King Abdalaziz St. Jiddah, tel. 32088
SAMESCO Riyadh

Proprietor Sh. Adnan Abdalrahman Abdalmajeed in partnership with Sh. Muhammad Ibrahim Al Hied.

Company History
Sh. Adnan began gaining his very wide business experience in 1960 and successively worked in the Ministry of Information gaining familiarity with broadcasting, advertising, marketing newspapers and fairs organisation. This last culminated in his organisation of the Jiddah Trade Fair in 1975, 76 and 77. Siaco itself specializes in all aspects of marketing and representation and the international fairs side of the business is handled by Sitifo.
Sh. Adnan is chairman of Samesco and he hold a 50% share with Sh. Muhammad Al Hied. The Saudi Medical Services Co. Ltd. specializes in the supply of medical equipment, the servicing of Government tenders, and operates a Flying Doctor Service as well as establishing specialized hospitals and clinics. Its capital is to be raised shortly to 45 million riyals. The Saudi International Transportation Co. Ltd, Siatraco, is chaired by Sh. Muhammad Al Hied and operates in the freight forwarding field.
The Saudi American Modern Agricultural Co. Ltd is a joint venture with a US company; participation is 70% Saudi and 30% US. The company is established to operate in the most advanced market-gardening techniques including hydroponics. The Saudi partners are:
President H.R.H. Prince Mansur bin Mishaal bin Abdalaziz al Sa'ud
Director General Sh. Adnan Abdalmajeed
Members Sh. Muhammad al Hied
        Sh. Muhammad bin Ghazi
        Sh. Abdullah bin Ghazi
        Sh. Hamdan bin Ghazi
        Sh. Abdalaziz bin Ibrahim al Hied

The two partners of Siaco are also in business in Rome in partnership with Dr Enzo Floramco in a company called Itasco, the Italian Saudi Co. Ltd. This company supplies construction materials, steel structures for turnkey jobs, and furnishings and decorations.
This commercial undertaking is one of many go-ahead concerns in Saudi Arabia with a really impressive track record. However what marks Siaco is a modern and enlightened approach to ideas and a terrific energy.

The Family of ABDALMAJEED

The old family of Mecca who for centuries have been responsible as guides (Mutawafiyin) to pilgrims making the Hajj (Pilgrimage) to the Holy Cities. This honoured profession is maintained by them to this day through Sh. Mahmud bin Ibrahim.

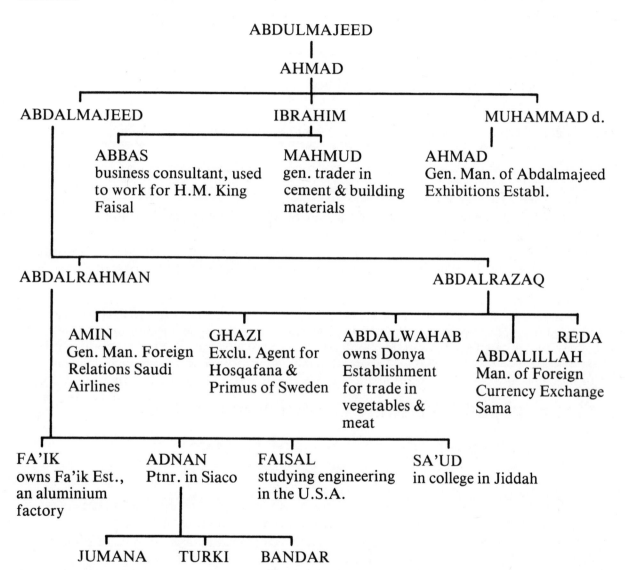

ABDULMAJEED
|
AHMAD

ABDALMAJEED — IBRAHIM — MUHAMMAD d.

ABBAS
business consultant, used to work for H.M. King Faisal

MAHMUD
gen. trader in cement & building materials

AHMAD
Gen. Man. of Abdalmajeed Exhibitions Establ.

ABDALRAHMAN — ABDALRAZAQ

AMIN
Gen. Man. Foreign Relations Saudi Airlines

GHAZI
Exclu. Agent for Hosqafana & Primus of Sweden

ABDALWAHAB
owns Donya Establishment for trade in vegetables & meat

REDA

ABDALILLAH
Man. of Foreign Currency Exchange Sama

FA'IK
owns Fa'ik Est., an aluminium factory

ADNAN
Ptnr. in Siaco

FAISAL
studying engineering in the U.S.A.

SA'UD
in college in Jiddah

JUMANA   TURKI   BANDAR

International Design Engineering and Architecture 'Idea Centre'

Address P.O. 1999 Jiddah

Telephone 40015, 46026

Telex 400220 IDEAMC

Cable MOHANDISZAIDAN

Branch office Riyadh P.O. 2824, tel. 62732, tx. 202093

Sole Proprietor Sh. Ziyad Ahmad Zaidan

Activities

This is probably the most go-ahead and exciting architectural firm in the Kingdom and it was founded in October 1974. Sh. Ziyad specializes in adapting Islamic and Arabian architectural themes to modern materials. He himself has had wide experience in the USA; having taken his degree at Detroit he gained practical experience by working with Wakely Kushner from 1968 to 1975, and Eggers and Higgins from 1967 to 1968. He is a member of the Board of the Prince Fawwaz Project for co-operative housing and the Idea Centre has already won two awards from the Ministry of Municipal Affairs.

Few architectural firms can see the whole job through but the Idea Centre has a Construction Supervision Department which ensures that both architect and client obtain satisfaction that work is executed in accordance with design. The following list of some of the projects awarded to this firm is not exhaustive but gives an accurate picture of the scope and versatility of its work.

The housing complex for the Yanbo Cement Company comprising 315 units; the Commercial Centre, Jiddah; the Fish Market Jiddah; the Foreign and Information Ministries complexes in Riyadh; a computerized information system for the Ministry of Municipal and Rural affairs; the Headquarters of the BETA company in Riyadh; the Riyadh Hotel in Jiddah and the Mecca Hotel in Mecca. Residences for H.R.H. Prince Misha'al bin Abdalaziz and H.R.H. Prince Hamoud bin Abdalaziz and Sh. Wabel Pharaon, the Okaz Printing and Publishing Centre, offices for the King Faisal Charitable Foundation in Dammam, complete designs for Royal Saudi Missions abroad, the Safwa Anik road in the Eastern Province, an interim building for the Ministry of Foreign Affairs in Jiddah, the Yanbu Master Plan and Design Study.

Electrical and Electronic Contracting Co. Ltd.

Address P.O. 1999 Jiddah

Telephone 690221, 690223

Telex 400477 EECCGO SJ

Cable MOHANDISZAIDAN

Proprietorship

Sh. Ahmad Muhammad Zaidan 50%

Sh. Muhammad Ahmad Zaidan 50%

Branch office

Riyadh P.O. 2824, tel. 62732, tx. 20293 IDEACN SJ, cable MOHANDISZAIDAN

The company was begun in 1978. The Managing Director, Sh. Muhammad Ahmad Zaidan, obtained his M.Sc. at Berlin in 1971 and gained experience with training courses at the Mechanical Institute Berlin, Ambig, Fritz Hanaman, Siemens, Institute of Computer Science Berlin, ITV Geneva and the Research Institute of Telefunken Germany. In addition he speaks three languages fluently, Arabic, English and German.

EECC are consultant contractors for electrical and electronic projects and the importation of teleprinter, telex and facsimile equipment. They effect sales to both the Government and the private sector of the market and cover installation operation and maintenance.

The company holds agencies for Datotek communications security equipment and Digital Facsimile Machines, for Data Source Office Computer Systems and Radio Stampa of Italy

Bankers National Commercial Bank, Al Jazira Bank.

The Family of ZAIDAN

Emanating from Mecca this family in itself characterizes the capacity for absorption of technology of the most advanced kind which is a feature of the Kingdom of Saudi Arabia.

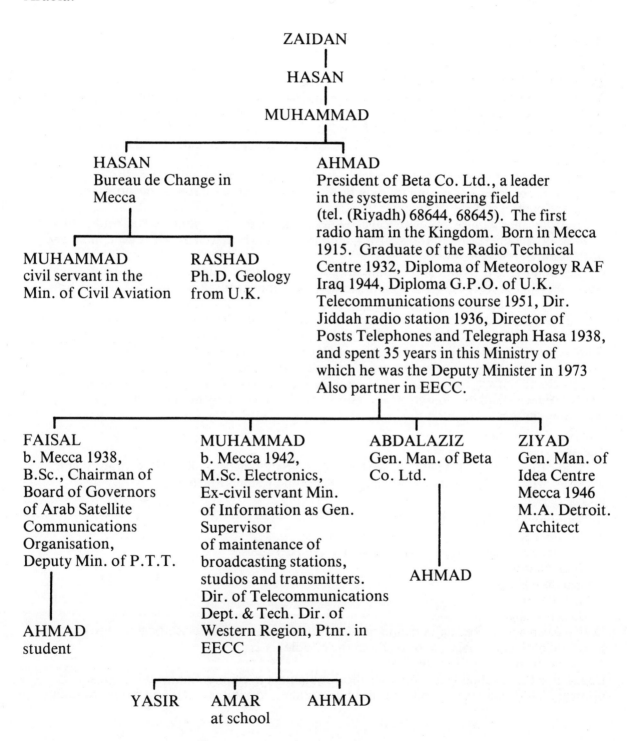

ZAIDAN

HASAN

MUHAMMAD

HASAN
Bureau de Change in
Mecca

MUHAMMAD
civil servant in the
Min. of Civil Aviation

RASHAD
Ph.D. Geology
from U.K.

AHMAD
President of Beta Co. Ltd., a leader
in the systems engineering field
(tel. (Riyadh) 68644, 68645). The first
radio ham in the Kingdom. Born in Mecca
1915. Graduate of the Radio Technical
Centre 1932, Diploma of Meteorology RAF
Iraq 1944, Diploma G.P.O. of U.K.
Telecommunications course 1951, Dir.
Jiddah radio station 1936, Director of
Posts Telephones and Telegraph Hasa 1938,
and spent 35 years in this Ministry of
which he was the Deputy Minister in 1973
Also partner in EECC.

FAISAL
b. Mecca 1938,
B.Sc., Chairman of
Board of Governors
of Arab Satellite
Communications
Organisation,
Deputy Min. of P.T.T.

AHMAD
student

MUHAMMAD
b. Mecca 1942,
M.Sc. Electronics,
Ex-civil servant Min.
of Information as Gen.
Supervisor
of maintenance of
broadcasting stations,
studios and transmitters.
Dir. of Telecommunications
Dept. & Tech. Dir. of
Western Region, Ptnr. in
EECC

ABDALAZIZ
Gen. Man. of Beta
Co. Ltd.

AHMAD

ZIYAD
Gen. Man. of
Idea Centre
Mecca 1946
M.A. Detroit.
Architect

YASIR

AMAR
at school

AHMAD

Dallah Establishment

Address head office P.O. 1438 Riyadh

Telephone 4641131

Telex 201036 DALLAH SJ

Cable DALLAH

Branch office Jiddah P.O. 2618, tel. 55422, tx. 401482 AVCO SJ

Proprietor Sh. Saleh Abdullah Kamel

Activities
The activities of this fast growing giant reflect an almost wholesale consumption of technology which justifies the great success of the company. Dallah is engaged in four main groups of activity and employs over four thousand people:

1. Contracting: road and civil construction and the erection and operation of driver training schools.

2. Måintenance and operation of air defence facilities, Government administration complexes, Government boarder centres and training facilities, pilgrimage air terminal facilities, traffic lights and control systems throughout the Kingdom.

3. Electronic, mechanical and electrical activities, which embrace weather surveillance, radar, runway visual range systems, transmitters, automatic stations as well as power generation and installation of power networks.

4. The commercial activities of the company cover the representation of leading international companies and procurement and commissioning for complete turnkey projects. These involve traffic and instrumentation, meteorology and electronics, radar, navigational aids, avionics, satellite systems and weather stations, air traffic control equipment, landing systems, telecommunications covering both public and private systems as well as microwave systems. They supply and market TV and videotapes. Dallah represent Doron of the USA for the production of simulator equipment and electronic teaching aids. They also represent Kongsberg of Norway for gas turbine generators and leading TV organisations in the Arab world producing and distributing programmes. Dallah also supply both light and heavy mobile workshops.

Affiliated Companies
Dallah Avco Trans Arabia
  Head office Jiddah tel. 55422, tx. 401158 ATTAS SJ; branches in Riyadh, Najran, Weijh, Qasim, Hail, Jouf, Medina, Talif, Tabuk, Bisha and Khamis Mushayt.

Board of Directors:
  Chairman Sh. Salem Kamel
  Sh. Omar Kamel
  Sen Vice President General Muhammad Tayyeb Al Tounisi
  Mr G. Newman
  General F Higgins
  Mr L Bogan
  Mr D F Walter

Dallah Avco undertakes major maintenance of civil, mechanical and electrical facilities in the Kingdom of Saudi Arabia and throughout the Middle East.

2. The Medical Centre Company Ltd
Engaged in the installation of electro-medical equipment in cooperation with Philips and Siemens. They also cover hospital furnishings, turnkey hospital projects and mobile hospitals.

3. The Arab Media Company
Representation of Arab TV organisations, production and distribution of programmes.
4. The Saudi Prefab and Precast Housing Co. Ltd
5. Dallah Industries Co. Ltd
Undertakes study, survey and implementation of medium and small scale industrial projects.
6. The Concrete Works Company
7. The Saudi Air Conditioning Company
8. Amartec Company Ltd
Specializes in environmental research.
9. Saudi Marketing and Trading Company
Engaged in the supply and marketing of chemicals and medicines.
10. Saudi Electro Mechanical Company
11. Trans Arabia Supply Company
12. National Employment Saudi Company

Dallah is also involved in the activities of the Tihama Advertising Corporation (q.v.), OKAZ Printing and Publishing and the Saudi Arabian Hotel and Tourism Company. Sh. Saleh Kamel also officiates as president of the Concrete Co., the Arab Media Co., Fast Co., the Saudi Pre-Fab Co. He is a member of the Board of DAR OKAZ Co. for Printing and Publishing, OKAZ Organisation for Press and Publication, OKAZ for Distribution, Tihama Advertising Corporation, the Services and Maintenance Co., Saudi Hotels and Resort Areas Co., the Saudi Overseas Marketing Co., the Saudi Construction Co., the Amartech Co., the Shobel Co. for Tourism (Egypt) and Shobel Switzerland and UK, the Arabian Investment Co. and the National Video Company in Egypt as well as Misr Investment and Development Co., the Faisal Islamic Egyptian Bank, the Faisal Islamic Sudanese Bank, the Red Sea Cement Co., Sudan Halad International, the Islamic Investment Co., Video Simen of the Bahamas, Simen Co. of Greece, the International Investment Group of the USA and the Oriental Production and Distribution Co. of Sharjah.

The Family of KAMEL

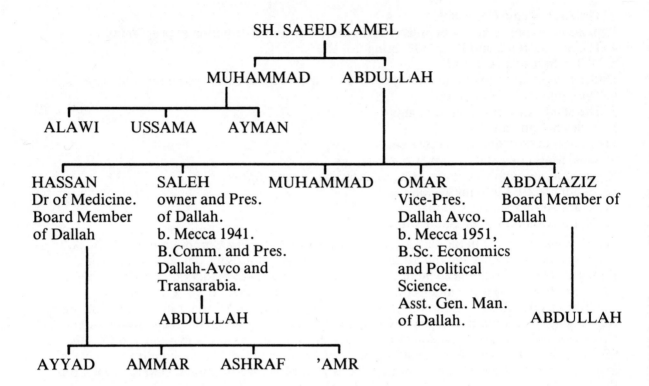

SH. SAEED KAMEL

MUHAMMAD — ABDULLAH

ALAWI   USSAMA   AYMAN

HASSAN
Dr of Medicine.
Board Member
of Dallah

SALEH
owner and Pres.
of Dallah.
b. Mecca 1941.
B.Comm. and Pres.
Dallah-Avco and
Transarabia.

ABDULLAH

MUHAMMAD

OMAR
Vice-Pres.
Dallah Avco.
b. Mecca 1951,
B.Sc. Economics
and Political
Science.
Asst. Gen. Man.
of Dallah.

ABDALAZIZ
Board Member of
Dallah

ABDULLAH

AYYAD   AMMAR   ASHRAF   'AMR

Economic Integration Company Limited

Address head office P.O. 6540 Riyadh

Telephone 60127

Telex 201505 SELECT SJ

Subidiary offices Jiddah P.O. 5096, tel. 22157

Ownership
The company is a partnership between H.R.H. Prince Saud ibn Na'if ibn Abdalaziz al Sa'ud, Sh. Mozhar Musallim Al Nowilaty and Sh. Muhammad Salahuddin Hussain Omar.

The company was formed in 1979 and is an example of the assimilation of modern management techniques in that its purpose is to provide management for a consortium of small companies who will be invited to join and benefit from the latest information and management methods. The company will specialise at first in the shipping, road construction and foodstuffs fields but is open to suggestions including the establishment of joint ventures.

Bankers Saudi British Bank, Riyadh Bank

The Family of NOWILATY

The family hails from the Holy City of Mecca and descends from clothmakers, a fact testified to in their name (Nuwayl means a loom). They branched out from manufacture, finally marketing their own product and latterly importing textiles.

all born in Mecca

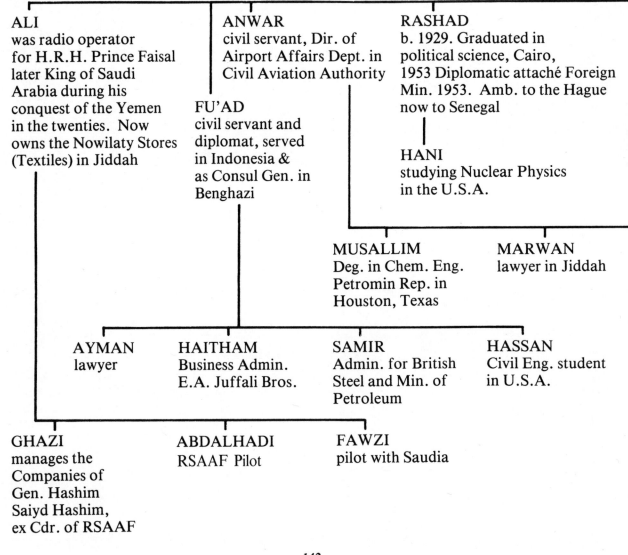

ALI
was radio operator for H.R.H. Prince Faisal later King of Saudi Arabia during his conquest of the Yemen in the twenties. Now owns the Nowilaty Stores (Textiles) in Jiddah

ANWAR
civil servant, Dir. of Airport Affairs Dept. in Civil Aviation Authority

RASHAD
b. 1929. Graduated in political science, Cairo, 1953 Diplomatic attaché Foreign Min. 1953. Amb. to the Hague now to Senegal

FU'AD
civil servant and diplomat, served in Indonesia & as Consul Gen. in Benghazi

HANI
studying Nuclear Physics in the U.S.A.

MUSALLIM
Deg. in Chem. Eng. Petromin Rep. in Houston, Texas

MARWAN
lawyer in Jiddah

AYMAN
lawyer

HAITHAM
Business Admin. E.A. Juffali Bros.

SAMIR
Admin. for British Steel and Min. of Petroleum

HASSAN
Civil Eng. student in U.S.A.

GHAZI
manages the Companies of Gen. Hashim Saiyd Hashim, ex Cdr. of RSAAF

ABDALHADI
RSAAF Pilot

FAWZI
pilot with Saudia

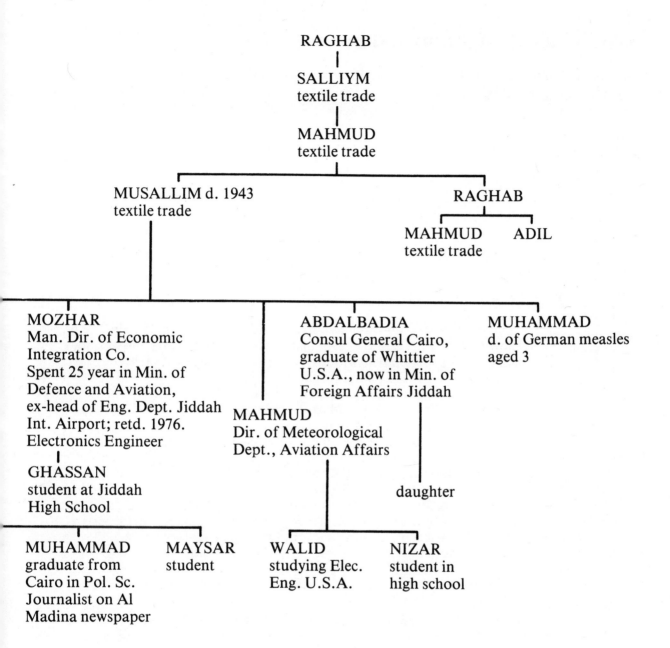

RAGHAB
|
SALLIYM
textile trade
|
MAHMUD
textile trade

MUSALLIM d. 1943
textile trade

RAGHAB

MAHMUD
textile trade

ADIL

MOZHAR
Man. Dir. of Economic
Integration Co.
Spent 25 year in Min. of
Defence and Aviation,
ex-head of Eng. Dept. Jiddah
Int. Airport; retd. 1976.
Electronics Engineer
|
GHASSAN
student at Jiddah
High School

MAHMUD
Dir. of Meteorological
Dept., Aviation Affairs

ABDALBADIA
Consul General Cairo,
graduate of Whittier
U.S.A., now in Min. of
Foreign Affairs Jiddah

MUHAMMAD
d. of German measles
aged 3

daughter

MUHAMMAD
graduate from
Cairo in Pol. Sc.
Journalist on Al
Madina newspaper

MAYSAR
student

WALID
studying Elec.
Eng. U.S.A.

NIZAR
student in
high school

Abdullah H Al Zamil and Sons

Address head office P.O. 9 Al Khobar and P.O. 285 Manama, Bahrain

Telephone 42567, 42784; Bahrain 53445

Telex 601114 ARI SJ; Bahrain 8381 ZAMIL GJ

Board of Directors
Chairman and Joint President Sh. Mohammed Abdullah Al Zamil (Bahrain)
Joint President Sh. Hamad Abdullah Al Zamil (Al Khobar)
Vice Chairman Sh. Abdalaziz Abdullah Al Zamil
President of Zamil Marine Sh. Zamil Abdullah Al Zamil
Man. Dir. of Arabian Refrigeration Sh. Ahmad Abdullah Al Zamil
President Zamil Aluminium Sh. Sulaiman Abdullah Al Zamil
President Zamil Soule Sh. Khalid Abdullah Al Zamil
President Bahrain Marble and Gulf Aluminium Sh. Fahd Abdullah Al Zamil
Director of Marketing Services, Arabian Refrigeration,
Sh. Adib Abdullah Zamil

Company History
Sh. Abdullah bin Hamad left Anaiza and after a short stay in Jubail settled in Bahrain where he became a well known merchant. He died in 1961 and his children returned to the Kingdom building on the commercial foundations laid by their father. This most remarkable and energetic family expresses the hopes and policies of the Royal Saudi Government and puts them into action with amazing vigour. To begin with they developed the commercial and real estate aspects of the family business finally founding the Industrial Division in 1972 with the establishment of Zamil Aluminium; in 1974 they began work on the first air conditioner factory in the Kingdom which began production in the following year and today this production is measured as giving a seven times growth rate. In 1976 the Soule joint venture for the manufacture of structural steel buildings was added to the list and this went into production in 1978 with an annual capacity of 30,000 tons. They operate the first and only factory in Jubail for meat processing and dairy products, they produce aluminium, marble and nails in Bahrain and their investments involve them in many other companies. On the service side Zamil Marine deals with Aramco serving offshore rigs with their supply boats and they own the only floating dry dock in the Kingdom which is used permanently by Aramco. They also operate a Commercial Division which handles their representation business, a travel agency and the Arab Gulf Construction Company.

The Commerical Division
This division is responsible for the management of the company's real estate investment, land development and property leasing business, marketing all A H Al Zamil and Sons products, both represented and manufactured, and other commercial activities which include:

Agencies
Allis Chalmers Services Inc: mineral processing equipment and cement manufacturing
    equipment, electrical switch gear, motors and voltage regulators.
Artex Investments Ltd: camp catering
Carl Freudenberg and Co: floor coverings, rubber needle felt and tufted carpeting.
Core Laboratories Inc: engineering and consulting services
English Rose Kitchens Ltd: kitchen furniture
Emerson Electric
Pacific Logistics SA: base vessels for banking services.
Teledyne Exploration, Teledyne Geotech, Teledyne Media: gas lift equipment, supervisory
    control systems and computer time sharing.

Texas International Company: drilling equipment and equipment for oil and gas well workover, rig manufacture.

Commercial Activities

Granada Jewellers (Orient Arts), P.O. 197 Al Khobar, tel. 41266

Al Zamil Opticians, P.O. 25 Riyadh, tel. 25265

Zamil Travel, P.O. 9 Al Khobar, tel. 45634, 45646, tx. 670132 ZAMIL SJ

The Industrial Division

Zamil Petroleum Services
P.O. 9 Al Khobar, tel. 42567, 42784, tx. 601115 ARI SJ
Oil well servicing and workover, water well drilling and development.

Arabian Refrigeration Industries
P.O. 294 Dhahran Airport, tel. 21939, 26529, tx. 601115 ARI SJ
Manufacture of Friedrich room air conditioners, central plant both split systems and packaged units. The company covers system design, duct manufacture and installation and its nationwide after-sales service includes a complete spare parts stock, all manufactured within the Kingdom.

Yamama Factories for Red Bricks and Clay Products
P.O. 4572 Riyadh, tel. 61343
Manufacture of red bricks, roof tiles and clay products.

Bahrain Marble Factory
Mina Sulman Industrial Estate P.O. 285 Manama Bahrain, tel. 713085, tx. 8381 ZAMIL GJ
Produces marble fascia and marble materials for floors and stairways.

Zamil Greatways Food Industries Ltd
P.O. 9 Al Khobar, tel. 42567, 42784, tx. 601115 ARI SJ
Food processing and refrigerated warehousing.

Zamil Marine Services
P.O. 9 Al Khobar, tel. 42567, 42784, tx. 601115 ARI SJ
Marine services and dry docking where they control the only manoevrable floating dock in the Middle East.

Zamil Soule Steel Buildings Co. Ltd
P.O. 9 Al Khobar, tel. 42567, 42784, tx. 601115 ARI SJ
Manufacture and fabrication of pre-engineered metal buildings for industrial, commercial, leisure and residential purposes.

Zamil Aluminium Factory and Gulf Aluminium Factory
P.O. 1633 Dammam, tel. 26679, tx. 601115 ARI SJ
Mina Sulman Industrial Estate P.O. 285 Manama, Bahrain, tel. 713725, tx. 8381 ZAMIL GJ
Both these factories produce aluminium doors and door frames and window frames; building and shop fronts, office partitions, handrails, banisters and balconies.

The Family of ZAMIL

A family originating from the Bani Thawr of Sbiya' and from the Qasim area and Anaiza.

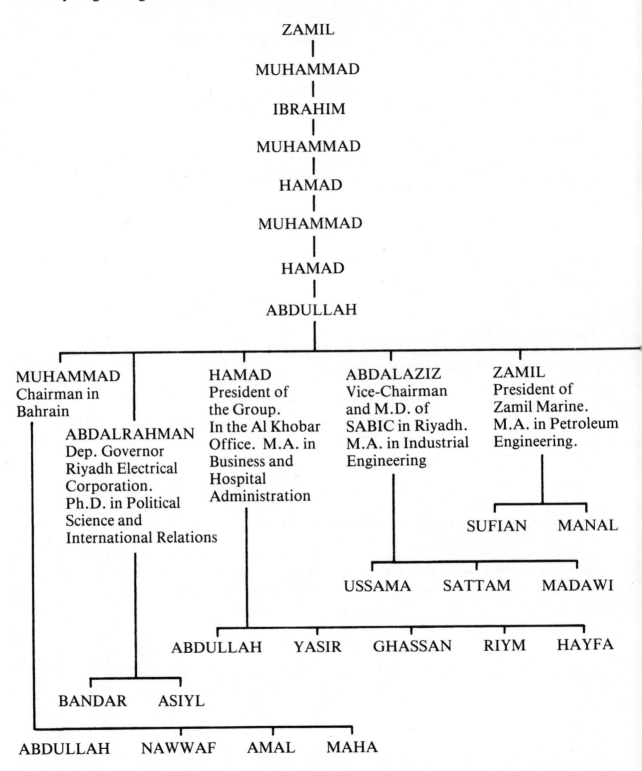

ZAMIL

MUHAMMAD

IBRAHIM

MUHAMMAD

HAMAD

MUHAMMAD

HAMAD

ABDULLAH

MUHAMMAD
Chairman in
Bahrain

ABDALRAHMAN
Dep. Governor
Riyadh Electrical
Corporation.
Ph.D. in Political
Science and
International Relations

HAMAD
President of
the Group.
In the Al Khobar
Office. M.A. in
Business and
Hospital
Administration

ABDALAZIZ
Vice-Chairman
and M.D. of
SABIC in Riyadh.
M.A. in Industrial
Engineering

ZAMIL
President of
Zamil Marine.
M.A. in Petroleum
Engineering.

SUFIAN   MANAL

USSAMA   SATTAM   MADAWI

ABDULLAH   YASIR   GHASSAN   RIYM   HAYFA

BANDAR   ASIYL

ABDULLAH   NAWWAF   AMAL   MAHA

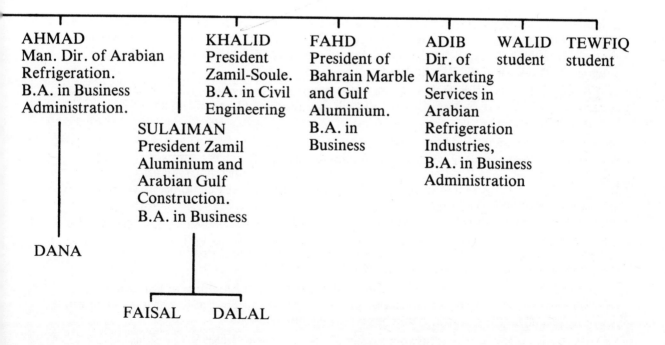

AHMAD
Man. Dir. of Arabian
Refrigeration.
B.A. in Business
Administration.

KHALID
President
Zamil-Soule.
B.A. in Civil
Engineering

FAHD
President of
Bahrain Marble
and Gulf
Aluminium.
B.A. in
Business

ADIB
Dir. of
Marketing
Services in
Arabian
Refrigeration
Industries,
B.A. in Business
Administration

WALID
student

TEWFIQ
student

SULAIMAN
President Zamil
Aluminium and
Arabian Gulf
Construction.
B.A. in Business

DANA

FAISAL   DALAL

Rolaco Trading and Contracting

Abdalaziz Al Abdullah Al Sulaiman and Company

Head Office P.O. 222 Jiddah
Telephone 51067, 54109
Cables ROLACO
Telex 401029 ROLACO SJ
Subsidiary offices Riyadh, Dammam, Paris and New York
Proprietor Sh. Abdalaziz Al Abdullah Al Sulaiman

Company History
Leaving the government service in 1954 Sh. Abdalaziz founded a company called Abdalaziz Al Abdullah Al Sulaiman Business Office which represented various Swedish and West German companies. Rolaco was formed shortly after this and soon became the largest importer of building materials in the Kingdom. Today the company deals in both bagged and bulk cement (Rolaco has its own silos in Jiddah Port with a capacity of 6000 tons), steel re-inforcement, heavy equipment including Nissan Diesel and Skania trucks, Kato cranes, Furukawa Drills, Champion motor graders and has in addition a contrasting department for carrying out the many and diverse interests of the family.

The family are the oldest hoteliers in the Kingdom owning the Kandara (P.O. 473 Jiddah, tel. 23155, tx. 401095 SJ), the Jiddah Palace Hotel (P.O. 473 Jiddah, tel. 32387, 32255, tx. 401095 SJ). A third hotel in Jiddah is under construction and the family also owns Intercontinental Hotels in Dammam, Cairo and Mecca. The Abdalaziz Al Abdullah Al Sulaiman and Brothers Company is also a part of the Arab Hotel Company in which the only other participants from the private sector are the Gosaibi family (q.v.), the remaining shareholders being the Arab Investment Company (a Saudi Kuwaiti group), the National Commercial Bank, and the Riyadh Bank.

Sh. Abdalaziz founded the Arabian Cement Company and today he is its chairman. Present capacity is 2,000 tons daily but when the Rabigh extension is fully operational this figure will be more than doubled.

Sh. Abdalaziz is a Member of the Board of the Saudi Arabian Refining Company (SARCO) of which 75% is owned by the Government, the Saudi National Electric Company (SNEC) FRAB Bank Paris and FRAB holdings of Luxembourg. He is the Chairman of the Al Jazira Bank, the Zahran Contracting Company, Siraj Zahran and Co. which holds the Datsun agency selling 90,000 cars a year and La Foncière Jiddah Insurance for which the brokers are Stewart Wrightson of the UK. He is also chairman of the Saudi Light Industry Corporation (SLIC) which runs two flexible foam factories, Saudi Arabian Barclay which operates a tyre re-tread factory producing 13,600 re-treads a year, and the Cement Products Industry Company as well as Al Sulaimaniyah Real Estate.

A further company within the family group is Saudicorp which functions as a screen for feasibility studies identifying and initiating industrial projects. The Saudi Capital Corporation is wholly owned by the group also and handles financial investment.

Sh. Abdalaziz represents the following as agent in the insurance field:
Nasco Karaoglan and Company, La Foncière, La Camat, Groupement Francais d'Assurances and Bankers Insurances.

The Family of AL SOLAIMAN

A family of Najd.

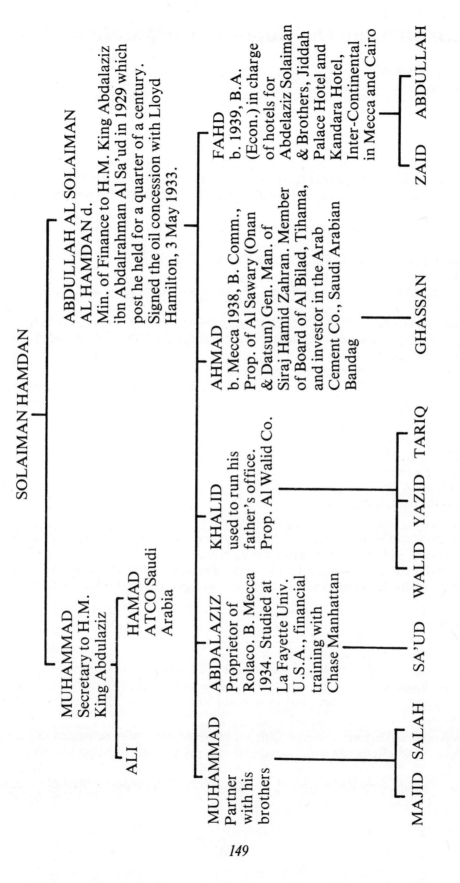

SOLAIMAN HAMDAN

MUHAMMAD
Secretary to H.M.
King Abdulaziz

ALI

HAMAD
ATCO Saudi
Arabia

ABDULLAH AL SOLAIMAN AL HAMDAN d.
Min. of Finance to H.M. King Abdalaziz
ibn Abdalrahman Al Sa'ud in 1929 which
post he held for a quarter of a century.
Signed the oil concession with Lloyd
Hamilton, 3 May 1933.

FAHD
b. 1939, B.A.
(Econ.) in charge
of hotels for
Abdelaziz Solaiman
& Brothers, Jiddah
Palace Hotel and
Kandara Hotel,
Inter-Continental
in Mecca and Cairo

ZAID   ABDULLAH

AHMAD
b. Mecca 1938, B. Comm.,
Prop. of Al Sawary (Onan
& Datsun) Gen. Man. of
Siraj Hamid Zahran. Member
of Board of Al Bilad, Tihama,
and investor in the Arab
Cement Co., Saudi Arabian
Bandag

GHASSAN

KHALID
used to run his
father's office.
Prop. Al Walid Co.

WALID   YAZID   TARIQ

ABDALAZIZ
Proprietor of
Rolaco. B. Mecca
1934. Studied at
La Fayette Univ.
U.S.A., financial
training with
Chase Manhattan

SA'UD

MUHAMMAD
Partner
with his
brothers

MAJID   SALAH

Saudi Research and Development Corporation (REDEC)

Address P.O. 1935 Jiddah

Telephone 52940

Telex 401122 REDEC SJ

Cable address REDEC

Subsidiary offices

P.O. 611 Riyadh, tel. 61357/8/9, cable REDEC RIYADH, tx. 201133

P.O. 998 Dammam, tel. 22011, 25421, cable REDEC DAMMAM, tx. 601019

P.O. 2514 Beirut, 408 Starco North, tel. 296703, 290424, cable INTEREDEC BEIRUT, tx. 20984 REDEC

61 Rue de la Boetie, 75008 Paris France, cable REDEC PARIS, tel. 256 3860, tx. 640997 REDEC

Via Della Camilluccia 697, 00135 Rome, cable INTEREDEC ROME, tel. 3279341-5, tx. 63067 REDEC

c/o Epirotiki Lines, Epirotiki Lines Building, 87 Andrea Mialuli, Piraeus, Greece, tel. 420648, tx. EPIR 212302

28 Al Jalaa Street (Al Yazigi), P.O. 3598, Damascus, Syria, tel. 332 588, tx. 11358 REDEC

60 Park Lane, Flat 29, London W.1., cable INTEREDEC LONDON, tel. 493 6595, 493 3580, tx. 21253 INTEREDEC

100 Rue du Rhine, Geneva, Switzerland, tel. 289811/2/3, tx. 28764 REDEC

Suite 2410, Pennzoil Place, 700 Milam Street, Houston, Texas 77002, tel. 713 237 9216, tx. 775022 ARAB CORP HOU

Proprietor

The company is owned as follows:

Dr Ghaith R Pharaon 61%

Shaikh Wabel R Pharaon 25%

Mrs Nada R Pharaon 7%

Shaikh Hattan R Pharaon 7%

Company History

Redec was incorporated with limited liability in January 1966 and since that date has developed into a highly diversified holding company whose pre-eminent position in Saudi commercial affairs has been due to imaginative and positive management. The company is one of the largest employers in the Kingdom and has made a tremendous contribution to the development of the country.

Business Activities

The Company operates through nine major divisions.

1. The Engineering and Contracting Division

This division has developed special capabilities in the following fields: airport construction, high quality buildings, irrigation and drainage projects, industrial construction, water distribution systems, sewage systems and treatment plants, highway construction, and city beautification projects.

This division is involved in joint ventures with a number of firms with related capabilities:

Incas Bona Saudi, 99% Redec owned, is involved with urban beautification and road construction.

Saudi Arabian Vianini, 60% Redec owned, designs and constructs ports, offshore facilities and irrigation projects.

Redec-Dailem, 50% Redec owned, and Saudi Arabian Parsons also 50% Redec owned, both design and construct heavy industrial and petrochemical complexes.

The activities of this division are supported by a very comprehensive training capacity operated in association with leading American and European firms. Its field operations are backed up by one of the world's largest and most up to date heavy equipment repair and parts supply facilities.

Lastly this division is fully integrated with International Systems Inc. of Mobile, Alabama. This company is 90% owned by Redec and specialises in the production of modular housing and solid concrete walled shipping containers.

2. The Industrial Division

This division, more than any of the others is responsible for Redec's contribution to the Saudi Arabian economy. This has been achieved by collaboration with leading international industrial companies, and this division manages Redec investment in enterprises that Redec itself has helped to create or that have especial promise. The division also works outside the Kingdom where Redec's investment programme can benefit research and development. Within the Kingdom the following areas of investment are managed by this division.

a. Water Bottling Plant producing under the brand name Safa with technical assistance from Evian.
b. Bus Assembly in Jiddah with Ward Industries of Conway, Arkansas
c. Two steel fabrication workshops for the production of steel structures, pressure vessels and metal panels for housing.
d. An offroad tyre re-treading plant in Jiddah with Brad Ragan Inc. of North Carolina
e. Pharmaceutical manufacturing with Sterling Drug International.
f. An industrial complex for manufacturing, construction and residential areas with full supporting services.

Among the heavy industry investments, where Redec's participation varies between 50% and 25%, made in collaboration with foreign companies within the Kingdom as well as abroad are the following:
a. A granular super phosphate plant
b. A petrochemical plant at Jubail
c. A reinforcing steel bar plant in Dammam
d. A lube oil plant in Riyadh
e. A salt extraction plant in Jubail
f. A magnesite plant in the Eastern Province
g. A white sugar syrup plant in Hofuf
h. An industrial gas plant in Jubail
i. Sulphur slating in the Eastern Province
j. A graphite and carbon industrial complex

3. The Commercial Division

This division serves as Middle East representative for foreign firms interested in turnkey projects or equipment supply to the Saudi Government. Major representations include those for Finmecannica and Montedison of Italy, Balfour Beatty of the UK, VACRS and Bes Engineering Corporation of Taiwan, Mitsui of Japan and Mowlem Construction Co. of the UK.

The division supports its principals with a sophisticated information bank and very superior liaison facilities. It also assists with customs clearance, bid preparation and immigration.

4. The Catering Division

Possessing a versatile inventory of specialist equipment this division has provided the very best in catering services to some of the world's largest companies in the most remote areas of the Kingdom.

5. Desalination Division

Operating Redec's Saudi Desalination Company this division plays a prominent part in the development of the vital resource, fresh water, in the Kingdom.

6. Electro-Mechanical Division

This division provides design, consultancy, supervision, installation, operation and maintenance services to the Group as well as to outside clients.

In addition to this primary function the division is involved in a 50% joint venture operation with Foley Electric and Sam P Wallace of Dallas and in other ventures with the following:
Balfour Kilpatrick International
China Technical Consultants
DRD Montagebau
Air et Chaleur

7. Maritime Shipping Division

This division was established to undertake general sea-transport through two Saudi based shipping companies and a wholly owned Panamanian subsidiary. The division transports crude oil and dry cargo in its own ships, as well as passengers. The operation is managed by International Shipping Inc.

8. Trading Division

Managed by Redec's Intertrade subsidiary this division supplies the Saudi building industry with timber, cement, steel, pre-fabricated buildings, construction machinery, furniture and appliances.

9. Computer Services Division

Operating one of the two largest systems in the Kingdom this division is operated by a joint venture with Demographics Inc. of the USA called Saudi Computer Services (Demographics). They use an IBM 370/135 with a 384,000 character memory and four 3330 type disc drives with a capacity of 400 million characters. Initially oriented towards the needs of the construction industry this division has readily accommodated itself to the fields of banking, distribution and manufacturing as well as offering financial and accounting services.

Bankers National Commercial Bank, First National City Bank.

The Family of PHARAON

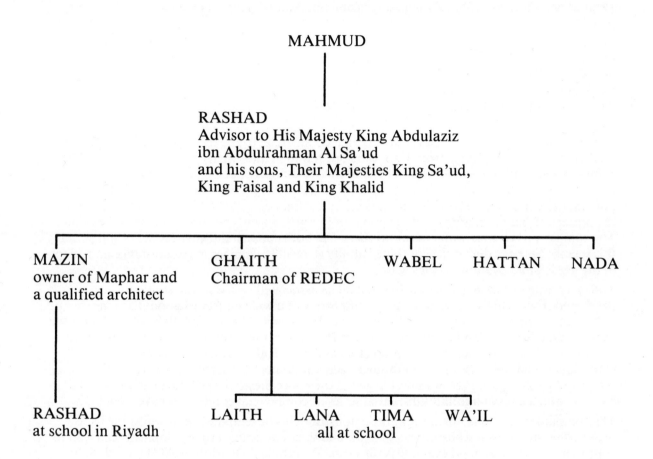

MAHMUD

RASHAD
Advisor to His Majesty King Abdulaziz
ibn Abdulrahman Al Sa'ud
and his sons, Their Majesties King Sa'ud,
King Faisal and King Khalid

MAZIN
owner of Maphar and
a qualified architect

GHAITH
Chairman of REDEC

WABEL   HATTAN   NADA

RASHAD
at school in Riyadh

LAITH   LANA   TIMA   WA'IL
all at school

Al Haj Abdullah Alireza Co. Ltd.

Head office P.O. 8 Jiddah

Proprietors The heirs of Sh. Zainal Alireza and Sh. Adullah Alireza extending to some forty people.

Board Members
President Sh. Muhammad Abdullah Alireza
Sh. Ahmad Yusuf Alireza
Sh. Muhammad Yusuf Alireza
Sh. Mahmoud Yusuf Alireza

Activities
Al Haj Abdullah Alireza Co. Ltd is the original commercial foundation of the Alireza family on their return to the Hidjaz from Iran some one hundred and twenty five years ago. Both the company registration number which is 1, and their low post office box number attest to their being part of the fabric of Saudi Arabian commercial history from its inception. Indeed their pre-eminence over such a long period indicates their financial and commercial acumen in both the present oil based economy and the previous import and entrepôt trade centred on Jiddah. The company has traded with enormous success in both commercial environments and perhaps this success has been due to the continued ability to react to changes in circumstance and adapt to the needs of innovations as they arise.

Today a centre of the shipping industry and all its associated concerns the company has developed from being simply, albeit large, importers of a wide variety of goods to being the hub of an enormous number of family interests. In the past Al Haj Abdullah Alireza imported generators, telephones and exchanges, foodstuffs, radios, tape recorders, paint, furniture, marine and fishing equipment, film projectors and electrical circuitry, batteries, air conditioners and refrigerators. Operating as general agents they acted for insurers and as travel and freight agents. Nowadays the goods they once merely imported have become the basis on which a very large and substantial series of commercial enterprises have been built.

The companies mentioned below amply demonstrate this development and whilst the list is incomplete show how the absorption of skills and their application to development can lead to continuing success. A good example is the General Technical Division of Al Haj Abdullah Alireza. This is called GENTEC for short.

Offices:
Jiddah P.O. 1531, tel. 22233, 22892, tx. 401037 ZENREZA
Riyadh P.O. 361, tel. 25676, tx. 201080 ZENREZA
Dammam P.O. 8, tel. 24133, tx. 601008 ALIREZA

Activities
Telecommunications Systems
PABX Intercoms, Key systems HF and VHF radio (fixed and mobile)
Automated telex switch systems and point to point equipment
Security systems
Fire detection, burglar alarms, surveillance systems, closed circuit TV
Sound systems
Industrial and professional sound products for hotels, airports, sports studio and shopping centres
Control systems
Environmental control and building automation systems

Gentec represent the following in the Kingdom: ADT Security Systems, The Acromedia Corporation, ALTEC Sound Products Division, Plantronics, I.T.T.

Laing Wimpey Alireza Ltd.

Head office P.O. 2797 Riyadh

Telephone 61361, 65995

Cable AIRCONSA

Branches
Elstree Way, Borehamwood, Herts, UK
P.O. 150 Dhahran Airport
P.O. 2059 Jiddah
P.O. 209 Abha

Proprietors
The Board of Directors:
Sh. Ahmad Yusuf Zainal Alireza
Sh. Muhammad Yusuf Zainal Alireza
Sh. Mahmud Yusuf Zainal Alireza
Mr. K. S. Bowden
Mr. D. G. Fitzgerald
Managing Director Mr. K. J. Gilder
Mr. W. D. Hewetson
Mr. J. Mason
Mr. B. Sanderson
Mr. J. M. Watt

Activities
Building and civil engineering. The company is a major subsidiary of Al Haj Abdullah Alireza. Whilst this is the major centre of the Alireza family interests the desire for independence and the attainment of achievement for oneself has motivated the formation of the following fully independent commercial enterprises by other family members. Indeed they often vie with each other in commercial competition.

Haji Husein Alireza and Co. Ltd.

Head office P.O. 40 Jiddah
Telephone 23509
Telex 401221 HUSREZA SJ
Activity
Under the management of the Sh. Husein Ali Alireza and operating the Mazda car agency amongst others. This company is one of the most modern and efficient in Saudi Arabia.

Lummus Alireza Co. Ltd.

Head office P.O. 2824 Riyadh
Telephone 60504
Cable LUMMUS RIYADH
Telex 201044 BETACOM SJ
Cable LUMMUS RIYADH
Board of Directors
Sh. Nabil Akbar Alireza Chairman
Sh. Mahmud Akbar Alireza Man. Dir.
Mr. W. P. Orr
Mr. J. O'Conner
Mr. H. O. Johansson
Activity
Construction and engineering of projects associated with the petrochemical and petroleum industries.

Xenel Industries

Head office P.O. 2824 Jiddah

Telephone 26466

Telex 401166 XENELEX SJ

Proprietors The Partners:
Chairman Sh. Muhammad Ahmad Alireza
Sh. Abdullah Ahmad Alireza
Sh. Hisham Ahmad Alireza
Sh. Khalid Ahmad Alireza
Sh. Yusuf Ahmad Alireza

The company is project oriented and designed to operate, as a first step, in the evaluation and specialisation fields. Implementation follows. To this end the partners follow their own areas of main interest and as a result the company operates in five loose divisions: services, contracting, finance, commerce and projects.

Xenel Industries control the following subsidiaries and joint ventures.

Saudi Cable Company
A joint venture with Anaconda of the US and Standard Oil. The first and only manufacturer of wire and cable in the Kingdom. The factory is located in Jiddah and the company can be reached at P.O. 4403 Jiddah, tel. 43976, 20377, 26466, 37619, tx. 401166 XENELEX, or Riyadh, tel. 67858, 64215, tx. 201175 XENELEX.

Saudi Bulk Transport
Situated in the Eastern Province they are engaged in bulk transport and bulk handling of cement on the largest scale in the area.

Other joint ventures are with Dravo of the USA for contracting, with Ret Ser of China, with Resource Sciences of the USA as Resource Science Arabia engaged in maintenance engineering and camp design with projects in Yanbo and Jubail. They represent UBM (United Builders Merchants) through Binex the materials subsidiary of Xenel and Arabian Bulk Trade which is another subsidiary.

The Arabian Maintenance Company
The maintenance operation of this Xenel company is fully comprehensive and covers ports, harbour and depot facilities, manufacturing and production plants, institutional and public buildings, airports and airlines as well as power, lighting, water, sewage, garbage collection and disposal, plumbing and air conditioning.
P.O. 2824 Jiddah, tel. 26466, 20377, 37619, tx. 401166 XENELEX SJ

Saudi Arabian Dames and Moore

Head office P.O. 2384 Riyadh

Telephone 62239

Telex 201127 ENGINEER SJ

Branch Office Jiddah P.O. 1238, te. 34992, 22236, tx. 401516 AMAL SJ, and Project Offices in Al Khobar and Yanbu

Proprietors
Dames and Moore of the USA 50%
Reza Investment Co. 25%
Industrial Services Co. 25%

Board of Directors
Mr. James W. Mitchell (Chairman)
Sh. Fahd Muhammad Alireza
Sh. Hamad Abdullah Linjazi
Mr. R. L. Lea
Mr. Farouk Ahmad

The company was established in 1977 and is engaged in planning engineering and the provision of quality control services, materials testing and geotechnical and environmental engineering. SADM have their own laboratories in Riyadh and operate site laboratories from this facility.

Rezayat Trading Establishment

Head office P.O. 90 Al Khobar

Telephone 41066

Telex 671006

Subsidiary offices
Rezayat Trading Co. P.O. 106 Safat, Kuwait, tel. 439596/7, tx. 2070.
Rezayat Europe Ltd. 52, Mount Street, London, W 1, tel. 01 499 6171, tx. 25997.
Rezayat Europe Ltd. 34 Avenue George V, Paris 75008, tel. 720 8656, tx. 641542.

Proprietor Sh. Taimur Abdullah Alireza

Activities

Mechanical and electrical engineering, trucking and plant hire, camp construction, heavy transport (off road), pipe and structural steel fabrication, precision engineering, camp management and industrial catering, shipping and container service, port handling, system built housing, general trading.

Wholly Owned Subsidiaries
1. In Saudi Arabia
Rezayat Trading Co. Ltd. Al Khobar
National Contracting Co. Ltd. Al Khobar and Riyadh
National Construction Co. Ltd. Al Khobar and Riyadh
2. In Kuwait
Rezayat Trading Co.
National Drilling Co. Ltd.

National Contracting Co. Ltd.
International Tank and Pipe SAK
3. In the United Arab Emirates
National Contracting Co. Ltd. in Abu Dhabi, Dubai and Ajman
4. In the Sultanate of Oman
National Contracting Co. Ltd.

Joint Ventures
 1. Saudi Arabian Engineering Co. Ltd, SAECO, Al Khobar.
 2. Saudi Arabian Fabricated Metals Industry Ltd, SAFAMI, Al Khobar.
 3. Arabian Mechnical Engineering Co. Ltd, AMEC, Al Khobar.
 4. Rezayat Williams Construction Co. Ltd, RAWCON.
 5. Brown and Root Alireza W.L.L. BRALCO.
 6. Lamnalco Ltd of Kuwait.
 7. Transmarine Transportation Services Co. Ltd, Kuwait.
 8. Rezcan Coatings and Linings Ltd.
 9. National Aggregate and Asphalt Co., Kuwait.
10. Crescent Transportation Co. Ltd.
11. National Aggregate and Asphalt Co. Ltd, Saudi Arabia.
12. The Arabian Badger Co. Ltd.
13. Corrosion Prevention Arabia Ltd.
14. Rezayat and Sparrows Crane Hire (M.E.) Ltd.
15. Saudi Arabian Port Handling Services Ltd.
16. Streif Arabia Ltd.
17. National Pipeline Company.
Ownership:
H.R.H. Sa'ud Ibn Naif Ibn Abdalaziz Al Sa'ud
Sh. Taimur Abdullah Alireza (majority shareholder)
Sh. Ahmad Hamad Al Gosaibi (q.v.)
Sh. Abdalaziz and Sh. Sa'ad bin Muhammad Al Mo'ajil (q.v.)
Sh. Jamal Hassan Jawa
Sh. Abdullah Taha Baksh
Sh. Abdullah Abdalaziz Al Sudeiri
Sh. Jamil Ibrahim Hujeilan
Sh. Abdalmajid Mahmud Zaher
Sumitomo Metals (Japan)
Sumitomo Chogi (Japan)
Activity
Manufacture of metal and spiral pipe for use in the petrochemical industry.

Capital 50 million riyals.

The Family of ALIREZA

The family originates in the Hidjaz and probably descends from tribesmen who migrated to the Khuzistan area of Iran in the early years of the Muslim era. Alireza returned to the Hidjaz some two hundred years ago.

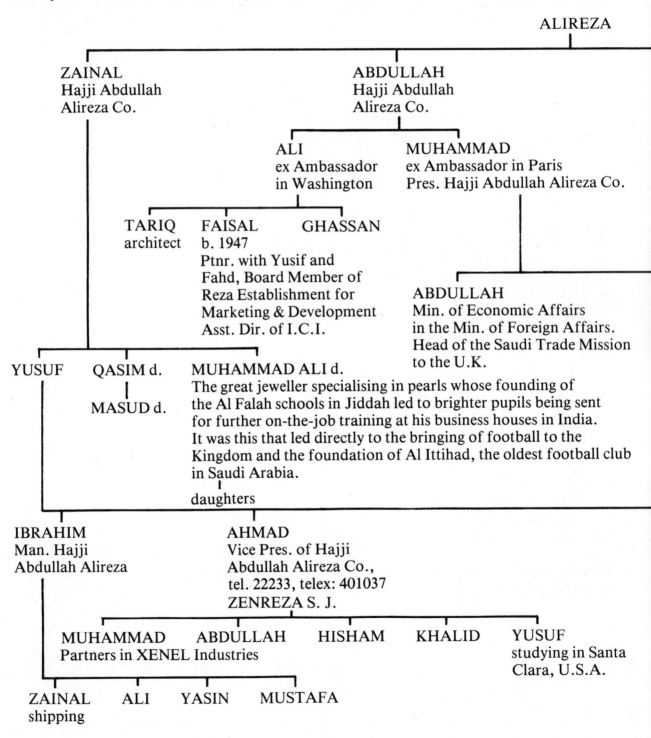

ALIREZA

ZAINAL
Hajji Abdullah
Alireza Co.

ABDULLAH
Hajji Abdullah
Alireza Co.

ALI
ex Ambassador
in Washington

MUHAMMAD
ex Ambassador in Paris
Pres. Hajji Abdullah Alireza Co.

TARIQ
architect

FAISAL
b. 1947
Ptnr. with Yusif and
Fahd, Board Member of
Reza Establishment for
Marketing & Development
Asst. Dir. of I.C.I.

GHASSAN

ABDULLAH
Min. of Economic Affairs
in the Min. of Foreign Affairs.
Head of the Saudi Trade Mission
to the U.K.

YUSUF

QASIM d.

MASUD d.

MUHAMMAD ALI d.
The great jeweller specialising in pearls whose founding of
the Al Falah schools in Jiddah led to brighter pupils being sent
for further on-the-job training at his business houses in India.
It was this that led directly to the bringing of football to the
Kingdom and the foundation of Al Ittihad, the oldest football club
in Saudi Arabia.

daughters

IBRAHIM
Man. Hajji
Abdullah Alireza

AHMAD
Vice Pres. of Hajji
Abdullah Alireza Co.,
tel. 22233, telex: 401037
ZENREZA S. J.

MUHAMMAD
Partners in XENEL Industries

ABDULLAH

HISHAM

KHALID

YUSUF
studying in Santa
Clara, U.S.A.

ZAINAL
shipping

ALI

YASIN

MUSTAFA

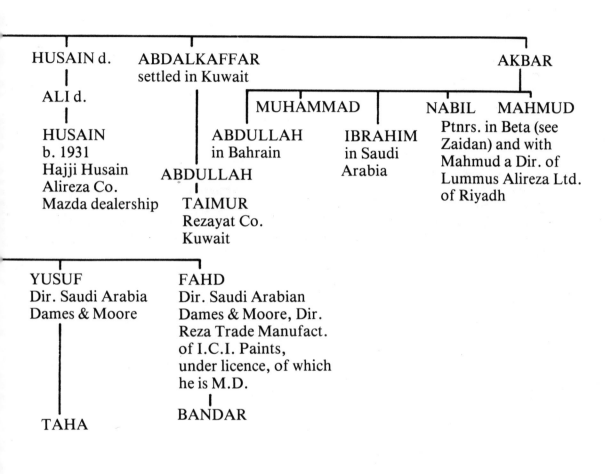

HUSAIN d.   ABDALKAFFAR   AKBAR
                settled in Kuwait

ALI d.   MUHAMMAD   NABIL   MAHMUD

HUSAIN   ABDULLAH   IBRAHIM   Ptnrs. in Beta (see
b. 1931   in Bahrain   in Saudi   Zaidan) and with
Hajji Husain   Arabia   Mahmud a Dir. of
Alireza Co.   ABDULLAH   Lummus Alireza Ltd.
Mazda dealership   of Riyadh
               TAIMUR
               Rezayat Co.
               Kuwait

YUSUF   FAHD
Dir. Saudi Arabia   Dir. Saudi Arabian
Dames & Moore   Dames & Moore, Dir.
                Reza Trade Manufact.
                of I.C.I. Paints,
                under licence, of which
                he is M.D.

                BANDAR
TAHA

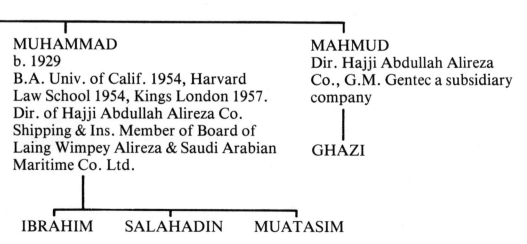

MUHAMMAD   MAHMUD
b. 1929   Dir. Hajji Abdullah Alireza
B.A. Univ. of Calif. 1954, Harvard   Co., G.M. Gentec a subsidiary
Law School 1954, Kings London 1957.   company
Dir. of Hajji Abdullah Alireza Co.
Shipping & Ins. Member of Board of
Laing Wimpey Alireza & Saudi Arabian   GHAZI
Maritime Co. Ltd.

IBRAHIM   SALAHADIN   MUATASIM

Al Rajhi Company for Exchange and Commerce

Address head office P.O. 28 Riyadh

Telephone 36922, 36606, 35644, 36977

Telex 201073 RAJHI SJ, 201630 RAJH SJ

Subsidiary offices
Jiddah P.O. 605, tel. 47674, 47675, tx. 401058 RAJHI SJ and nearly eighty other branches throughout the Kingdom of Saudi Arabia

Board Members
Sh. Salih Abdalaziz Al Rajhi
Abdullah Abdalaziz Al Rajhi
Sulaiman Abdalaziz Al Rajhi Managing Director
Muhammad Abdalaziz Al Rajhi

Company History
The company was formed in 1978 by merging the banking interests of Sh. Salih, Sh. Abdullah and Sh. Sulaiman with the contracting business of Sh. Muhammad. The resulting company is the giant of the family concerns and controls enormous real estate holdings and huge interests spanning investment in the national industries and factories. The company is engaged in currency exchange, dealing in currencies throughout the world and also deals in bullion. There is hardly a country in the world with which the company does not correspond.

Capital Six hundred million riyals.

Al Rajhi Commercial and Exchange Establishment

Address head office P.O. 4514 Jiddah

Telephone 42590, 31182

Telex 401602 ARAJHI SJ

Cable address RAJHI LIMITED

Subsidiary offices Two branches in Jiddah, and in Abha, Khamis Mushait, Jizan, Medina, Yanbo, Riyadh, Mecca, Al Khobar.

Proprietor Sh. Abdalrahman Abdalaziz Al Rajhi

The company, formed in 1975, is licensed as a Currency Exchange Bank and also operates a full range of banking services including deposits. However they do not usually operate as a source of loans and if at all these are on very short terms.

The company has the following correspondents:
Yemen Bank for Reconstruction and Development, Sana'a
Arab Bank, Beirut
National Bank of Yemen, Aden
Halim Sulfiete Bank, Ammam
Delta Bank, Cairo
Arab Bank, Jordan
Banque du Caire and the National Bank, Egypt
Trade Development Bank, London
Korea Exchange Bank, Seoul
The Republic National Bank of New York
National Westminster, London
Bank of America, New York and Bombay
Indian Bank, Madras
Habib Bank, Pakistan
Bank Misr, Cairo
Deutscher Bank, Frankfurt and Dusseldorf
Banca Commerciale, Milan

Sh. Abdalrahman is a partner with Abdullah Salih Rajhi and Abdalrahman Salih Rajhi in the Alrajhi Financial Corporation in Geneva. This organisation holds 45% of the IFA Bank in Paris where another 45% is held by Sh. Nasir Sabah al Ahmad al Sabah of Kuwait. The remaining 10% is shared by a number of other Arabian companies.

Sh. Abdalrahman also owns two other companies which at present share the premises and credentials of the Head Office in Jiddah.
1. Rayac, a trading and contracting company.
2. Gem Jewels, a company which manufactures jewellery.

Capital The Al Rajhi Commercial and Exchange Establishment has a capital of ten million Saudi riyals.

Abdullah Salih Al Rajhi Establishment

Address head office Jizan, but General Administration Office P.O. 968 Dammam

Telephone 20331, 28765 (Dammam)

Telex 601158 AL RAJHI SJ

Subsidiary offices
Jiddah, tel. 27451, P.O. 6727, tx. 401861 JMSRAF SJ.
Branches in Riyadh, Mecca, Al Khobar, Buraydah, Khamis Mushait, Al Thuqba, Al Qatif, Dhahran Airport, Jubail and Hafi al Batin

Proprietor Sh. Abdullah Salih Al Rajhi

Company History
The company was founded in 1972 and engages in currency exchange and dealing. In this activity they correspond with banks in most countries throughout the world.

Joint Ventures
Al Jassar and Al Rajhi, P.O. 24461 Kuwait.
Al Hariri and Al Rajhi Co., P.O. 20 Sana'a, Yemen Arab Republic.

Bankers National Commercial, Saudi British Bank, Riyadh Bank.

Al Rajhi Trading Establishment

Address head office Jiddah

Telephone 23336, 25158

Subsidiary Offices
Al Khobar, tel. 43628
Mecca tel. 34643
Dammam tel. 25801
Ta'if tel. 20987
Hasa tel. 21489

Proprietor Sh. Abdalrahman Saleh Al Rajhi

Activity
Foreign currency exchange. Correspondents world-wide.

Rajhi Consulting Engineers

Address head office P.O. Box 7669 Riyadh

Telephone 68853

Telex 201249 NASIR SJ

Cable address RAJ CONSULT

Proprietor Sh. Hamad bin Nasir Al Rajhi

Sh. Hamad was born in Mecca in 1948 and holds a B.Sc. and an M.Sc. in Civil Engineering from the University of California. He is a member of the American Society of Civil Engineers and was a member of conference at San Francisco in 1973 on Water Pollution in California Coastal Waters and in 1974 in Miami on Computer Use in Water Resources Engineering. He has contributed to professional journals and represents the younger generation of highly qualified professionalism which is emerging in the Kingdom.

Business Activity
The consultancy specializes in water supply projects for the Government but also handles a certain amount of architectural work.

The consultancy has an association with TCB Morris International of Houston and the J.E. Sirrien Company of Greenville, South Carolina.

Turnover 27 million Saudi riyals

Bankers National Commercial Bank

Rajhi Development Co. Ltd.

Address head office P.O. 4301 Riyadh

Telephone 65116, 60576

Telex 201249 NASIR SJ

Cable address RAJ CONSULT

Subsidiary Offices
Representatives and associates in Jiddah, Dammam, Khamis Mushait, Ta'if, Yambo, Medina, Mecca and Tabuk.

Proprietor The Board

Board Members
The Board consists of the sons of Sh. Nasir bin Hamad Al Rajhi. The Managing Director is US educated Sh. Abdullah bin Nasir.

Company History
The company was established in 1975 and its youth indicates a drive and energy that may be lacking in older and larger corporations. The company is comprised of a building materials import and supply division, a transportation division, a contracting division and a bio-medical division. They also, reflecting the social development needs of the Kingdom, operate a landscape gardening division.

Joint ventures A joint venture is operated with Hydrosoil BV of Holland and called Al Rajhi Hydrosoil.

Bankers National Commercial Bank

The Family of AL RAJHI

In 1979 it is estimated that there are seven hundred male members of this family. Originating from Al Bukariya in Qasim they are Bani Zayd of Qahtan

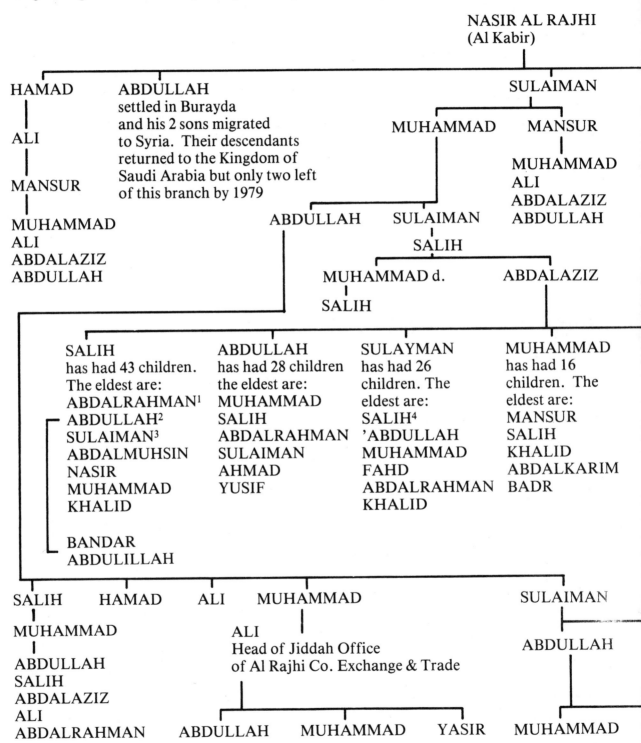

NASIR AL RAJHI (Al Kabir)

HAMAD

ABDULLAH
settled in Burayda
and his 2 sons migrated
to Syria. Their descendants
returned to the Kingdom of
Saudi Arabia but only two left
of this branch by 1979

SULAIMAN

ALI

MUHAMMAD   MANSUR

MANSUR

MUHAMMAD
ALI
ABDALAZIZ
ABDULLAH

MUHAMMAD
ALI
ABDALAZIZ
ABDULLAH

ABDULLAH   SULAIMAN

SALIH

MUHAMMAD d.   ABDALAZIZ

SALIH

SALIH
has had 43 children.
The eldest are:
ABDALRAHMAN[1]
ABDULLAH[2]
SULAIMAN[3]
ABDALMUHSIN
NASIR
MUHAMMAD
KHALID

BANDAR
ABDULILLAH

ABDULLAH
has had 28 children
the eldest are:
MUHAMMAD
SALIH
ABDALRAHMAN
SULAIMAN
AHMAD
YUSIF

SULAYMAN
has had 26
children. The
eldest are:
SALIH[4]
'ABDULLAH
MUHAMMAD
FAHD
ABDALRAHMAN
KHALID

MUHAMMAD
has had 16
children. The
eldest are:
MANSUR
SALIH
KHALID
ABDALKARIM
BADR

SALIH   HAMAD   ALI   MUHAMMAD   SULAIMAN

MUHAMMAD

ALI
Head of Jiddah Office
of Al Rajhi Co. Exchange & Trade

ABDULLAH

ABDULLAH
SALIH
ABDALAZIZ
ALI
ABDALRAHMAN

ABDULLAH   MUHAMMAD   YASIR   MUHAMMAD

[1]owner of Al Rajhi Trading Establishment
[2]owner of Abdullah Salih Al Rajhi Est.
[3]Foreign Exchange Department of Al Rajhi Co. in Riyadh for Exchange and Trade
[4]in Riyadh

continued

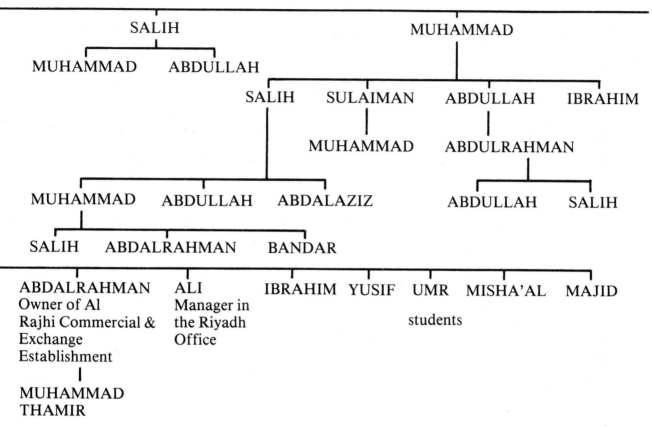

```
SALIH                          MUHAMMAD
  |                               |
MUHAMMAD   ABDULLAH        SALIH  SULAIMAN  ABDULLAH  IBRAHIM
                            |       |          |
                            |    MUHAMMAD  ABDULRAHMAN
                            |                  |
          MUHAMMAD  ABDULLAH  ABDALAZIZ   ABDULLAH  SALIH
             |
     SALIH  ABDALRAHMAN  BANDAR
```

ABDALRAHMAN   ALI   IBRAHIM YUSIF UMR MISHA'AL MAJID
Owner of Al   Manager in
Rajhi Commercial &   the Riyadh   students
Exchange   Office
Establishment
    |
MUHAMMAD
THAMIR

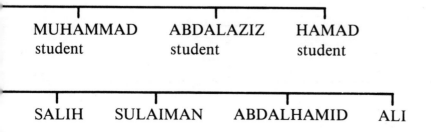

```
MUHAMMAD      ABDALAZIZ      HAMAD
student       student        student

SALIH   SULAIMAN   ABDALHAMID   ALI
```

continued

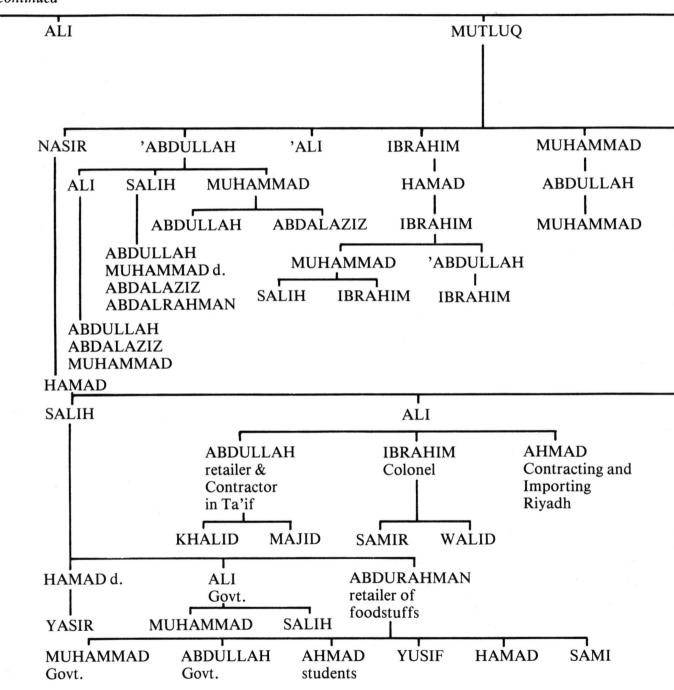

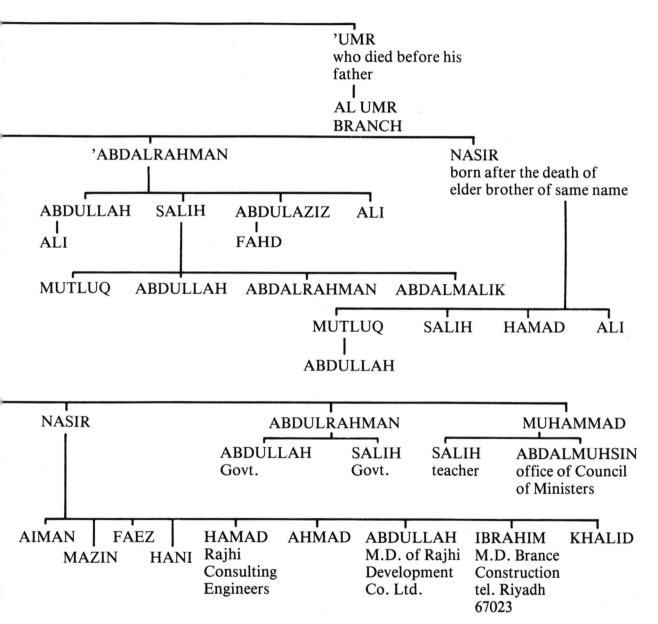

'UMR
who died before his
father

AL UMR
BRANCH

'ABDALRAHMAN

NASIR
born after the death of
elder brother of same name

ABDULLAH   SALIH   ABDULAZIZ   ALI

ALI   FAHD

MUTLUQ   ABDULLAH   ABDALRAHMAN   ABDALMALIK

MUTLUQ   SALIH   HAMAD   ALI

ABDULLAH

NASIR   ABDULRAHMAN   MUHAMMAD

ABDULLAH   SALIH   SALIH   ABDALMUHSIN
Govt.   Govt.   teacher   office of Council
of Ministers

AIMAN   FAEZ   HAMAD   AHMAD   ABDULLAH   IBRAHIM   KHALID
MAZIN   HANI   Rajhi   M.D. of Rajhi   M.D. Brance
Consulting   Development   Construction
Engineers   Co. Ltd.   tel. Riyadh
67023

All these brothers are members of the Board of the Rajhi Development Co. Ltd.

Sh. Khalid Fatany

Address head office Apartment 311 Azizia Building, King Faisal St. Riyadh, P.O. 376.

Telephone 25459, 4780459

Telex 200175 FATANI SJ

Cable address MORAGUIN

Subsidiary Offices
Jiddah P.O. 445, tel. 26446
Dammam P.O. 1122, tel. 25137

Proprietor Sh. Khalid Fatany

Accountant and Auditor
The first partnership was established in 1965 between Sh. Abdalwahab Abdalwasi who is now the Minister of Hajj and Sh. Abdalaziz Daghestani presently Deputy Minister of the Audit Bureau. Sh. Khalid joined the partnership in 1970 and took over in 1972 when the other partners relinquished their work to take up government appointments. The assisting partner in Riyadh is Abdalatif Othman.

Bankers National Commercial Bank.

The Family of FATANY

This is a typical professional and learned family which has its recent origins in the Holy City of Mecca. However, they relate that in Abbasid times an ancestor who was of the Thaqiyf tribe in the Ta'if region and named Isma'iyl became a soldier and fought in the East. He married a local girl and his son Muhammad stayed in his mother's country as did his descendants until Da'uwd returned to Mecca some 170 years ago. The family thus has many relatives in Malaysia and Thailand where there is today a district called Fatani after them.

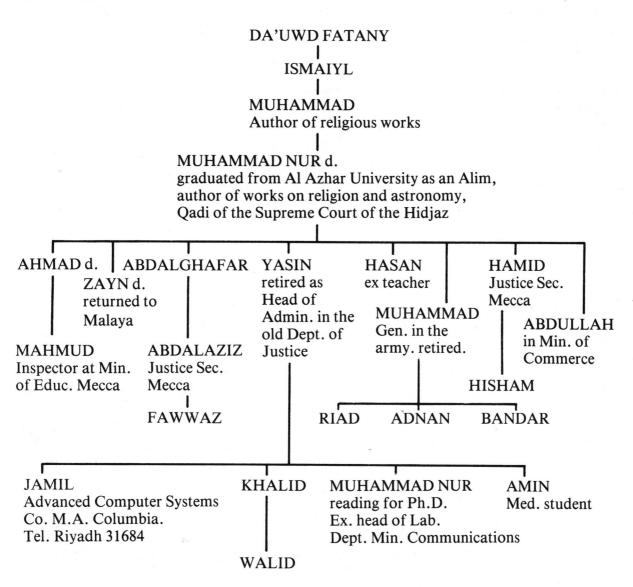

DA'UWD FATANY

ISMAIYL

MUHAMMAD
Author of religious works

MUHAMMAD NUR d.
graduated from Al Azhar University as an Alim,
author of works on religion and astronomy,
Qadi of the Supreme Court of the Hidjaz

AHMAD d.

ZAYN d.
returned to
Malaya

ABDALGHAFAR

YASIN
retired as
Head of
Admin. in the
old Dept. of
Justice

HASAN
ex teacher

HAMID
Justice Sec.
Mecca

MAHMUD
Inspector at Min.
of Educ. Mecca

ABDALAZIZ
Justice Sec.
Mecca

MUHAMMAD
Gen. in the
army. retired.

ABDULLAH
in Min. of
Commerce

FAWWAZ

HISHAM

RIAD   ADNAN   BANDAR

JAMIL
Advanced Computer Systems
Co. M.A. Columbia.
Tel. Riyadh 31684

KHALID

MUHAMMAD NUR
reading for Ph.D.
Ex. head of Lab.
Dept. Min. Communications

AMIN
Med. student

WALID

Abdalmajid Ahmad Mohandis

Address head office P.O. 524 Jiddah

Telephone 32805

Telex 400329 MANDIS

Subsidiary Office Riyadh

Proprietor Abdalmajid Ahmad Mohandis

Abdalmajid Mohandis is an extremely professional public accountant and auditor whose seventy odd clients testify to his success and quality. He obtained his academic qualifications at Cairo University and polished this achievement by deliberately working in a professional concern, SABA, for eight years to gain experience. During this period he refined his skills by taking Arthur Anderson Training Courses. Feeling then that he was equipped to enter private practice he established his independence and founded the present firm in 1970. His smart and efficient offices overlook the growing city of Jiddah from the twelfth floor of the Nashar Building from where he can watch the building activities of many of his clients. The firm corresponds with a major European company.

The Family of MOHANDIS

Family tradition relates that the ancestor of the family came to Jiddah on the Hajj some two hundred years ago and they still possess a deed dated 1841 **AD** giving them title to one of the coral block houses of old Jiddah. The same house is still standing today. The family originally came from the Sulaimaniya of Afghanistan.

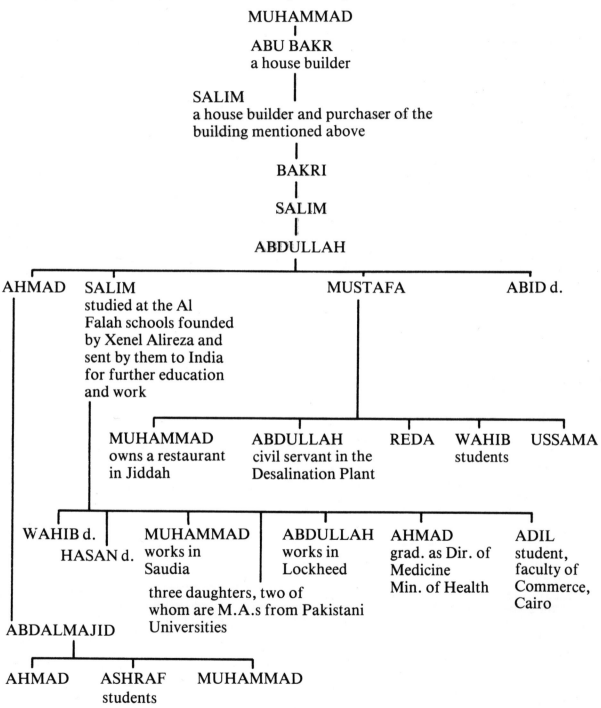

MUHAMMAD

ABU BAKR
a house builder

SALIM
a house builder and purchaser of the
building mentioned above

BAKRI

SALIM

ABDULLAH

AHMAD   SALIM   MUSTAFA   ABID d.
studied at the Al
Falah schools founded
by Xenel Alireza and
sent by them to India
for further education
and work

MUHAMMAD   ABDULLAH   REDA   WAHIB   USSAMA
owns a restaurant   civil servant in the   students
in Jiddah   Desalination Plant

WAHIB d.   MUHAMMAD   ABDULLAH   AHMAD   ADIL
     HASAN d.   works in   works in   grad. as Dir. of student,
                Saudia   Lockheed   Medicine   faculty of
                                              Min. of Health   Commerce,
                three daughters, two of   Cairo
                whom are M.A.s from Pakistani
ABDALMAJID   Universities

AHMAD   ASHRAF   MUHAMMAD
           students

The National Commercial Bank

Address head office P.O. 3555 Jiddah

Telephone 33580/4

Telex 401102, 401086 SJ

Cable address BANK SAUDI

Head office
King Abdulaziz St., Jiddah, P.O. 3555, tel. 33580/4, tx. 401102, 401086, cable BANKSAUDI

Major branches
Al Khobar, P.O. 1, tel. 42266, tx. 67023
Beirut, P.O. 2355, tel. 240508
Dammam P.O. 13, tel. 21566
Jiddah (main) P.O. 3555, tel. 23121, tx. 401102
Mecca P.O. 228, tel. 21405
Medina P.O. 26, tel. 25344
Riyadh P.O. 34, tel. 25082, tx. 20009
Ta'if P.O. 19, tel. 21022, tx. 45006

Major International Corporate Finance Offices
International Division Jiddah, P.O. 3555, tel. 23794, 49149, tx. 401102, 401086
Regional Development Riyadh, P.O. 34, tel. 34100, 34746, 34625, tx. 20009

Branches (cable address for all: MOWAFFAK)
 1. Jiddah Main Branch, P.O. 104, tel. 23122
 2. Bab-Sharief, Jiddah, P.O. 710, tel. 26352, 26353, 34946
 3. Ta'if, P.O. 19, tel. 21021, 22022, tx. 450006 ALAHLI
 4. Medina, P.O. 26, tel. 25344, 25345, tx. 470010
 5. Riyadh, P.O. 34, tel. 34100, 34128, 34229, tx. 201009, 201296
 6. Al Khobar, P.O. 1, tel. 42266, 42489, tx. 670023
 7. Dammam, P.O. 13, tel. 21717, 21577, tx. 601116
 8. Tabuk
 9. Khamis Mushait
10. Al Ahsa, P.O. 1, tel. 21441, 21442
11. Abha, tx. 901009
12. Yanbu
13. Arar
14. Najran
15. Buraydah
16. Hail, P.O. 85
17. Jizan
18. Al Gurrayat
19. Turaif
20. Al Jubail
21. Sharoorah
22. Baljorashi
23. Beirut, P.O. 2355, Kaaki Bldg. Sakiat, El Ganzir, tel. 314680, tx. 20642
24. Raffh
25. Hafir Al Batin
26. Al Konfodah
27. Al Dawadmy

28. Al Hadithah
29. Al Bahah
30. Al Magma'a
31. Affif
32. Al Bakyria
33. Anaiza
34. Shagdam
35. Al Kharj
36. Al Dariyah
37. Mecca, P.O. 228, tel. 45513, 45523, tx. 440005

Offices
38. Mecca Road, Jiddah, P.O. 3436, tel. 39656, 39957, tx. 40
39. Hindawiya, Jiddah, tel. 48624
40. Sharafiya, Jiddah, tel. 36791, 44763, 44764
41. Bab Mecca, Jiddah
42. Medina Road, Balishain Sq., Jiddah, tel. 59765
43. Al Shubekka, Mecca, P.O. 328
44. Aziziyah, Mecca, P.O. 228, tx. 440005
45. Al Ataebiyah, Mecca, P.O. 228
46. Al Gummaizah, Mecca
47. Al Shuwmasy, Riyadh, P.O. 34
48. Airport Road, Riyadh, tx. 201732
49. Al Nasriah, Riyadh, tx. 201657
50. Industrial City, Riyadh
51. Dhahran, Al Khobar
52. Military City, Tabuk
53. Al Gazzah, Mecca
54. Hallah Bin Dayal, Riyadh
55. Industrial City, Dammam
56. Al Faisaliyah, Najran
57. King Abdalaziz St. Al Khobar
58. Midan Al Khamis, Al Ahsa
59. Hidjaz St., Riyadh
60. Riyadh Airport
61. Al Dirah, Riyadh, P.O. 34
62. Mallaz, Riyadh, P.O. 34
63. Thogbah, Al Khobar

Seasonal branches
64. Sea Pilgrims' City Branch, Jiddah
65. Airport Pilgrims' City Branch, Jiddah
66. Mona Branch, Mecca

Company History
The National Commercial Bank has its origins in 1939 and assumed its present name in 1954.
It was founded by Sh. Salih Mousa Al Kaki, Sh. Abdalaziz Muhammad Al Kaki, Sh. Abdullah
Mousa Al Kaki and Sh. Salim Ahmad bin Mahfouz.

Business Activity

In all aspects of the economic development of Saudi Arabia NCB's presence is evident. For example, within the Saudi business sphere large scale project financing has been granted or arranged for the Jiddah, Riyadh and Eastern Province power expansion programmes, Jiddah Cement expansion, the Dammam Cement and the new Yanbo Cement Plants. NCB continues to recognise the importance to the country of trade and inventory build-up to face the continuing increase in demand and consumption. Financing to this sector of business represents the biggest share in the bank's total credit extension. Changes in trade patterns and the substantial growth in consumer demand for goods and services have placed new demands on the banking system and NCB is the first to recognise the importance of assisting young and small business ventures. The demand for project financing from local and foreign corporate customers has increased and is expected to grow. To satisfy these needs NCB devised improved methods of raising finance and the International Corporate Finance Group has completed several large medium term financings for housing complexes required by Saudia, Bechteb, Juffali and Mitsui Saico. The bank continues its programme of modernising and updating its operations procedures and equipment and has introduced new offices with corporate banking facilities especially to serve foreign corporate customers. The plan for a new headquarters for NCB envisages the choice of a prime site and the building when completed will comprise a modern banking hall with an area of about 2,500 square metres and will include twenty seven storeys of office space. The building will be equipped with the most modern equipment and communication systems available. The bank currently has 1,800 employees including many of the finest Saudi bankers, but needs a rapidly increasing number of highly trained and professional personnel, especially in the international sphere. The investment of the Government in higher education is beginning to bear fruit in the form of a reservoir of university trained Saudis capable and interested to develop a career in banking, but until they are available in quantity it is necessary for the bank to recruit qualified bankers from the United States, Europe, and elsewhere. The bank is proud of its record in assisting Saudi entrepreneurs with venture capital with a view to building up an infrastructure of business enterprise within the Kingdom. The bank is the major participant in the country's trade finance and opened SR 6.7 billion in letters of credit in 1977.

The National Commercial Bank is claiming for itself a place among the world's leading banks and is involved in note issues, syndicated medium term credits and performance guarantee facilities, very often in a lead management position. It is the bank's intention to continue to compete in the highest circles of international banking and to enhance its reputation as one of the world's most professional financial institutions. NCB is making considerable progress in implementing an electronic data processing system. The selected system will be based on four centres, Jiddah, Riyadh, Dammam and Mecca and will utilise NCR Hardware. In Jiddah and Riyadh the most recent of NCR's equipment, the NCR 8550 Criteria, is planned to be installed whilst the NCR 8250 Century is planned for Dammam and Mecca. At present they have 31 NCR 299/200 electronic accounting machines for accounting within individual branches which will be used for data capture for computer centre processing once the centres are operative. The configuration will be controlled from Jiddah and will cost SR 12.5 million, and will ultimately employ over 100 personnel.

An overview of the bank's financial results reflects the health of the Saudi Arabian economy as a whole. On balance, liquidity reserves accumulate at a rate faster than the banks ability to identify profitable uses for these funds although SAMA continues to maintain high reserve requirements which necessitates a high degree of liquidity.

Investment and Real Estate

The following is a list of companies owned or partially owned by the bank.

Name of Company	Location	Value in SR
United Arab Company	Mecca	1
Al Ahsa Electric Company	Al Ahsa	150,000
Badana Electric & Water Company	Arar	210,000
The National Gas & Manufacturing Company	Riyadh	4,667,065
The Electric Company of Riyadh	Riyadh	26,579,708
Yemama Cement Company	Riyadh	23,078,550
Saudi Provisions Company	Riyadh	1
The National Gypsum Company	Riyadh	292,500
Medina Electric Company	Medina	108,750
The Saudi Preaching Press Establishment	Jiddah	30,000
The Electric Company of Dhahran District	Dhahran	12,512,150
Jiddah Electric Company	Jiddah	21,727,440
The Arabian Fertilizer Company (SAFCO)	Dammam	632,000
The Arabian Cement Company	Jiddah	42,277,200
The Electric Company of Mecca	Ta'if	355,220
Tabuk Electric Company	Tabuk	286,500
Balgrishy Electric Company	Balgrishy	25,000
Red Sea Insurance Company	Jiddah	500,000
The Saudi Hotel Services Company	Jiddah	6,000,000
The Saudi Real Estate Company	Jiddah	20,000,000
Yanbu Cement Company	Yanbu	3,500,000
		165,310,085

NCB participates to the extent shown in the following banks:

Saudi International Bank Ltd.	1.25%
European Arab Holding S.A.	4.39%
Compagnie Arab et International d'Investissement	7.2%
The Arab Jordan Investment Bank	5%
Saudi Investment Banking Corporation	8%
Arab Malaysian Development Bank Berhad	12%
Arab Latin America Bank	3.33%
Saudi Spanish Bank	16%

The Bank has overseas investments in the Pan Islamic Navigation Company (SR 147,300), Arab Bank Ltd (SR 385,000) and the Beirut Riyadh Bank (SR 14,300).

Affiliates of NCB

European Arab Bank
European Arab Holding SA Luxembourg
14 rue Aldringer
Luxembourg-Ville
Grand Duchy of Luxembourg
(Subsidiary banks in Frankfurt, Brussels and London)

BAII
Banque Arabe et Internationale d'Investissement
12 Place Vendôme
75001 Paris
France
tel. 260 3401, tx. 680 330 F

SIBL
Saudi International Bank
99 Bishopsgate
London EC2M 3TB
tel. 638 2323, tx. 8812261/2/9

Saudi Investment Banking Corporation
P.O. 3533
Riyadh
Saudi Arabia
tel. 60300, 60401, tx. 20170

Arab Jordan Investment Bank
P.O. 8797
Amman
Jordan

Arab Malaysian Development Bank
8th Floor
Hong Leung Building
117 Jalan Bandar
P.O. 233, Kuala Lumpa 01-22, Malaysia
tel. 200033, tx. 31167/9

Arab Latinamerica Bank
Huallaga 320
Lima 1
Peru
tel. 286038/9, tx. 25138

Saudization

Saudization of foreign banks operating in the country has now become mandatory. All branches of foreign banks were subject to conversion and 60% of their share capital must be owned by Saudi individuals. Algemene Bank Nederland and Banque de l'Indochine et de Suez, The British Bank of the Middle East and Banque du Caire have all completed this process.

The National Commercial Bank feels that the move towards Saudization has been a significant one in the right direction. Saudi Arabia has a larger and more meaningful banking system which can play an even more important role in the development of the economy. This development will create greater competition to provide better and wider customer service in view of the increased branch banking authority granted to the converted banks. NCB already enjoys a very broad base across the country and looks forward to meeting its new competition on equal terms. The new banks, as Saudi entities, must submit to the Saudi Banking Control Regulations and thus cannot base their lending limits on the capital pool of their parent bank.

The Capital Market

With the Saudization programme fully implemented, the total Saudi capital contribution in all the ten previously fully owned foreign banks is estimated to be about SR 600 million. This contribution when added to the value of other corporate shares and the upgraded capital of existing joint stock companies will make a handsome capital market. Major existing share companies with their capitalisation are listed below:

Joint-Stock Companies

Name of Company	Authorized capital in SR	Year
Jiddah Cement Co. Jiddah	150,000,000	1960
Yamama Cement Co. Riyadh	750,000,000	1962
Dammam Cement Co. Dammam	850,000,000	1970
Yanbu Cement Co. Yanbu	700,000,000	1977
Southern Region Cement Co.	700,000,000	1977
Jiddah Electric Co. Jiddah	100,000,000	1973
Riyadh Electric Co. Riyadh	540,000,000	1973
Dhahran Electric Co. Dammam	100,000,000	1973
Badana Electric & Water Co. Arar	4,104,850	1972
Jizan Electric Co. Jizan	3,000,000	1973
Saudi Electric Co. Mecca & Ta'if	120,000,000	1973
Medina Electric Co. Medina	30,000,000	1973
Al Hassa Electric Co. Al Hassa	20,000,000	1973
Tabuk Electric Co. Tabuk	2,500,000	1975
National Gas & Industrial Co. Riyadh	116,651,200	1961
National Gypsum Co.	36,000,000	1961
Saudi Arabian Fertilizers Co.	100,000,000	1965
Red Sea Insurance Co. Jiddah	13,000,000	1975
Saudi Hotel Services Co.	60,000,000	1977
Saudi Real Estate Co. Jiddah	350,000,000	1977
Saudi Investment & Banking Corp. Jiddah	90,000,000	1977
Bank Aljazira Jiddah	50,000,000	1977
Bank Al Saudi Al Hollandi Jiddah	90,000,000	1977
Bank Al Saudi Al Faransi Jiddah	100,000,000	1977

Common stocks are the main instruments in the capital market. A few private placements of notes issued mainly by foreign borrowers in Saudi riyals have been made but purchases are mainly by institutional investors. The total amount of private placements issued since the first financing in 1973 in SR 692 million and is shown here:

1. Autopistas Del Mare Nostrum 'AUMAR', 8.25% 1975-80/82
SR 100,000.000
2. Banque Nationale Pour le Developpement Economique 'BNDE'
8.5% 175-1980/84
SR 100,000,000
3. Australian National Hotels 8.75% 1978-80
SR 27,000,000
4. Banque Nationale d'Algerie 9% 1977-1980/84
SR 80,000,000

5. Société Anonyme Marocaine de l'Industrie du Raffinage 'SAMIR'
8.5% 1977-1982/87
SR 100,000,000
6. Compagnie Nationale Algerienne de Navigation 'CNAN' 8.75% 1977-1987
SR 100,000,000
7. Interedec 'Bermuda' 9% 1977-1982
SR 35,000,000
8. Compagnie Nationale Algerienne de Navigation 'CNAN' 8.5%
1978-1983/88
SR 100,000,000
9. Korea Exchange Bank 7.75% 1983
SR 50,000,000

NCB has been the lead manager in most of these issues and continues making a market for all of these notes. It is gratifying to note there has been some active trading between the banks despite the very limited number of these issues and the international characteristics of participants and investors. The demand for these instruments is surprisingly large and the Saudi riyal capital market will easily absorb a much larger volume. Maturities of debt securities in the Saudi riyal capital markets, however, have been shorter than in other major capital markets. Institutional investors, as well as individuals, are reluctant to invest in securities with longer maturities than 5-7 years, while maturities in other capital markets, especially the Euro-capital market have been stretched to 10 and 15 years. Maturities are shorter in the Saudi riyal sector but the low cost and stability of the Saudi riyal for the foreseeable future is more than off-setting for the potential borrower. As the leading bank in Saudi Arabia they are making a great commitment and anticipate a greater contribution in the future in creating and encouraging the country's capital markets.

Letters of Credit
Number of correspondents and letters of credit in important countries (figures for 1977). The letters of credit opened by the bank are analysed by country in the following table:

Country	Number of correspondents	Number of documentary letters of credit	Value in SR (000)
Japan	30	9,230	1,693,172
USA	76	2,600	754,780
W Germany	29	2,091	596,224
Italy	25	3,143	500,661
Korea	18	2,307	486,638
Taiwan	14	3,821	44,135
Switzerland	12	482	336,582
UK	38	1,583	297,116
Belgium	14	392	141,475
India	16	1,185	141,143
Hong Kong	20	1,684	124,467
total	292	28,518	5,472,393

Industrial Investments

At the end of 1975 the responsibility for developing basic industries other than petroleum refining was shifted to the Ministry of Industry and Electricity which in turn created the Saudi Basic Industries Company (SABIC). The basic responsibilities of SABIC are the preparation of public sector projects, project evaluation (along with joint venture partners where appropriate) to provide project financing and the supervision of successful implementation of such projects. Industrial development made considerable advances during the year. Industrial estates in Jiddah and Riyadh are now in operation, with new consumer light industry developing consistently and constantly. Investment in this sector is gaining momentum.

Review of Banking and Finance

The year was very active in banking and finance within the Kingdom continuing the trend of recent years. The Government pursued the policy of encouraging investment through specialized credit institutions operating in the Kingdom.

Real Estate Development Fund (REDF)

By the end of the fiscal year 1976/77 the cumulative disbursement of the REDF since its inception in 1974 reached SR 23 billion. From mid'77 no new loans were extended. New procedures for real estate financing set the maximum loan for private residences at SR 350,00 or 70% of the cost whichever is lower and set limits on construction location beyond which the property will not qualify for financing. This restriction is intended to avoid developments in areas where utilities are not yet available. Commercial development will continue to benefit from fund financing as before but with more regulated disbursement scheduling to avoid heavy and irregular demand on available labour and services. The locations eligible for commercial development financing are also regulated in that only properties in main cities and towns will be subsidised with the objective of increasing the supply of apartment houses and office blocks. Loan approvals are now solely processed at the headquarters of the fund to enforce disbursement planning. These new procedures are expected to achieve rapid and successful property development without the inflationary impact seen in the past.

Saudi Industrial Development Fund

This fund, created to stimulate and facilitate industrial investment by the private sector experienced a sharp increase in both new loan applications and fundings since its inception in 1974. Total loans committed reached SR 2,234 million by the end of 1976.

The Family of BIN MAHFOUZ

Originating in Kharaikhar near the Wadi Du'an in Hadramawt, the Saudi branch descend from Salim Ahmad Bin Mahfouz who first worked in the Kaki household until he was able to establish his own business which developed into the banking colossus seen today. They come from Al Mahfouz, a separate section of the Sai'ar (see Binzagr).

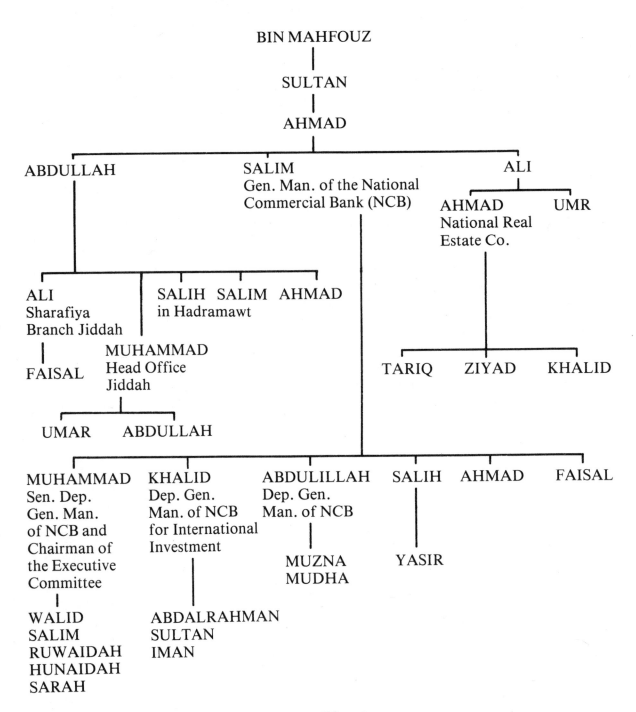

BIN MAHFOUZ

SULTAN

AHMAD

ABDULLAH — SALIM Gen. Man. of the National Commercial Bank (NCB) — ALI

ALI Sharafiya Branch Jiddah — SALIH SALIM in Hadramawt AHMAD

AHMAD National Real Estate Co. — UMR

FAISAL — MUHAMMAD Head Office Jiddah

TARIQ ZIYAD KHALID

UMAR ABDULLAH

MUHAMMAD Sen. Dep. Gen. Man. of NCB and Chairman of the Executive Committee

KHALID Dep. Gen. Man. of NCB for International Investment

ABDULILLAH Dep. Gen. Man. of NCB

SALIH AHMAD FAISAL

MUZNA MUDHA

YASIR

WALID SALIM RUWAIDAH HUNAIDAH SARAH

ABDALRAHMAN SULTAN IMAN

Government organisation in the Kingdom as it effects financial and commercial affairs

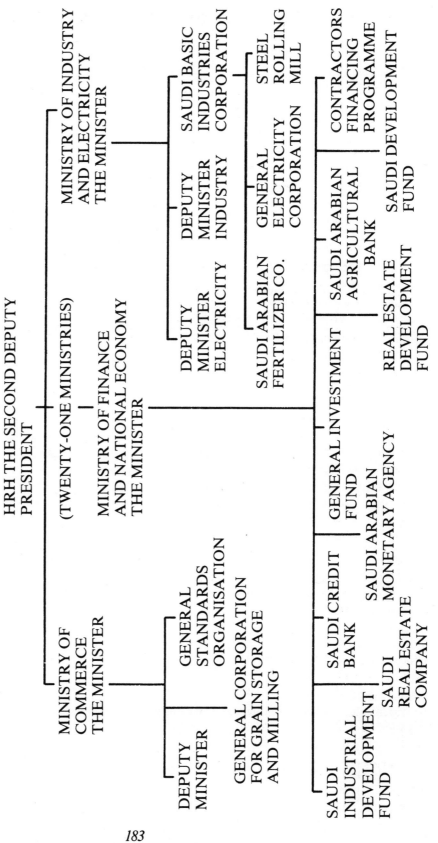

HIS MAJESTY THE KING PRESIDENT

THE FIRST DEPUTY PRESIDENT HRH THE CROWN PRINCE

HRH THE SECOND DEPUTY PRESIDENT

(TWENTY-ONE MINISTRIES)

MINISTRY OF COMMERCE THE MINISTER

DEPUTY MINISTER

GENERAL STANDARDS ORGANISATION

GENERAL CORPORATION FOR GRAIN STORAGE AND MILLING

MINISTRY OF FINANCE AND NATIONAL ECONOMY THE MINISTER

SAUDI CREDIT BANK

SAUDI ARABIAN MONETARY AGENCY

SAUDI REAL ESTATE COMPANY

GENERAL INVESTMENT FUND

SAUDI INDUSTRIAL DEVELOPMENT FUND

SAUDI ARABIAN AGRICULTURAL BANK

REAL ESTATE DEVELOPMENT FUND

MINISTRY OF INDUSTRY AND ELECTRICITY THE MINISTER

DEPUTY MINISTER ELECTRICITY

DEPUTY MINISTER INDUSTRY

SAUDI BASIC INDUSTRIES CORPORATION

SAUDI ARABIAN FERTILIZER CO.

GENERAL ELECTRICITY CORPORATION

STEEL ROLLING MILL

CONTRACTORS FINANCING PROGRAMME

SAUDI DEVELOPMENT FUND

REAL ESTATE DEVELOPMENT FUND

Addresses and Details of some Saudi Institutions

SABIC

The Saudi Arabian Basic
Industries Corporation

Chairman H. E. Dr. Ghazi A Al Gosaibi.
Minister of Industry and Electricity
Vice Chairman Sh. Abdalaziz al Zamil (q.v.)
Members
Dr Faisal Bashir,
The Dep. Min. of Planning.
Dr Mansual Turki,
The Dep. Min. of Finance.
Sh. Ahmad Tuwaijari,
The Dep. Min. of Industry.
Sh. Yousif Alireza (q.v.)

Paid up capital ten thousand million riyals
Riyadh tel. 60040/69954
tx. 2001177 SABIC SJ, cables SABIC

Saudi Development Fund
President H. E. The Minister of Finance
Sh. Muhammad Aba Al Khail
Vice President Sh. Khalid Al Masud
Riyadh tel. 38268, 38202, 38212
tx. 201145 SUNDUQ SJ

General Investment Fund
Chairman H. E. The Minister of Finance
Sh. Muhammad Aba Al Khail
Riyadh tel. 27000 ext. 202

Saudi Real Estate Development Fund
Riyadh tel. 33500, 33523
Jiddah tel. 34148

SAMA

Governor Sh. Abdalaziz Al Quraishi (q.v.)
Riyadh tel. 27923, 30150, 30161
Mecca tel. 29045, 26105, 29046
Medina tel. 21217, 21216
Jiddah tel. 31306, 31130, 31122
Dammam tel. 23771, 22375
Ta'if tel. 23019, 21019

Saudi Agricultural Bank
President Sh. Abdalaziz Muhammad Al Mansur
Riyadh tel. 23934, 23911, 39303
Jiddah tel. 24279, 21188
Qatif tel. 51984
Ahsa tel. 21662, 24567
Ta'if tel. 23159
Medina tel. 21142, 221141

Saudi Industrial Development Fund
Dir. General Sh. Muhammad Al Sayyari
(Chairman of SIBC)
Riyadh P.O. 4143
tel. 33755, 33306, 33219
tx. 201065 SIDFUND SJ

Saudi Investment Banking Corporation
Riyadh P.O. 3533, tel. 60300, 60401
tx. 201170 SIBCOR SJ
Jiddah, P.O. 6330, tel. 56741/2,
tx. 401413 SIBJED SJ
Al Khobar P.O. 1581, tel. 42311, 47506
tx. 671333 SIBALK SJ

Chambers of Commerce and Industry
Riyadh
Al Khazzan Street. P.O. 596, tel. 22700, 22600.
Jiddah
Sea Port Street. P.O. 1264, tel. 31059, 23535, 25659.
Dammam
P.O. Box 719, tel. 21134.

The money supply is controlled by the Saudi Arabian Monetary Agency which is accountable to the Minister of Finance. Government involvement is not confined to pure financing however, and its direct intervention in economic development is through the medium of SABIC, the Saudi Arabian Basic Industries Corporation, which operates under the chairmanship of the Minister of Industry and Electricity. SABIC controls the huge hydrocarbon and mineral based projects at Yanbu and Jubail through the medium of a Royal Commission. At Yanbu an area of 150 square kilometres is being developed and to date contracts of over 182 million riyals have been awarded. At Jubail the immediate site covers an area of 170 square kilometres though a further 730 square kilometres are available for expansion. SABIC itself was established in 1976 and apart from the Yanbu and Jubail projects is involved in establishing joint ventures with major international concerns in order to develop the industrial sector of the economy. The government also has direct involvement in cement, electricity, steel and fertilizers (SAFCO). The picture of business in the Kingdom given by the foregoing accounts of family businesses and their development from simple and often very small importing operations into huge corporations would be incomplete without some consideration of the enormous role that the Government itself plays. This part is not just one of implementing a policy of free enterprise but also of direct involvement and encouragement in pursuit of the goal of independence from the strictures of a purely oil based economy.

The Government provides financing through the following State Funds which receive control and guidance from the relevant ministry according to the diagram.

The Saudi Industrial Development Fund

Established in 1974 the SIDF provides funds for private industry operating outside the field of hydrocarbon based projects. The fund is managed by the Chase Manhattan Bank and provides up to 50% of the capital requirements of a project. To be eligible a business must have not less than 25% Saudi participation and loans are interest free. Applications must be accompanied by feasibility studies.

The Public Investment Fund

The fund was set up in 1971 to provide finance on a commercial basis and relieve the Ministry of Finance from financing state industries in which the private sector can invest. This fund is now exhausted having provided money in the main for Petromin and Saudi Arabian Airlines.

The Real Estate Development Fund

Starting in 1974 REDF was used to provide funding of up to 50% of the cost of putting up commercial buildings and apartment blocks. It has also had another role in the financing of private home construction where up to 70% of a maximum cost of 300,00 RS was provided. The activities of this fund were suspended in 1977.

The Credit Bank

The object of this fund is to provide financial resources for citizens of meagre means to purchase capital equipment and to help them with medical treatment and marriage expenses.

Contractors Fund

This has not been a very active fund. Its purpose since its inception in 1974 has been to provide funds for the provision of modern tools and equipment and materials to individuals. Money will not be allocated to joint ventures and grants of up to 75% of the equipment cost or 20% of contract value have been provided.

General Investment Fund

Set up in 1971 the fund acquires shares in newly established businesses for resale at minimal prices to individuals of low income. The fund also finances investment in projects involving commercial production.

The Saudi Arabian Agricultural Bank

Established in 1962 the bank provides loan and credit facilities for the promotion and development of agriculture.

The Saudi Investment Banking Corporation

The objective of this institution, founded in 1976, is to provide loans to companies and individuals in order to promote new projects in agriculture and industry.

The Saudi International Bank

Set up in 1975 the bank has it headquarters in London and its object is to participate in international merchant and commercial banking. The principal shareholder is SAMA with 50%, the National Commercial Bank and the Riyadh Bank each hold 2.5% and the remaining 45% is held by six international banks.

Morgan Guaranty Trust Company of New York	20%
The Bank of Tokyo Ltd	5%
Banque Nationale de Paris	5%
Deutsche Bank AG	5%
National Westminster Bank	5%
Union Bank of Switzerland	5%

The General Organisation of Social Insurance

The Board of Directors consists of representatives of the Government, the insured and employers. The organisation invests its funds in public limited companies.

Private financing rises to meet the funds thus provided by the State through the private banking system, the doyen of which in the Kingdom is the National Commercial Bank. Private and short term loans are injected into the system by the Saudi Investment Banking Corporation which contains both a direct Government as well as national Saudi commercial interest and international involvement.

The establishment of companies in the private sector takes its legal base from Islamic Sharia Law and a body of Arab custom and tradition. In Saudi Arabia this is expressed mainly by two sets of laws which are of interest to the foreigner. The first of these is the Foreign Capital Investment Code published by Royal Decree in Feburary 1964; the second is the Companies Regulations published similarly in July 1965. These two laws establish the method of obtaining licences and delineate various privileges which can be obtained. In addition they define the various kinds of company permitted in the Kingdom. These are:

1. A General Partnership
Where an association is formed between two or more persons who are jointly or severally liable to the extent of their entire assets for the partnership's debts.

2. A Limited Partnership
Where one partner is a general partner and the second is a limited or sleeping partner who is liable to the extent of his capital in the business.

3. A Joint Stock Company
Where the minimum number of shareholders is five and the business is a limited liability company in a classical sense. Such a company in the public sector must have a capital of at least one million Saudi riyals; if in the private sector two hundred thousand riyals.

4. A Partnership Limited by Shares
In this case there is a general partner and four other partners who are only responsible to the extent of their equity in the company.

5. A Limited Liability Partnership
It is this form of company which is of most interest to non Saudis. Here the company consists of two or more partners who are responsible to the extent of their interest in the capital of the company. The partners may not exceed fifty in number. The minimum capital is fifty thousand Saudi riyals and the company may not take up public subscriptions or engage in banking and insurance operations.

The Family of SABIC

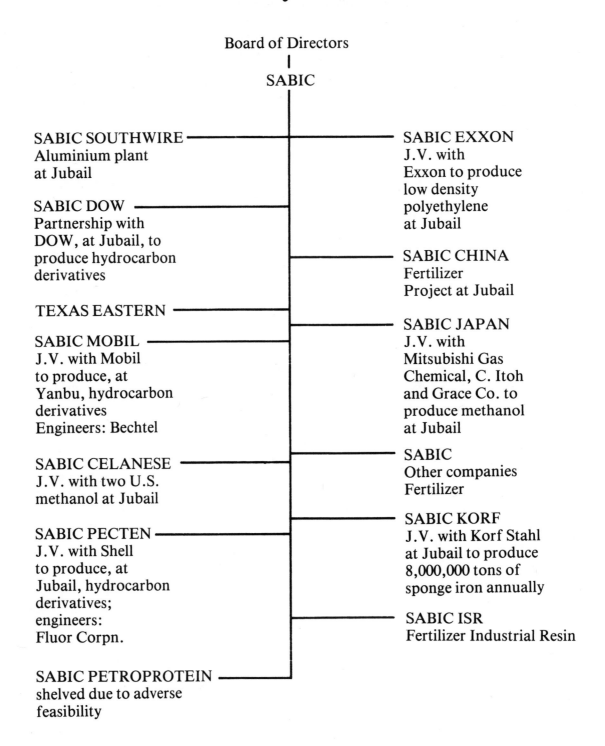

Board of Directors
|
SABIC

SABIC SOUTHWIRE
Aluminium plant
at Jubail

SABIC DOW
Partnership with
DOW, at Jubail, to
produce hydrocarbon
derivatives

TEXAS EASTERN

SABIC MOBIL
J.V. with Mobil
to produce, at
Yanbu, hydrocarbon
derivatives
Engineers: Bechtel

SABIC CELANESE
J.V. with two U.S.
methanol at Jubail

SABIC PECTEN
J.V. with Shell
to produce, at
Jubail, hydrocarbon
derivatives;
engineers:
Fluor Corpn.

SABIC PETROPROTEIN
shelved due to adverse
feasibility

SABIC EXXON
J.V. with
Exxon to produce
low density
polyethylene
at Jubail

SABIC CHINA
Fertilizer
Project at Jubail

SABIC JAPAN
J.V. with
Mitsubishi Gas
Chemical, C. Itoh
and Grace Co. to
produce methanol
at Jubail

SABIC
Other companies
Fertilizer

SABIC KORF
J.V. with Korf Stahl
at Jubail to produce
8,000,000 tons of
sponge iron annually

SABIC ISR
Fertilizer Industrial Resin

Saudi Investment Banking Corporation

Shareholders

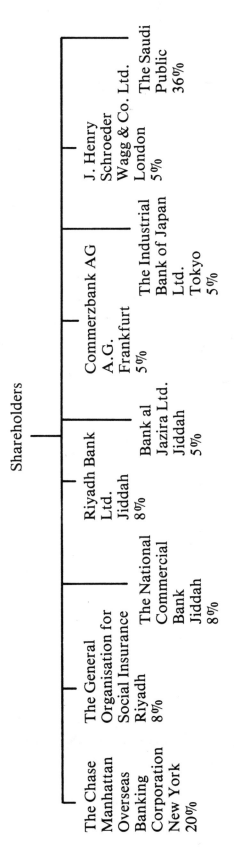

| The Chase Manhattan Overseas Banking Corporation New York 20% | The General Organisation for Social Insurance Riyadh 8% | The National Commercial Bank Jiddah 8% | Riyadh Bank Ltd. Jiddah 8% | Bank al Jazira Ltd. Jiddah 5% | Commerzbank AG A.G. Frankfurt 5% | The Industrial Bank of Japan Ltd. Tokyo 5% | J. Henry Schroeder Wagg & Co. Ltd. London 5% | The Saudi Public 36% |

Medium Term Finance and Banking Services; Deposits; Investment Banking, Syndications and Portfolio Management.

Chairman: Hamad Saud Al Sayari (D.G. of Saudi Industrial Development Fund)

General Manager: Richard F. Stacks representing Chase Manhattan Overseas Banking Corporation

Faisal Muhammad al Bassam

Wahib Said Binzagr (q.v.)

Mussaid al Sannani representing the General Organisation of Social Insurance

Omar Abdulqadir Bajamal representing the National Commercial Bank

Rashid al Mubarak al Ruweshid representing the Riyadh Bank

George W. Mallinckrodt representing Commerzbank, Industrial Bank of Japan and J. H. Schroeder Wagg

Peter Nice representing Chase Manhattan Overseas Banking Corporation and one further director to be appointed by the Saudi Arabian Monetary Agency.

Board of Directors

Bibliography

The Arab News Business Weekly

Corporate Development in the Middle East, ed. Robert Nelson, Oyez Publishing, 1978

A Guide to Industrial Investment in Saudi Arabia, 5th edition, Industrial Studies and Development Centre

A Hundred Million Dollars A Day by Michael Field, Praeger Publishers, 1976

Philby of Arabia by Elizabeth Monroe, Faber and Faber, 1973

The Riyadh Chamber of Commerce and Industry Directory 1979

Saudi Arabia by H St John Philby, Ernest Benn, 1955

Saudi Arabia. A Case Study in Development by Sh. Fouad Farsy, Stacey International, 1978

Saudi Arabia in the Nineteenth Century by R B Winder, St Martins Press, 1965

The Saudi Arabian Monetary Agency Annual Report 1978

The Saudi Economic Survey

The Saudi Gazette

The Telephone Directory of the Kingdom of Saudi Arabia

The Tihama Economic Directory 1978

Who's Who in Saudi Arabia 1978-9, 2nd edition, Tihama and Europa Publications